Lisp

by

Paul M. Chirlian
Stevens Institute of Technology

Weber Systems, Inc.
Cleveland, Ohio

The authors have exercised due care in the preparation of this book and the programs contained in it. The authors and the publisher make no warranties either expressed or implied with regard to the information and programs contained in this book. In no event shall the authors or publisher be liable for incidental or consequential damages arising out of the furnishing or performance of any information and/or programs.

Published by:
Weber Systems, Inc.
8437 Mayfield Road
Chesterland, OH 44026
(216) 729-2858

For information on translations and book distributors outside of the United States, please contact WSI at the above address.

Lisp

Contents

To Barbara, Lisa, Peter and Jerry

Preface

This is a book that discusses the Lisp programming language. This text is appropriate for readers who have little or no knowledge of any other programming language, because the basic concepts of programming will be introduced. On the other hand, the coverage will be thorough enough so that experienced programmers can use this book to add Lisp to their repertoire of programming languages.

Lisp is widely used for the programming of artificial intelligence applications. Data and instructions can be intermixed in Lisp. Indeed, instructions can be part of the data. Lisp can easily manipulate symbols and lists. Using Lisp, it is easy to associate information with symbols. A wealth of data structures can be established using Lisp. These aspects of Lisp are discussed to enable the reader to program artificial intelligence applications. Lisp, however, is by no means restricted to these applications. The use of Lisp for more familiar programming applications is also discussed.

We start by considering simple examples that all readers should be able to follow. The ideas of simple arithmetical operations are familiar to almost all people. For this reason, we start by discussing the Lisp programming of simple arithmetic applications. Once the reader has gained some experience using Lisp, we consider more traditional Lisp applications.

Although Lisp is as old as FORTRAN, it is a constantly evolving language. This is both an advantage and a disadvantage. Because of its evolution, Lisp can be considered to be a modern language. On the other hand, such evolution has resulted in many varieties of Lisp. One standard that is being developed is that for Common Lisp. We shall discuss Common Lisp in this book. At times, however, we shall consider the variations that occur in other dialects of Lisp. The author has been fortunate to have worked with several excellent Lisp systems. One is Golden Common Lisp that, in large part follows the Common Lisp standard. As it evolves it should come to be a full implementation of this standard. Another excellent Lisp system is TLC lisp. Although is is not exactly Common Lisp, anyone familiar with Common Lisp should be able to use TLC Lisp after studying the TLC Lisp manual. The writers of TLC Lisp have a thorough understanding of the underlying philosophy of Lisp, and their Lisp system reflects this understanding. In addition, the TLC Lisp manual presents this philosophy in a very clear and concise manner.

The book is organized so that the beginner can start writing programs almost immediately. Numerous exercises are included at the end of each chapter. A manual containing the solutions to the exercises is available for instructors.

The author would like to thank his colleague Dr. Derek Morris for his many helpful discussions. Loving and heartfelt thanks are due my wife Barbara who provided me with many in depth, discussions about Lisp and who greatly influenced the book. She also made important comments about the book's style and wrote the solutions manual.

1

Introduction to Lisp Programming

This book will show you how to write programs using the Lisp programming language. We shall start by discussing some very simple ideas of programming and then build up to complex concepts. Because Lisp is very powerful and versatile, it can be used to write powerful programs. On the other hand, because Lisp has is not difficult to learn a beginner can start to program in Lisp without much difficulty. Lisp is specifically designed to process lists. Indeed its name stands for "list processing." Lisp can be used in a wide variety of programming applications. It is especially suited for those applications that fall under the general heading of "artificial intelligence."

The modern digital computer can do remarkable things. It can control the operation of a complete manufacturing process, monitor the patients in a hospital recovery room, and perform calculations in seconds that would take days or years to perform by hand. The computer can appear to think while doing things such as performing medical diagnoses after being supplied with a set of symptoms, or it can control the operations of a robot. However, the computer cannot think. Every one of its operations must be controlled by a set of instructions called a *program*. In this book we shall discuss the Lisp programming language and show how it is implemented.

1-1. Some Computer Fundamentals

Before we start discussing programming with Lisp we shall look at some fundamentals of computer operation. This discussion is applicable to a small microcomputer, a minicomputer, or to a large mainframe computer.

The operations of the computer are directed by a *central processor* that performs the basic arithmetic and logical operations. For instance, the central processor can add two numbers or compare them to see if they are equal. The central processor receives instructions from a program and it directs the operation of the computer in accordance with those instructions.

Computers have a *main memory* that stores both the data and the program that direct the operation of the computer. (Note that sometimes supplied data can also contain instructions.) The main memory can store a relatively large amount of information. It usually stores the instructions and data for the program that is being run. However, the main memory is not large enough to store all the programs and data that most programmers have. In addition, the information stored in the main memory is usually lost when the computer is turned off. For these reasons there is provision for storing data and programs outside of the main memory of the computer. The appropriate information is then read back into the main memory when it is needed. Such information is usually stored in what is called *external memory*, usually on magnetic disks or tapes. Disk storage is much faster than tape storage. However a great deal of data can be stored on a tape. Most computers use *floppy disks* and/or *hard disks* to store data. The transfer of data between the central processor and the main memory is much faster than such data transfer from disks or tapes. However, much more data can be stored on magnetic media.

If a computer is to be useful, then there must be a way to enter and output data and programs. Most computers use a *video terminal* for this. When using such a terminal, the programmer types on a keyboard that resembles an ordinary typewriter keyboard. The terminal generates the electric signals that supply information to the computer. The output appears on a screen that resembles an ordinary television receiver. There are other devices used for input/output. If a *hard* or printed copy is desired, then the data can be output to a *printer*.

The program that actual directs the operation of a computer is written in what is called a *machine language*. The statements in a machine language program are in the form of binary numbers and consist of very simple instructions such as: add two numbers, compare two numbers to see if they are equal, or fetch some data from memory. Programming in machine language is usually very tedious because long sets of instructions have to be written to perform simple tasks such as the division of two numbers. Special languages called *programming languages* make the job much easier for the programmer. In this book we shall discuss the Lisp programming language. To illustrate the relative simplicity of Lisp let us consider a simple arithmetic example. (We use arithmetic here because most people are familiar with it.) Suppose that we want to write a statement in Lisp that corresponds to the algebraic equation:

x=a+b/c   (1-1)

The Lisp statement that corresponds to this is:

(SETQ X (+ A (/ B C)))   (1-2)

The Lisp statement is much shorter than the set of machine language instructions that are needed to perform the operations of eq. (1-1). Note that (1-2) does not appear in the same form as the algebraic equation. However do not let this disturb you. This notation is the same as the *reverse Polish* or *prefix* notation that can be used to describe the way data is entered in some simple calculators. After we describe the Lisp arithmetic operations in detail, the notation of (1-2) will not be confusing. The SETQ will be explained in sec. 1-4. Note the parentheses in (1-2). Lisp has many parentheses and it can be annoying to keep track of them. However, we shall discuss procedures that eliminate most of the problems associated with parentheses. Do not let the strange notation, parentheses or anything that you may have heard frighten you. Lisp is not hard to learn. We shall start very slowly and explain each new concept thoroughly.

The program that actually directs the operation of the computer is written in machine language. The programs written in a programming language must be translated into machine language. There are programs called *interpreters* or *compilers* that translate programs written in programming languages into machine-language programs. The programmer who writes in Lisp, or in any other programming language, need not be concerned with the inner workings of the interpreter or compiler, because they function automatically. A compiler translates a program into a machine-language program that will run on its own, without any other programs. An interpreter does not produce a complete machine-language program. The interpreter translates each line, or set of lines, in a programming language program into a set of machine language instructions while the program is running. However, the individual instructions are not saved nor is a complete machine language program is ever generated. Complied programs generally *run* faster than interpreted programs. This is because the compilation process need be performed only once to generate the machine-language program, while the interpreter must be run each time that the program is run. On the other hand, it may take several minutes for the compiler to be run. While a program is being developed, it may have to be compiled over and over again for the purpose of testing and error correction. The time required for these multiple compilations can seriously increase the time required to *develop* programs.

Actually, there are two processes that must be carried out in order to convert a program written in a programming language into a complete stand-alone machine-language program. Most programming languages come with a collection of *library routines* that perform various operations such as those that control the input or the output of data. The compiled program must be combined with the appropriate library routines. This operation is called *linking* and it is performed by a program called a *linker*. A (compiled) program must first be compiled and then be linked before it can be run. On the other hand, when a program is interpreted, it can be run almost immediately so that the time required to develop interpreted programs is often considerably shorter than that required for compiled programs. Note however, that compilation and linking times are becoming shorter as computers become faster.

Some interpreted languages are *extensible*. That is you can add to the programming language, thus extending its capabilities. This is true of Lisp and is one of its outstanding features. That is, you can add your own features to your Lisp system. Essentially every Lisp system is available with an interpreter. In addition, some Lisp systems also include a compiler. Remember that you do not have to know the details of the internal operations of the interpreter or of the compiler and linker. However, you must know the proper sequence of commands required to run them. These instructions are not standard. However, they are simple and straightforward. Proper instructions will be listed in the manual that comes with your Lisp system.

Because Lisp is an evolving language, there is no one standard Lisp system. However, Common Lisp is becoming a standard. In this book we shall discuss Common Lisp. We also shall consider Golden Common Lisp and other Lisps such as TLC Lisp, Zata Lisp, Mulisp and Maclisp. We shall indicate any departures of these Lisps from the Common Lisp standard.

1-2. Some Fundamentals of Lisp Programming

In this section we shall discuss some basic ideas that you must understand if you are to program in Lisp. After you finish reading the next sections of this chapter, you will be able to run your own Lisp programs.

LISP CHARACTERS

No matter what language is used, information must be written in a particular set of characters. For instance, the English language uses the 26 letters of the alphabet, the digits, and the punctuation marks. Similarly, there is a set of allowed characters in the Lisp language. Let us consider these characters. There are the 26 lowercase letters of the alphabet:

a b c d e f g h i j k l m n o p q r s t u v w x y z

the 26 uppercase letters of the alphabet,

A B C D E F G H I J K L M N O P Q R S T U V W X Y Z

the digits,

0 1 2 3 4 5 6 7 8 9

and the following symbols:

! " # $ % & ' ( ) = - { } [ ] | \ ` @ + ; * : > < , . ? / ~ ^ _
The blank space is also a valid character.

Certain of these characters are reserved and should be used for special purposes only. These are:

( ) { } [ ] ? ! ^ ~ _ $ %

In particular, these symbols should not be included in names that you define. (We shall discuss names later in this section.)

There are also some special characters that are used. These consist of combinations of the above characters. These may vary from implementation to implementation, these are:

#\SPACE, which represents the blank space
#\NEWLINE, which represents the newline character

Note that the text written after a newline character will appear on a new line. There are other special characters that are included with most Lisp systems. Consult your Lisp manual to find the special characters for your system.

NAMES - IDENTIFIERS

In (1-2) we illustrated a simple Lisp statement. In that statement the terms X, A, B and C were all *names*, or *identifiers* for Lisp atoms. We shall discuss atoms in sec. 1-4; for the time being just consider that X, A, B, and C each identify or name a variable. Names can consist of more than one letter in Lisp. For instance, a valid Lisp statement is:

(SETQ DISTANCE (/ VELOCITY TIME))   (1-3)

The use of names with English meanings helps explain the program to human readers. Because they make the program easier to read, descriptive names make programmer mistakes less likely.

Note that we used capital letters in (1-3). In some Lisp systems, lowercase letters will be converted to capital letters when they are read by the Lisp system. In such cases it does not matter how you enter Lisp instructions or names. For instance, First, FIRST, and FIrSt will all be equivalent. In other Lisp systems, you must enter all standard Lisp words using capital letters. Note that a standard Lisp word is a word that is recognized by the Lisp system to mean that some particular act should be performed.

ATOMS AND LISTS

An *atom* is an indivisible set of characters. For instance, the name VELOCITY is an atom. Similarly the number -23456 is also an atom. Standard Lisp words are themselves atoms. Lisp is concerned with the manipulation of *lists* . Lists can be collections of atoms. For instance,

(The book is on the table)   (1-4)

is a list that contains six atoms. They are The, book, is, on, the, and table. The list starts with a left parenthesis and ends with a right parenthesis. List (1-4) is a collection of six atoms. Lists can contain other lists. For instance,

(A BD (THE HOUSE) TOY)   (1-5)

is a list containing the atoms A, BD, and TOY and the list (THE HOUSE). We could extend these ideas further. For instance,

(A BD (THE HOUSE (HELLO LISP USERS)) (TOY BOAT))   (1-6)

is a list that contains the atoms A and BD and two other lists. One of the lists, (THE HOUSE (HELLO LISP USERS)) contains two atoms, THE and HOUSE, and the list (HELLO LISP USERS).

Atoms in lists can represent data such as text or numbers. In addition, the atoms can represent Lisp instructions. One of the differences between Lisp and most other programming languages is that data and instructions can be intermixed. However, we shall see that this is not necessarily confusing. In the next sections you will learn how to write a simple Lisp program.

1-3. Running Some Very Rudimentary Lisp Programs

In this section we shall discuss some very simple Lisp operations. They can be considered to be rudimentary programs. They could be called one-line programs or simply Lisp expressions. In the next two sections we shall start writing programs that are somewhat more complex. The Lisp interpreter is almost always used for program development. A very simple program could be written in the following way: A list is typed in at the terminal. Remember that all lists start with a left parenthesis and end with a right parenthesis. Next the RETURN key is pressed. (Some Lisp systems do not require this step, but will automatically proceed after the right parenthesis is entered.) The Lisp system then reads the list that was entered. Next the list is *evaluated*. This is called an EVAL operation. In its simplest form, evaluation consists of examining the list. The first atom is assumed to be a keyword that supplies the Lisp system with an instruction. This instruction is applied to the rest of the list. The result of the evaluation is then output to the screen. This operation is called a *READ-EVAL-PRINT* loop. It is said to be a loop because the interpreter keeps repeating the operation so that additional lists can be entered and evaluated, and their results output. We have oversimplified the operations here. They shall be discussed in greater detail in subsequent chapters.

Because everyone is familiar with arithmetic, we shall start with simple examples illustrating arithmetic operations. In subsequent chapters we shall discuss more complex Lisp operations. Lisp was designed to process lists. Usually lists containing general information are processed. However Lisp can process lists of numbers. For instance, a list of numbers can be added with a single Lisp expression. This is easier to do in lisp than in other programming languages. As an example of this let us write a Lisp expression that adds the numbers 4, 6, 11, 25, and 40. This can be accomplished by entering the following list:

$$(+ 4\ 6\ 11\ 25\ 40) \hspace{4cm} (1\text{-}7)$$

After you press RETURN, or simply type the right parenthesis on some systems, the number 86 will appear on your screen. The atom + indicates that the remainder of the list is to be added. In this case, after the list is read, the EVAL operation interprets the + to mean that the remaining atoms in the list represent numbers that are to be added. After this operation is performed the desired sum is obtained and output. If the remaining atoms do not represent numbers, then an error will result. Most Lisp systems will output an error message that will help you diagnose the error.

Of course, we assume that you have a Lisp system running on your computer. The Lisp manuals that come with your Lisp system will tell you how to start up your Lisp system. Each time that you start your Lisp system, a "banner" will appear announcing such things as the name of the system and copyright information. Next a *prompt* will appear. This is simply an indication that the Lisp system is ready to accept additional information. For instance, the asterisk is a commonly used prompt. If the asterisk is used as a prompt then, when (1-7) was entered, your screen would appear as:

$$*(+ 4\ 6\ 11\ 25\ 40) \hspace{4cm} (1\text{-}8)$$

Prior to your entering of (1-7), the asterisk would be the only character on the line. Note that you do *not* type the prompt; it is output by the Lisp system. In the remainder of this book we shall not indicate prompts nor shall we discuss the termination of lines with a RETURN.

Note that each number in (1-7) is separated from the next by a blank space. In this case the blank is said to be a *delimiter*. The + atom in (1-7) represents a *procedure*. Lisp systems are supplied with a number of procedures. There is no single standard set of Lisp procedures, although there are some procedures that are supplied with practically all Lisp systems. Note that, the names used for particular procedures may vary from one system to another. For instance, in some Lisp systems, the procedure that we have called +, is called PLUS. If you were using such a system, then (1-7) would be written as:

$$(\text{PLUS}\ 4\ 6\ 11\ 25\ 40) \hspace{4cm} (1\text{-}9)$$

Note that the operation of the procedures is not the same in all Lisp systems. For instance, the + function that we have described is that given in the Common Lisp Standard. However, with some Lisp systems, there can be only two numbers following the + atom. You should consult your Lisp manual to learn the names and operations of the procedures that come with your Lisp system.

SUBTRACTION, MULTIPLICATION, AND DIVISION

We have considered the operation of addition. Now let us discuss subtraction, multiplication and division. The Lisp procedures that perform these functions are also designed to process lists of numbers. The atom - indicates that each atom in the list following the second atom is to be subtracted from the second atom. For instance,

$$(-20\ 4\ 5\ 7) \hspace{4cm} (1\text{-}10a)$$

will result in 4 being output on your screen. In this case 4 is subtracted from 20, resulting in 16; then 5 is subtracted from 16, resulting in 11; finally 7 is subtracted from 11 resulting in 4. This value is output on the screen. We assume that each atom except the first represents a number. If there is only one number in the list following the - atom, then the number output on the screen will be the negative of that number. For instance,

$$(-34) \hspace{4cm} (1\text{-}10b)$$

will result in -34 being output on the screen. Negative numbers can be used in all lists. For instance,

$$(-50\ -20) \hspace{4cm} (1\text{-}10c)$$

will result in 70 being output. Note that 50 -(-20) = 70. The name of the procedure that we have just discussed is -, in some Lisp systems this procedure is named MINUS or DIFFERENCE. Again some Lisp systems allow only one or two numbers in the list.

The procedure that performs multiplication is called *. Do not confuse this with your prompt, which also may be an asterisk. This procedure results in the product of all the numbers in the list. For instance,

$$(*\ 3\ 4\ 5) \hspace{4cm} (1\text{-}11)$$

will result in 60 being output. Note that this is the product of 3, 4, and 5. Some Lisp systems use the name TIMES for this procedure. Remember that in some Lisp systems there can be only two numbers following the *.

The procedure that performs division is /. The atom / indicates that the second atom is to be divided, successively by the following atoms in the list. For instance,

$$(/\,30\,3\,5) \qquad\qquad (1\text{-}12)$$

will result in 2 being output. That is 30 will be divided by 3, yielding 10, then 10 will be divided by 5 yielding 2. It is assumed that all the atoms following the / represent numbers. (Note that in some Lisp systems only two numerical atoms may follow the / atom.) Again we shall extend these ideas in the next section.

If there is only one atom following the slash, then the operation is somewhat different. In this case, the result is the reciprocal of the number. For instance,

$$(/\,10) \qquad\qquad (1\text{-}13)$$

results in an answer of 0.1. Of course, this assumes that your Lisp system can work with floating-point numbers.

The reader should note that two different types of numbers are generally handled by computers, namely *integers* and *floating-point* numbers. An integer is a number with no fractional part, that is, it is a whole number. For instance, 1, 5, -22, and 244 are integers. A floating-point number has a fractional part. For instance, 10.0, -22.4, 367.89, and -244.0 are floating point-numbers. Computers store and manipulate integers and floating-point numbers in very different ways. When you input data, some Lisp systems will automatically assume that you are working with floating-point numbers, while other Lisp systems will assume that you are working with integers. Indeed, some Lisp systems can work only with integers, while others can work with both integers and floating point numbers. If a system can work with both types of numbers then you can indicate that an input number is a floating point number by including a decimal point, even if there is no fractional part, that is, input 10.0 rather than 10. Consult the Lisp manual that comes with your system to determine whether floating-point numbers and/or integers can be used, and how they are to be represented.

When floating-point numbers are divided, the results are as expected. However, when integer arithmetic is used, the results can be surprising. Fractional parts of the numbers are discarded. For instance, let us consider the division:

$$(/ 7.0 3.0) \qquad\qquad (1\text{-}14a)$$

The result will be 2.33333. On the other hand if integer arithmetic is used as in:

$$(/ 7 3) \qquad\qquad (1\text{-}14b)$$

the result will be 2. That is the fractional part will be lost.

There are other Lisp procedures that are used with integer division. One such is QUOTIENT. It will yield the same result as (1-14b) when applied to two integers.

Number types and the maximum allowable size for numbers will also be discussed in greater detail in the next chapter. This discussion of this section is intended to demonstrate some of the results of integer arithmetic.

1-4. Binding - Assignment

In the last section we considered some extremely simple Lisp operations that manipulated specific numbers. These operations would be much more versatile if the result of a calculation could be stored and then retrieved using a specific name. This name could then be used whenever the result was desired. Operations such as these are needed when most programs are written. Consider that the sum of a twenty numbers were to be used at several places in a program. It would be very tedious to have to type a list consisting of a plus sign and the twenty numbers each time that the sum was needed. Fortunately Lisp allows values to be assigned to atoms. The value is now stored under the name of the atom and can be referred to by that name. (In this sense atoms can play the same role as do variables in many other programming languages.) Atoms can also take on other roles in Lisp. We shall subsequently demonstrate that in addition to values atoms can represent lists as well.

The Lisp function SETQ is used to assign a value to an atom. In this case the atom is said to be *bound* to the value or the value is *assigned* to the atom. For instance, if we enter,

$$(SETQ ABC 55) \qquad\qquad (1\text{-}15)$$

the atom ABC will be bound to 55. If subsequently we enter,

(+ 20 ABC 10)   (1-16)

the value 85 will be output. The atom ABC will be treated as 55. The use of the SETQ function creates an atom that the Lisp system recognizes and it also stores a value for this atom. We shall consider additional details of this storage subsequently.

Calculations can be included in the binding operation. For instance, if we have,

(SETQ ZZZ (+ 3 4 5))   (1-17)

the EVAL procedure will be applied to the inner list so that ZZZ will be bound to 12.

It often is desirable to bind an atom to something other than a number. For instance, you might want the atom to represent an entire list. However, as we have just seen in (1-17) the list is evaluated before the atom ZZZ was bound. A procedure is needed to inhibit the EVAL procedure. In almost all Lisp systems the single quotation mark or equivalently the apostrophe can be used for this purpose. The apostrophe signifies that the list or atom following it is to be considered literally. For instance, the following will bind the atom DEFG to the list (+ 3 4 5):

(SETQ DEFG '(+ 3 4 5))   (1-18)

Note that because the list was not evaluated before the atom was bound, DEFG is bound to the list (+ 3 4 5).

The bindings of atoms can be determined simply by entering the atom's name followed by RETURN. For instance, if ABC is typed, and then RETURN is pressed, 55 will appear on the screen. On the other hand if DEFG is typed, followed by RETURN, (+ 3 4 5) will appear on the screen. Note that because the apostrophe is not present in (1-17), the inner list is evaluated and ZZZ is bound to the result of the evaluation. On the other hand, in (1-18), the apostrophe prevents evaluation of the inner list and DEFG is bound to the actual list itself.

Suppose that both (1-17) and (1-18) have been entered. It now would be proper to write:

(+ 20 ZZZ 5)   (1-19)

The result 37 would then be output. Note that it would be *improper* to replace ZZZ by DEFG in (1-19) since the + procedure expects that the remaining atoms represent numbers, not lists.

There are times when it an atom is bound to a list and we want to use the result of the evaluation of that list. Remember that the Lisp procedure EVAL causes the evaluation of a list. Thus we can write:

(EVAL DEFG)   (1-20)

This would result in 12 being output, because DEFG is bound to the list (+ 3 4 5). In a similar way we could write:

(+ 20 (EVAL DEFG) 5)   (1-21)

There can be many parentheses in complex Lisp expressions and this can tend to be confusing. Take care to have the proper number of parentheses in the proper position. Most Lisp systems provide an *editor* that is used to write programs that are more than several lines long. An editor is itself a program that allows you to enter text and modify it. Some Lisp editors have features that associate each right parenthesis with the corresponding left parenthesis. For example, the GMACS editor of Golden Common Lisp causes the left parenthesis to blink after the corresponding right parenthesis has been typed.

Let us consider some additional details of binding. If we enter the sequence,

(SETQ AAA 55)   (1-22a)
(SETQ BBB AAA)   (1-22b)

then BBB will be bound to 55. Note that (1-22b) causes BBB to be bound to whatever AAA is bound to. On the other hand if (1-22b) had been replaced by,

(SETQ BBB 'AAA)   (1-23)

then BBB would be bound to the sequence of characters AAA. Note that characters can also be data.

Let us consider some aspects of the notation that we have used. Examine (1-22a). On the basis of the previous discussion, this seems to indicate that AAA is bound to the value to which the atom named 55 is bound. Strictly speaking (1-22a) should be written as:

(SETQ AAA '55)   (1-24)

However, almost all Lisp systems will interpret an atom that consists only of numbers to be a number and not to be the name of an atom. Thus, it is not necessary to include the apostrophe with numbers. Lisp could become very tedious if this were not the case.

Note that if statements (1-22a) and (1-22b) are entered, BBB will be bound to 55. If AAA is *subsequently* bound to a new value, the binding of BBB will *not* be changed.

If an atom is bound to a value, and subsequently that atom is bound to another value, then its old value is lost. For instance, if we have,

(SETQ AAA 'house)   (1-25a)

AAA is bound to the string of characters that spell house. If we subsequently enter,

(SETQ AAA 55)   (1-25b)

now AAA is bound to the number 55 and its old value 'house' is lost.

Let us consider some additional examples. Suppose that (1-25b) has been entered. Then, if we enter AAA followed by RETURN, 55 will be output. On the other hand, if we enter 'AAA followed by RETURN, AAA will be output. The single quote (apostrophe) causes the string of characters following it to be interpreted literally. Such character strings are delimited (ended) by a blank space. Therefore, the string can be no longer than a single word. (When we discuss strings in chapter 8 we shall consider strings that include blank spaces.)

SETQ is used to bind atoms to values. The SETQ procedure was not available in older versions of Lisp. The procedure that was used was called SET. The form of its use was:

(set 'AAA 55)   (1-26)

The atom's name was preceded by an apostrophe. Statement (1-26) indicates that the atom whose name is (literally) AAA is to be bound to 55.

The SETQ procedure is included to eliminate the need for writing the apostrophe. If the apostrophe were omitted from (1-26) then the Lisp system would apply EVAL to AAA. This is not what is desired and the apostrophe is included to inhibit the evaluation of AAA.

It can be convenient to use SET in some circumstances. Suppose that AA is bound to an atom, for example (SETQ AA 'TEST), and we want to bind the atom to which AA is bound to 5. That is, we want to bind TEST to 5. Evaluation of the following expression will achieve the desired result:

(SET AA 5)   (1-27)

When (1-27) is evaluated, the system will automatically apply EVAL to AA, resulting in the value TEST. Hence, TEST will be bound to 5, as desired. Of course, the evaluation of (SETQ TEST 5) would accomplish the desired result directly. However, we shall see that there are circumstances where the value of the atom to which AA is bound is not known. In such cases an expression such as (1-27) should be used.

The use of the apostrophe is also a relatively new construction. It is an abbreviation for the Lisp procedure called QUOTE. For instance, 'AAA is equivalent to:

(QUOTE AAA)   (1-28)

The use of the QUOTE procedure can make some Lisp statements very long and hard to read. Lisp systems that do not let you use the apostrophe can be very tedious to use. Fortunately, almost all Lisp systems provide for the use of the apostrophe.

Some Lisp systems also include a procedure called SETF. This is a more general procedure than SETQ. However, at this stage we can use SETF and SETQ interchangeably. We shall discuss SETF subsequently.

1-5. An Introduction to Procedures and Functions

So far we have discussed some of the procedures that are supplied with your Lisp system. You can also write your own Lisp procedures. Actually most Lisp programs consist of a collection of such procedures. One of the advantages of the Lisp system is that it is *extensible*. That is, you can extend the system by adding your own procedures. Once these procedures are added to your Lisp system, you can use them just as you use the procedures that are supplied with your system.

In this section we shall discuss writing simple Lisp procedures. Later, additional ideas about procedures and techniques for writing more complex procedures will be discussed.

```
(DEFUN AVE-FOUR(A B C D)
   (/ (+ A B C D) 4.0)
)
```

Figure 1.1. A function that averages four numbers

The Lisp procedure named DEFUN is used to establish a procedure. For instance, suppose that we want to write a procedure that averages four numbers. That is, we want to add four numbers and then divide the resulting sum by four. Let us call the procedure AVE-FOUR. This procedure is illustrated in figure 1-1. To help explain this procedure let us write a Lisp expression that averages four numbers. The ideas used in writing this expression will then be incorporated into the procedure AVE-FOUR. Suppose that we wanted to average the numbers 100, 90, 95, and 97. The following would accomplish this:

$$/ (+ 100\ 90\ 95\ 97)\ 4) \tag{1-28}$$

Now consider figure 1.1. The first line consists of a left parenthesis followed by the atom DEFUN followed by the name of the procedure that we are writing. In this case it is AVE-FOUR. The procedure name is followed by a list enclosed in parentheses. The list contains atoms. Each atom in the list corresponds to a value that is to be supplied to the procedure. We say that the values are *passed* to the procedure. Because four numbers are to be averaged, then four values must be passed to the procedure and there are four atoms in the list. Note that the list of atoms enclosed in the parentheses *must* follow the procedure name. It is possible to write procedures that are designed to be passed no values. In such cases, the list is empty. That is, there simply will be a left parenthesis followed by a right parenthesis (). The list contained within the parentheses is called a *formal parameter list*.

The second line of the procedure of figure 1.1 consists of the operations described in (1-29). Note that the formal parameters are used in place of the specific numbers of (1-29). Actually each of the formal parameters can be considered to be an atom that has been bound to the appropriate value passed in the formal parameter list. These atoms *cannot* be used outside of the procedure. We shall discuss this in much greater detail in chapter 5.

The last line of the procedure consists of a right parenthesis. This corresponds to the left parentheses at the beginning of line one. Note the indentation. This is included to make the procedure readable to people. The Lisp interpreter ignores the indentation. When a very simple procedure is written, indentation may not seem too important. However, when complex procedures are written, then we shall see that proper indentation will make the program much more readable. Actually the entire procedure could be written on one line. Its form would be:

(DEFUN AVE-FOUR(A B C D) (/ (+ A B C D) 4.0))   (1-30)

Even in this simple case, it is obvious that the form of figure 1.1 is easier to read.

When a procedure is used, that procedure is said to be *called*. Let us see how the procedure AVE-FOUR would be used to average the numbers 90.0, 95.0, 91.0, and 100.0. You would simply enter:

(AVE-FOUR 90.0 95.0 91.0 100.0)   (1-31)

Note that the values passed to the procedure are not enclosed in parentheses when that procedure is called. After the user presses RETURN, the average 94.0 would be output. The procedure is said to have *returned* the value 94.0. Note that the values 90.0, 95.0, 91.0, and 100.0 correspond to A, B, C, and D, respectively, in the formal parameter list. That is, each value in the calling expression is passed to the corresponding formal parameter in the formal parameter list.

Either atoms or lists that evaluate to a number can be passed to AVE-FOUR. For instance, the following sequence is valid:

(SETQ TEST1 90.0)   (1-32a)
(AVE-FOUR 85.0 TEST1 (* 2 50) 100)   (1-32b)

The atom names in the formal parameter list were A, B, C, and D. This is a satisfactory choice for a simple procedure. However, when more complex procedures are written, the formal parameters should be given descriptive names.

AVE-FOUR is a special type of procedure called a *function*. A function is a procedure that simply returns a single value and has no other effect on the Lisp system. For instance SETQ is not a function because, in addition to returning a value, it has an effect on the Lisp system. Let us consider this. If we have,

(SETQ X 45)   (1-33)

the value 45 will be returned. In addition, an atom called X will be established and bound to the value 45. Because of these are additional effects, SETQ is not a function. These additional effects are called *side effects*.

When you write a procedure, it must become included as part of your Lisp system. This process is called *evaluation*. If the procedure is typed in response to the prompt, then the evaluation will take place after the last parenthesis is typed and RETURN is pressed. (Remember some Lisp systems do not require the RETURN.) If the procedure is short, then this type of operation is satisfactory. However, if the procedure consists of more than one or two lines, you should use an editor to enter it. The procedure can then be stored and modified if needed. Your Lisp manual will indicate techniques that will allow you to read in a procedure produced by the editor and then to evaluate that procedure. If the editor is one that is integrated into the Lisp system, this technique can be as simple as pressing a single key. In any case the procedure will be described in the manual that accompanies your Lisp system.

When a complex procedure is written, it is desirable to include *comments* that describe its operation. A comment is text that is ignored by the Lisp system, but is a part of the program that can be read by programmers. In Lisp the *comment character* is the semicolon (;). If a semicolon appears on a line, any text on that line following the semicolon will be ignored by the Lisp system. In figure 1.2 we have added comments to the program of figure 1.1. The comment on the first line describes the overall operation performed by the procedure. The comment on the second line describes the operation performed on that line. Remember that when the comment character (;) is included, any text beyond it to the end of that line is ignored by the Lisp interpreter.

```
(DEFUN AVE-FOUR(A B C D)    ; function averages four numbers
    (/ (+ A B C D) 4.0)    ;add four numbers and divide by four
)
```

Figure 1.2. Comments added to figure 1.1.

1-6. Programming Errors - A First Discussion

Almost all programs contain some errors when they are first written. The experienced programmer knows this and assumes that correcting errors, or *bugs* as they are commonly called, is a natural part of the programming process. Do not be discouraged if your programs contain bugs. We shall discuss debugging in detail subsequently. In this section we shall simply consider some simple debugging procedures.

One type of error is a mistake in *syntax*. In this case the rules of Lisp have not been followed. For instance, you may have written an atom that represents a list into an expression that expects a number. Syntax errors are usually caught by the interpreter and an error message will be output. You might have more than one error and there could be several error messages. Various Lisp systems have different procedures that can help you with debugging. Your Lisp manual will describe these procedures. At this time let us consider the simplest of debugging procedures. Reread your program carefully. The error message(s) will often give you an idea of where to look. It should be pointed out that the quality of error diagnostics will vary from system to system.

A program can be written with perfect syntax, but still have *logical* errors. In this case, the program does not generate any error messages and runs, but the answers are wrong. For instance, suppose that you type a minus sign instead of a plus sign. The program will be perfectly good Lisp but you will not calculate what you intended. Whenever you write a program, you must *always* check it by running several sets of test data for which you already know the correct answers. This should be done with *several* sets of data. This cannot be emphasized too strongly. *Always check your program.*

We shall discuss procedures for debugging logical errors in a later chapter. For the time being start by rereading your program carefully. If this does not uncover the error, then go through the calculations step-by-step just as the computer would. This often shows up logical errors because in doing so you may find that the program is not performing the calculations that you want it to.

Exercises

1. Describe the components of a computer.

2. What is the function of a interpreter?

3. What is the function of a compiler?

4. List all the valid Lisp characters.

5. List the special Lisp characters.

6. Use your Lisp system to average 6 numbers.

7. Use your Lisp system to obtain the value of factorial 6.

    6(5)(4)(3)(2)(1)

8. Bind an atom called FACT6 to the value of factorial 6.

9. Write a function that computes the sum of six numbers.

10. Write a function that computes the average of six numbers.

11. Write a function that computes the following mathematical expression:

$(a + b)(a - 2b)$

12. Write a function that computes the following mathematical expression:

$(a + b)(a-b)/(c +d)$

13. Write a function that computes the following mathematical expression:

$(a^2 + b^2)(c + d)$

14. Write a function that computes the square of a number. Use that function in another function that computes:

$(a^2 + b^2)/(c^2 + d^2)$

2

Some Preliminary Discussions

In this chapter we shall continue the discussion of arithmetic operations and discuss some simple ideas of input and output. The reader may question the discussions of arithmetic at the beginning of a book on Lisp which, after all was designed to process lists and which is being applied to artificial intelligence applications. At this point we could start with a discussion of list manipulation and the manipulation of symbols. We shall defer this discussion until chapter 3.

We begin with a discussion of arithmetic for several reasons: Because everyone is familiar with it, arithmetic provides a logical introduction to a programming language, especially for those people who do not know any other programming language. Programmers who have been programming in languages other than Lisp are probably familiar with arithmetic operations. They might want to "try out" some simple Lisp operations using familiar programs of their own. Thus, it makes sense to use arithmetic operations as an introduction to Lisp for experienced programmers. Finally, because many programs that are not arithmetic in nature often require some arithmetic calculations, it is desirable to discuss such calculations at an early stage of the book.

We shall also discuss some simple ideas of input and output in this chapter so that the programmer can write programs that do such things as place prompts on the screen and call for the reading of data.

2-1. Integer Arithmetic

Integers were introduced in sec. 1-3. We shall now extend the ideas discussed there. Some Lisp systems only perform integer arithmetic. As we discussed in sec. 1-3, the fractional parts of arithmetic operations are discarded when integer arithmetic is performed. This means that when we are dealing with integer division, unexpected results can be obtained. For example, consider the following:

$$(/\ 9\ 4) \tag{2-1a}$$

If this is an integer calculation then this expression will will yield the result 2, and the remainder of 1 will be lost. Note that:

$$9/4 = 2 + 1/4$$

In this case the quotient is 2 and the remainder is 1. In a similar way,

$$(/\ 3\ 4) \tag{2-1b}$$

will yield 0, because the remainder of 3 will be lost. Note that in some Lisp systems the function DIV, rather than 1, is used for integer division.

Lisp provides procedures that return the remainder of an integer division. One of these is called MOD. For instance, if we have,

$$(MOD\ 9\ 4) \tag{2-2}$$

the remainder, 1 in this case, will be returned. Thus, the quotient can be obtained using the / function and the remainder can be obtained using the MOD function.

When the dividend and/or the divisor are negative, the results of the / and MOD operations must be described in detail. In general, different Lisp systems may apply somewhat different rules here. The Common Lisp standard is the one which will be given here. The sign of the integer returned by MOD will be the same as the sign of the divisor. Let us consider the implications of this. If we have,

$$17/3 = 5 + 2/3 \tag{2-3a}$$

the quotient is five, and the remainder is two. Now suppose that we have:

$$17/(-3) = -6 + (-1)/(-3) \tag{2-3b}$$

The result of the corresponding MOD operation would be -1. Because we are using the rule that the sign of the remainder must be the same as that of the divisor, the quotient must be increased in magnitude from -5 to -6. Now consider:

$$(-17)/3 = -6 + 1/3 \qquad (2\text{-}3c)$$

The result of the MOD operation would be 1. Note that in (2-3a) the quotient appears to be -5 while in (2-3b) and (2-3c) it appears to be -6. Finally,

$$(-17)/(-3) = 5 + (-2)/(-3) \qquad (2\text{-}3d)$$

The result of the MOD operation would be -2. The manipulations of the previous examples can be used with any integers to determine the result of the MOD operation.

Next let us consider the result returned by the / procedure. Equations (2-3a) to (2-3d) indicate that the quotients will be 5, -6, -6, and 5 respectively. These values may or may not conform to the results returned by the / function. There is no Common Lisp standard for this operation with integers. Common Lisp has a standard which states: When two integers are divided, and there is a nonzero remainder, then the result returned will be a ratio. For instance,

$$(/ \ 17 \ 3) \qquad (2\text{-}4)$$

will return the ratio 17/3. Unfortunately most Lisp systems do not have a provision for working with ratios at the present time. If you are going to utilize the division of negative integers, you should study your Lisp system manual carefully, and do a number of sample problems. This should help you understand how your system works with division of negative integers.

There is another Common Lisp standard function called REM. This function will return the same result as MOD for positive numbers. For negative numbers however, the sign of the returned number will be the same as that of the dividend. Thus, the results for negative numbers may differ from those returned by MOD. For instance, if we recompute Eqs. (2-3) now using the fact that the sign of the remainder must be the same as the sign of the dividend, we obtain:

$$17/3 = 5 + 2/3 \qquad (2\text{-}5a)$$
$$17/(-3) = -5 + 2/(-3) \qquad (2\text{-}5b)$$

$$(-17)/3 = -5 + (-2)/3 \qquad (2\text{-}5c)$$
$$(-17)/(-3) = 5 + (-2)/(-3) \qquad (2\text{-}5d)$$

The results of the REM operation will be 2, 2, -2, and -2 respectively. Some Lisp systems provide other procedures for obtaining the quotient and remainder of integer division. In general, these procedures will all function in the same way when positive integers are divided. However, the results may be different for negative integers.

MAXIMUM MAGNITUDE OF INTEGERS

In many Lisp systems an integer is stored in a fixed number of memory bits. This limits the maximum allowable range for integers. For instance, if integers are stored in 16 bits then the integers can range between -32768 and 32767. The range of integers will vary from system to system. Your Lisp manual should indicate the maximum range for integers that you can use. Some Lisp systems do not fix the amount of memory that is used to store an integer. In those systems the maximum magnitude of integers is limited simply by the amount of available memory. Computer arithmetic operations take more time when the size of the integers is not fixed. The most versatile Lisp systems allow you to work with two classes of integers: those called FIXNUM having a fixed size and, consequently, a fixed range, and the class of those integers whose storage size is not fixed, called BIGNUM. The use of class FIXNUM will result in faster operation and use less memory, but there are occasions where the integers must be of class BIGNUM. In some Lisp systems operations integer operations will be of class FIXNUM, but will switch automatically to class BIGNUM when the integer size becomes too large. Consult your Lisp manual to determine what class of integers your system supports.

2-2. Floating-Point Operations

In sec. 1-3 we discussed the Lisp procedures +, -, *, and / that signify addition, subtraction, multiplication, and division, respectively. When floating-point numbers are involved the problems discussed in the last section in regard to integer division do not arise. Because floating-point numbers have a fractional part there are no "lost" remainders.

Floating-point numbers can have a very large range, but the number of significant figures is limited. Let us consider this. Suppose that the number of significant figures is limited to seven.

Some examples of floating point numbers with seven significant figures are:
    23.45678
    -123.4567
    9999999
    0.1234567

The limitation on the number of significant figures does not restrict the range of the figures with which you can work because most programming languages accommodate *exponential notation,* in which the numbers are multiplied by an integral power of 10. The letter E is commonly used to indicate that 10 is to be raised to the power that follows. For instance, 5.324567E8 represents 5.234567 times 10^8. Thus,

    5.234567E8 = 523456700.0   (2-6)

Similarly:

    E3 represents 1000
    E9 represents 1,000,000,000
    E-4 represents 0.0001

Note that very large, or very small, numbers can be represented in exponential notation without exceeding the limit on significant figures. The maximum magnitude of the exponent is limited. Typically, it can range between -38 and 38, although these numbers are system dependent and we shall see that Lisp systems often provide several allowable ranges. Check your Lisp System manual to determine the allowable range of exponents.

If the maximum range of exponents ranges from -38 to 38, exponential notation can be used to represent very large and very small numbers. However, it is conceivable that the result of a calculation could become too large to be represented, even by exponential notation. This is said to cause an *overflow.* If the number in question is so small that it cannot be represented using an exponent of -38, then an *underflow* is said to result. Overflows and underflows result in errors. Different Lisp systems will respond in different ways to such errors. Some Lisp systems will abort computation and output an error message. In other systems however, computation will proceed and wrong answers will be output, without warning. This is a dangerous situation. If the system does not warn about errors, then the programmer should include some error-checking provision in the program. This is not easy to do, although statements can be included in your programs that check for the size of numbers. We shall discuss such procedures in subsequent chapters. It would be preferable for the system to report on overflow and underflow errors. Note that although integer operations may also cause overflow and underflow, a Lisp system that automatically switches to type bignum will usually not encounter these problems.

Lisp provides for several types of floating-point numbers. They are called SHORT, SINGLE, DOUBLE, and LONG. Each type provides a different degree of *precision*, i. e., the number of significant figures, and each provides different allowable exponent range. In general, SHORT will have the fewest number of significant figures and the smallest range of allowable exponent values. On the other hand, LONG will have the greatest number of significant figures and the largest range of allowable exponent values. SINGLE and DOUBLE will provide precision and allowable ranges that lie between SHORT and LONG. Not every Lisp system provides all four types of floating-point numbers. The number of significant figures and allowable exponent values for each floating-point type will vary with the computer. On a small computer, SHORT may provide a precision of as few as four significant figures and an exponent range of -16 to + 16 while LONG might provide 64 significant figures and an exponent range of -308 to 308. On a large computer there could be greater precision and exponent range in corresponding types of floating-point numbers.

When a number is written, its type can be specified by replacing the E in the exponential notation by another letter. These letters are S, F, D, and L for SHORT, SINGLE, DOUBLE, and LONG respectively. For instance we could write,

    2.345L17

to specify type LONG. If the letter E is used for the exponent, the Lisp system will assume that it is one of S, F, D, or L. That is there is a default floating-point type that will be picked by the Lisp system if no specific type is specified.

If less than four floating-point types are supplied by a Lisp system then two, or more, names will be used for the same type. For instance, if there is only one type then, no matter whether S, F, L, or D is used to indicate the exponent, the effect will be the same. Check your Lisp Manual to see how many floating-point types are supported and to determine their precisions and allowable exponent ranges.

A COMPARISON OF OPERATIONS

In a computer, there are significant differences between integer and floating-point operations. In general, FIXNUM operations will require less memory and will be faster than floating-point operations. Similarly, the speed of floating-point operations will decrease and the memory requirements will increase as the precision of the floating point numbers is increased. Thus, the minimum precision consistent with the accuracy of the computation should be used for any particular job.

All floating-point calculations are subject to some small error. For instance, suppose that we divide 1 by 3. The answer is 0.3333333.... There should be an infinite number of 3's following the decimal point, but the computer can work with only a finite number of digits. Thus, the answer will slightly in error. This is called a *roundoff error*. Actually, all floating-point calculations, including addition and subtraction, can generate roundoff errors. The roundoff error produced by any one calculation is usually small enough to be ignored. However, because computer programs often involve very many calculations, the roundoff errors can accumulate, resulting in a significant total error. If the precision of the floating-point numbers were increased, by using type LONG for example, then the roundoff errors would be reduced. Thus, there is often a tradeoff between accuracy and speed of calculation.

Integer arithmetic is not subject to roundoff error. However, there are occasions when integers cannot be used. For instance, integers cannot be used to represent numbers with fractional parts. At times, integers can be used in what appear to be floating-point calculations. For instance, if your program deals with financial calculations, then there should be two significant figures following the decimal point. If all numbers were multiplied by 100, then they would become integers and integer arithmetic could be used. This type of operation in which floating-point numbers are all multiplied by a constant, so that they can be represented by integers, is called *scaling*.

2-3. Simplification of Complicated Expressions - Hierarchy

There are certain rules about the order in which ordinary algebraic operations are performed. These are so familiar that most people do not think about them. For instance, consider the algebraic equation:

$$x = a + b/c \qquad (2\text{-}7)$$

This states that x is computed by dividing b by c and then adding a to the resulting quotient. If we wanted to add a and b and *then* divide the resulting sum by c we would write:

$$x = (a+b)/c \qquad (2\text{-}8)$$

No parentheses were needed in the first case because there is a certain *hierarchy* or *precedence* that specifies the order in which the operations are performed. In ordinary algebra, the hierarchy rules state that multiplication or division is performed before addition or subtraction. Thus, in Eq. (2-7), the division is performed first. If we want to perform operations in an order that is different from those specified by the hierarchy rules we must use parentheses to group terms.

Most programming languages have rules of hierarchy. If you make a mistake in interpreting these rules then incorrect results will be obtained. Lisp does not have these problems. The use of lists, which are incidentally enclosed in parentheses, and the reverse Polish (prefix) notation provide an almost automatic implementation of hierarchy. For example, suppose that the following computation is to be performed:

$$[a + b/(c + d + e) + f][g - h(i+j)] \qquad (2\text{-}9)$$

An equivalent Lisp expression is:

$$(*(+ A (/ B (+ C D E)) F) (- G (* H (+ I J)))) \qquad (2\text{-}10)$$

The only hierarchy rule that we must use is that innermost lists are evaluated before the lists that enclose them. For instance, in (2-10) the order of evaluation is:

```
(+ C D E)
(/ B (+ C D E))
(+A (/B(+ C D E)) F)
(+ I J)                                              (2-11)
(* H (+ I J))
(- G (* H (+ I J)))
(* (+ A (/ B (+ C D E)) F) (- G (* H (+ I J))))
```

Expression (2-10) may appear to be confusing. However, if you remember that the evaluation starts with the innermost list and works outward, the expressions can be easily understood. Later in this section we shall discuss techniques that are used to make such expressions more readable.

As an example of the evaluation of a relatively complex expression, let us write a function that calculates the following equation:

$$f(x) = \frac{(x^3 - x^2)[2x + x^3(x + 3)]}{x + x^2(x - 1)} \qquad (2\text{-}12)$$

A Lisp function that evaluates f(x) is shown in Fig. 2-1. Actually, three functions are shown there. The first is called SQUARE and it returns the square of the value passed to it. Note that square simply causes X to be multiplied by X. The second function is called CUBE and returns the cube of X. We could have replaced the second line of this function with the Lisp expression:

$$(* X X X) \qquad (2\text{-}13)$$

Instead, we used the function SQUARE as a part of the function CUBE. That is, the cube of X is obtained by using the expression:

$$(* X (SQUARE X)) \qquad (2\text{-}14)$$

The function FOFX computes f(x). (*See* Eq. (2-12).) The / at the start of the second line of the function is equivalent to the fraction bar in (2-12). The numerator of eq. (2-12) is computed in the second line of the function FOFX and the denominator of eq. (2-12) is computed in the third line of the function. (Remember that a list can extend over more than one line.)

```
(DEFUN SQUARE(X)
    (* X X)
)

(DEFUN CUBE(X)
    (* X (SQUARE X))
)

(DEFUN FOFX(X)
    (/ (* (- (CUBE X) (SQUARE X)) (+ (* 2 X) (* (CUBE X) (+ X 3))))
       (+ X (* (SQUARE X) (- X 1))))
    )
)
```

Figure 2.1. The functions SQUARE, CUBE, and FOFX. FOFX is defined in eq. (2-12)

If the expression that is being computed is not simple, the Lisp expression that is used to evaluate it can become hard to read and, therefore, hard to understand. Such expressions are prone to errors. There are several techniques that can be used to make the expressions more readable. One is to write different parts of the expression on separate lines. This was done in figure 2.1 where the denominator was written on a separate line. Indentation can be a help here, because it helps the reader keep track of how the lists are nested within each other. For instance, the third line of the function FOFX is indented more than the second line and the closing parenthesis on the fourth line is at the same indention level as the parenthesis at the start of the second line.

```
(DEFUN N1(X)
    (- (CUBE X) (SQUARE X))

)


(DEFUN N2(X)
    (+ (* 2 X) (* (CUBE X) (+ X 3)))
)


(DEFUN D1(X)
    (+ X (* (SQUARE X) (- X 1)))
)

(DEFUN F1OFX(X)
    (/ (* (N1 X) (N2 X)) (D1 X))
)
```

Figure 2.2. The function N1, N2, D1, and F1OFX. F1OFX is a modification of FOFX (see figure 2.1) that uses functions N1, N2, and D1.

```
(DEFUN F2OFX(X)
    (SETQ A (- (CUBE X) (SQUARE X)))
    (SETQ B (+ (* 2 X) (* (CUBE X) (+ X 3))))
    (SETQ C (+ X (* (SQUARE X) (- X 1))))
    (/ (* A B) C)
)
```

Figure 2.3. The function F2OFX which is a modification of FOFX (see figure 2.1). Function F2OFX uses intermediate atoms.

Another technique that can be used to make Lisp procedures more readable is to write procedures in terms of simpler procedures. For instance in figure 2.1, we wrote the functions SQUARE and CUBE. Because these functions were available, FOFX was shorter and easier to read. Note that SQUARE and CUBE were also written to avoid repeating identical operations. In figure 2.2 we have extended this technique by writing three functions. Each function is used to compute one of the major factors of eq. (2-12). That is, function N1 returns the result of the computation of $(x^3 - x^2)$, function N2 returns the result of the computation $(2x + x^3 (x + 3))$, and function D1 returns the result of the calculation $(x + x^2 (x - 1))$. The final result is returned by the function F1OFX. Note that functions N1, N2, and D1 are each simple and readable. The technique of breaking a complicated procedure into simple subprocedures is often used in Lisp programming. It is relatively easy to write and debug simple procedures. Breaking a complicated procedure into simpler ones will often substantially reduce the time required to write complex programs. Note that subprocedures can themselves be broken into simpler procedures. This is illustrated in figure 2.2 where the functions N1, N2, and N3 make use of the functions SQUARE and CUBE.

Still another technique that can be used to make Lisp programs more understandable is to compute parts of the function separately and then bind a different atom to each part. This is illustrated in figure 2.3. The function F2OFX also computes f(x) as defined in eq. (2-12). Now the three atoms A, B, and C are each bound to one of the three major factors of eq. (2-12). That is atom A is bound to the result of the computation of $(x^3 - x^2)$, atom B is bound to the result of the computation $(2x + x^3 (x + 3))$, and atom C is bound to the result of the calculation $(x + x^2 (x - 1))$. Each of these bindings is on a separate line and is relatively easy to read. The final result is calculated in the fifth line of the function. When atoms are bound you should be careful that you are not inadvertently changing the value of a previously bound atom.

The techniques illustrated in figures 2.2 and 2.3 involve extra computer operations when the programs are run. For instance, in figure 2.2 there are additional functions that must be called while in figure 2.3 there are additional bindings of atoms. This requires additional memory to store the information about the functions and/or the atoms. In addition, the operation is also slowed by the time required for the retrieval of values to and from memory. If memory usage and speed are at a premium, then these techniques should be avoided. However, in most cases, the advantages gained by making the program more readable offset any of the disadvantages. An understandable program is much less prone to errors and much easier to debug if errors do occur. Remember that debugging time can represent a substantial amount of total programming time. The techniques that we have discussed to make the program more readable often do not increase execution time or memory usage substantially. Thus, the use of subprocedures and/or intermediate atoms should be used to make your program more understandable. In particular, subprocedures should be used to break your program into small, relatively simple tasks.

2-4. Primitive Procedures and Functions

In the last section we wrote procedures that were called by other user-written procedures. Lisp systems include many built-in procedures that can be used for a variety of applications. We have already considered some of these. For instance, DEFUN, SETQ, +, -, *, /, and MOD are some typical procedures that are supplied with most Lisp systems. Procedures that are provided by the Lisp system are called *primitive procedures* or simply *primitives*. In a similar way we can speak of *primitive functions*. Throughout this book we shall discuss many primitive procedures. In this section we shall discuss some of those that relate to numerical operations.

CONVERSION OF NUMBER TYPE

There are several primitive functions that convert between number types. For instance, FLOAT is used to convert an integer into a floating-point number. There are two forms of its use. For instance,

$$(FLOAT\ 15) \qquad (2\text{-}15)$$

returns 1.5F1, which is of type SINGLE. (In this case type SINGLE is designated by the F. Some Lisp systems will return 15.0 in this case. That is, the exponential notation will not be used unless it is necessary.) If a second number is passed to FLOAT, then the returned number will be of the same type as that second number. For instance,

$$(FLOAT\ 15\ 2L1) \qquad (2\text{-}16)$$

will return 1.5L1, because the second number is of type LONG (note the L). Note that only the type of the second number is considered; its size is of no consequence.

There are several primitive functions that can be used to convert floating-point numbers into integers. These functions not only convert a floating-point number into an integer, but they also can optionally perform division before performing the conversion. One of these functions is TRUNCATE. If TRUNCATE is used with a single argument then it returns an integer simply by discarding the fractional part of the number. (The values supplied to functions or procedures as formal parameters are called *arguments*.) For instance,

(TRUNCATE 6.7)   (2-17a)

will return the integer 6. In addition,

(TRUNCATE -6.7)   (2-17b)

will return the integer -6.

If two floating-point numbers are supplied as arguments to TRUNCATE then the first is *divided* by the second and then TRUNCATE is applied to the resulting floating-point quotient. For instance,

(TRUNCATE 5.6 2.0)   (2-18)

will return the result 2. Note that (2-18) is equivalent to:

(TRUNCATE (/ 5.6 2.0))   (2-19)

Another function that is used to convert from floating-point to integer type is ROUND. This function converts to the nearest integer using the usual rules of rounding. For example,

(ROUND 6.3)   (2-20a)
(ROUND 6.5)   (2-20b)
(ROUND -7.6)   (2-20c)
(ROUND -8.1)   (2-20d)

will return 6, 7, -8, and -8, respectively. ROUND also can be used with two arguments in the same manner as TRUNCATE is. For example, the following two expressions will return the same result:

(ROUND 5.6 3.1)   (2-21a)
(ROUND (/ 5.6 3.1))   (2-21b)

The function FLOOR is similar in its operation to TRUNCATE except that the returned number is the *largest* integer that is not *larger* than a single argument to FLOOR, or the result of the division of two arguments to FLOOR. For instance,

(FLOOR 6.7)	(2-22a)
(FLOOR 7.1)	(2-22b)
(FLOOR -3.6)	(2-22c)
(FLOOR -2.1)	(2-22d)

will return 6, 7, -4, and -3, respectively. (Remember that -3 is larger than -3.6.) Again, FLOOR can be used with two arguments and the following are equivalent:

(FLOOR 3.5 2.1)	(2-23a)
(FLOOR (/ 3.5 2.1))	(2-23b)

Finally the function CEILING is also similar to TRUNCATE except that the returned number is the *smallest* integer that is not *smaller* than a single argument to CEILING, or the result of the division of two arguments to CEILING. For instance,

(CEILING 6.7)	(2-24a)
(CEILING 7.1)	(2-24b)
(CEILING -3.6)	(2-24c)
(CEILING -2.1)	(2-24d)

will return 7, 8, -3, and -2 respectively. Again CEILING can be used with two arguments and the following are equivalent:

(CEILING 5.8 2.1)	(2-25a)
(CEILING (/ 5.8 2.1))	(2-25b)

The functions TRUNCATE, ROUND, FLOOR, and CEILING actually return two numbers. One is the number that we have discussed and the other is the remainder. For instance,

(TRUNCATE 5.2 2.0)	(2-26)

will return 2 and 1.2. Note that the first number returned will always be an integer. The type of the second number will be a floating-point number if either argument is a floating-point number. The precision of the floating-point number will be equal to the higher of the precisions of the arguments. Actually, the four functions that we are discussing can take floating-point, integer, or rational arguments. (A rational argument is in ratio form.) The type of the first returned number will always be an integer. If both arguments are integers then the second returned number (remainder) will be an integer. If both arguments are rational then the remainder will be rational. If a and b are the values of the first and second arguments and q and r are the returned numbers, where r represents the remainder, then the following equation will be satisfied:

$$a = QG +r \hspace{4cm} (2\text{-}27)$$

The second returned number is not available for most operations. For instance,

$$(+ 2 \text{ (TRUNCATE 6.3 2.0))} \hspace{3cm} (2\text{-}28)$$

will return 5. That is, the first returned number of the TRUNCATE operation is 3 and, therefore 3 is used as the value returned by the function. The second returned number is ignored. The second returned number will be output to the screen when the function is entered directly from the keyboard. That is if you type in (TRUNCATE 6.3 2.0) then both results (3 and 0.3) will be output to the screen.

There are four other functions FTRUNCATE, FROUND, FFLOOR, and FCEILING that are equivalent to TRUNCATE, ROUND, FLOOR, and CEILING, respectively. The only difference is that the (first) returned number will be a floating-point number.

MATHEMATICAL FUNCTIONS

There are Lisp primitives that perform many of the standard mathematical operations. For instance, EXP takes a single argument and returns e raised to that power. Note that e is the base of the natural logarithms. EXPT takes two arguments and returns the first argument raised to the power of the second argument. For instance,

$$(\text{EXPT 2.3 4.6}) \hspace{4cm} (2\text{-}29)$$

will return 46.1262 which is equal to $2.3^{4.6}$. There are other functions that compute logarithms and trigonometric functions. Consult your Lisp manual to determine all the mathematical functions that are supplied with your Lisp system.

Type Conversion

Sometimes it is desirable to make one type appear as another for the purpose of a particular computation. We shall discuss such applications in the next section. The primitive function COERCE can be used for this purpose. The form of its use is:

(COERCE 23 'LONG-FLOAT)   (2-30)

The value returned will be 23D0. The second argument is called the RESULT-TYPE. It specifies the type of the returned value. Note that the apostrophe precedes the RESULT-TYPE. Some typical result types that apply to numerical types are:

FLOAT
SINGLE-FLOAT
SHORT-FLOAT
DOUBLE-FLOAT
LONG-FLOAT
T

These names are largely self explanatory. The type T is called the identity type. It returns the same type as the type of the first argument. That is, no type conversion takes place when T is used as the RESULT-TYPE. Note that there is no RESULT-TYPE for integer. Use one of the previously discussed functions for that purpose. There are other types that we shall discuss throughout the book and COERCE can be used with many of them. Your Lisp manual will describe the RESULT-TYPEs that can be used with COERCE in your Lisp system.

2-5. Mixed-Mode Operations

An arithmetic operation involving numbers or variables of more than one type is termed a *mixed-mode operation*. Most Lisp systems will temporarily convert the numbers, or the values of the variables, in accordance with the following scheme. (In the following we shall use numbers to mean actual numbers or values of variables.) If all the numbers are integers, some being of type FIXNUM and others being of type BIGNUM, then all the numbers will be converted to type BIGNUM. If any of the numbers is a floating-point type then all the numbers will be converted to the highest precision floating point type that is present.

For instance consider:

(* 2 3.0F1 5.0L3)   (2-31)

This represents the product of an integer, a floating-point number of type SINGLE, and a floating-point number of type LONG. Thus, all the numbers will be converted to type LONG, because LONG is the highest precision of all the floating-point types that are present. The value returned as a result of (2-31) will be 3.0L5.

Some Lisp systems will perform an automatic conversion. For instance, suppose that the allowable range of FIXNUM is -32768 to 32767 and that the following is entered:

(+ 30000 3000)   (2-32)

If there is automatic conversion, the correct answer 33000 will be output as a BIGNUM. On the other hand, if there is no automatic conversion, then either an error message or an incorrect answer will be output. Automatic conversion can also occur with floating-point numbers. For instance, suppose that the exponent range for type SINGLE is -38 to +38, while that for type LONG is -308 to 308. Now consider the following:

(* 1.0F30 2.0F20)   (2-33)

If there is automatic conversion, then 2.0L50 will be output. If there is no automatic conversion, then either an error message or an incorrect answer will be output.

There are other conversions that are produced by some systems, but not by others. For instance consider:

(/ 5 4)   (2-34)

If this is an integer division, then the result 1 should be returned. Some Lisp systems will automatically convert this division to a floating-point operation and return 1.25.

The rules for mixed-mode operations may vary greatly from system to system. Your Lisp manual should indicate how your system performs mixed-mode calculations. It probably is best to perform a number of simple calculations of the type discussed here in order to determine how your system handles them.

2-6. Atoms, Variables, and Constants

In this section we shall briefly discuss some terminology. An atom can be either a *number* or a *symbol*. Numeric atoms represent numbers. For instance, as we have discussed, 55 represents the number 55 and not an atom named 55. An example of a symbolic atom is + or HOUSE. Numeric atoms can contain one of the letters E, S, F, D, or L, in the appropriate position, to represent exponential notation. We also have used atoms to store values. Such atoms are referred to as *variables*. For instance, consider:

    (SETQ RATE 5)   (2-35)

Here RATE is a symbolic atom that is bound to 5. Thus, RATE is a variable. It is also both an atom and a symbol. Note that many Lisp systems do not allow the names of symbolic atoms to start with a number.

Some Lisp systems are such that an atom can be the name of both a procedure and a variable. For instance, consider figure 2.4. There we have written a function called FOO that adds its two arguments. We have also bound FOO to 5. This means that a function and a variable each named FOO exist simultaneously. These are two completely different entities and the system will not confuse them. The Lisp system will know which is meant by how it is used in the Lisp expression. For instance, if you enter,

    (FOO 20 30)   (2-36)

the value 50 will be returned, because FOO was interpreted as a function. On the other hand if you simply type FOO followed by RETURN, 5 will be output, because FOO is interpreted as a variable. You can even use,

    (FOO 20 FOO)   (2-37)

and 25 will be returned. The Lisp system will consider that the first FOO is the function, while the second FOO is the variable. We have included this example only to show that the same name can be used for two different kinds of atom, without confusing the Lisp system. It certainly will confuse people, however. In general, do not use the same name for variables and procedures. Some Lisp systems will function in a different manner. In some systems if the operations of figure 2.4 are performed, the second FOO will hide the first one. In such systems, the operations of Fig. 2-4 would result in a variable called FOO. If you attempt to use FOO as a function an error would result. Again, you should generally not use the same name for a procedure and a variable. The discussions of the previous paragraphs are included to indicate a potential source of error.

```
(DEFUN FOO(A B)
    (+ A B)
)


(SETQ FOO 5)
```

Figure 2.4. An illustration of a function and a variable with the same name

CONSTANTS

There is a primitive function called DEFCONSTANT, which is similar to SETQ in its action. That is, it is used to bind an atom to a value. The binding can be changed subsequently. DEFCONSTANT is usually used only to bind atoms whose values will not be changed throughout the program. Such atoms are called *constants*. For instance, we could write:

(DEFCONSTANT PI 3.1415926)   (2-38)

Now PI could be used throughout the program in place of 3.1415926. Note that with some Lisp systems, a subsequent SETQ or DEFCONSTANT could be used to change the value of PI, so that it is not truly constant. In this case, the purpose of DEFCONSTANT is to indicate to all *people* who read the program that this value is intended to be a constant and should not be changed. *Remember that many Lisp systems will not protect constants from change.* If such changes are made inadvertently, erroneous result will be produced.

We shall subsequently discuss primitive functions that perform a test and return one of two values, true or false. A function called CONSTANTP tests to see if an atom represents a constant. Atoms bound using DEFCONSTANT will test as true if CONSTANTP is applied to them. Other entities also are considered to be constants in Common Lisp. For instance numbers, characters, and lists whose first atom is QUOTE are all considered to be constants. Your Lisp manual should list all the entities that are considered to be constants in your system.

2-7. Simple Reading and Printing of Data and Text

Data is passed to a procedure in a list. That is, a list consisting of the name of the procedure followed by the parameters is entered. This technique is satisfactory for programmers to use. However, when programs are designed to be run by people who have no programming experience, the user should be prompted to enter the required data from the keyboard, and the results should be output with suitable explanatory statements.

When a procedure is executed, the Lisp system will output the returned value. However, a program may consist of one procedure that calls other procedures. Only the *last* returned result will be output by the Lisp system. If a program is to compute many results, provision must be made to display those results on the screen. In this section we shall discuss procedures that are used to output text and data. In addition, we shall discuss a procedure that will allow a person running a program to enter data from the keyboard.

The procedure PRINT will output data to the screen. For instance if, after the atom X has been bound to 5, you enter,

(PRINT X)   (2-39)

the output that will appear on the screen is,

5
5

That is, when PRINT is passed a variable, the current value of that variable will be output. Notice that the value is output twice. This is because the procedure PRINT both produces the printed output *and* returns the value that it has output, which is then output by the Lisp system.

PRINT can be used to output text. A collection of characters is called a *string*. In Lisp a string is enclosed within double quotation marks. For instance,

"The book is on the table"

is a string. If PRINT is passed a string, that string will be output. For instance, if you enter,

(PRINT "The book is on the table")   (2-40)

the output will be:

"The book is on the table"
"The book is on the table"

Note that the quotation marks are themselves output and that the string is output twice. The first output is a result of the action of the procedure PRINT. The second output occurs because PRINT returns its evaluated input and then the system outputs it. Note that the string is interpreted literally and output just as is.

The printing of the quotation marks around strings is often not desirable. For instance, if your program outputs text, you probably would not want it embedded within quotation marks. We shall discuss a method for eliminating the quotation marks later in the section.

Actually, Lisp has a number of special characters and these will be output exactly as they are written when PRINT is used. We shall discuss these special characters in a subsequent chapter. The reason that PRINT is constructed in this way is so that its output can be used as input to the Lisp system. In particular, if PRINT is passed a list, that list will be evaluated prior to its being printed. System commands can be included in that list. The result, not the list, will occur just as if it were input from the keyboard. For example,

        (PRINT (* 2 3))   (2-41)

will result in the output:

        6
        6

Again, the first 6 is due to the *action* of the PRINT procedure, while the second 6 is due to the fact that the list (* 2 3) has been evaluated and then *returned* by the PRINT procedure. (Note that we have not included any special characters here.) If you want to output an unevaluated list then precede it with an apostrophe. This will inhibit evaluation. Thus,

        (PRINT '(* 2 3))   (2-42)

will result in the output:

        (* 2 3)
        (* 2 3)

PRINT precedes all its output by a newline character, so that data that is actually output on the screen will be on a new line. In many systems, a newline consists of a carriage return followed by a line feed. The output of PRINT is followed by a blank space.

There is another procedure named PRIN1, that operates in essentially the same way as does PRINT except that the output is not preceded by a newline nor is it followed by a blank space.

The procedure PPRINT is similar in its action to print. It is used to format printed special text, such as Lisp programs, in order to make them more readable. PPRINT does not return the value of its evaluated input, instead it returns the value NIL. For instance if, in the previous examples, PPRINT had been used in place of PRINT the second output would have been NIL. Note that NIL is a Lisp constant. It represents an empty list, that is a list with nothing in it. NIL also represents the logical value false. We shall discuss this further in a subsequent chapter.

The procedures that we have discussed thus far in this section are not ideal for providing output to users of the program. For instance, the double quotation marks that enclose quotes are output. As previously noted PRINT outputs data in a form that can be read by the Lisp system. The procedure PRINC outputs data in a form that is more appropriate for people to read. For example,

(PRINC "The book is on the table")   (2-43)

will result in the output:

The book is on the table
"The book is on the table"

The first output, due to the action of PRINC is not enclosed in quotes. The second output is the value returned by PRINC which is then output by the system. The appearance of the two outputs on the screen is not as cumbersome as it may seem. This is because Lisp programs usually consist of procedures that in turn, call other procedures. The Lisp system will output only the value returned by the outermost procedure.

Another primitive that is useful in the output of data is TERPRI. Its action is to generate a newline character. This is used to space the output appropriately. TERPRI returns NIL.

```
(DEFUN AVE-FOUR(A B C D)
    (TERPRI)
    (PRINC "The average of the four grades is ")
    (PRINC (/ (+ A B C D) 4.0))
    (PRINC " ")
)
```

Figure 2.5. A procedure that averages four numbers

To illustrate the ideas that we have discussed in this section, we have rewritten AVE-FOUR of figure 1.2 so that it now outputs explanatory text (*see* figure 2.5.) Let us consider this procedure. The TERPRI causes any subsequent output to start on a new line. Then the first PRINC expression causes,

The average of four grades is

to be output. Note that the last character output is a blank space (*see* figure 2.5.) The next PRINC expression causes the evaluation of:

(/ (+ A B C D) 4.0)

and the output of the result. Note that PRINC does not generate any newlines so that the answer will be output on the same line as the text. The procedure could terminate at this point, but then the value returned by the second PRINC would be output. This would result in the average being output again. To avoid this, we have added the last PRINC. This causes a blank space to follow the output. The value returned by the last PRINC statement, a blank space enclosed in quotes, will be output by the system. For instance, if the input is,

(AVE-FOUR 100 90 90 100)

the output will be:

The average of four grades is 95.0

Many programs are designed to be run by people who have no programming experience. In such cases it would be desirable to have the program output text that prompts the user for appropriate input. The person running the program could then type in the necessary data. The READ procedure is used to accept this type of input. As an example of its use, consider:

(+ 2 (READ) 3)   (2-44)

When this expression is executed, the system will pause when the READ is encountered and wait for input from the keyboard. A number should be entered followed by a RETURN. The entered number takes the place of the (READ) in (2-44). For instance if the user types 5, followed by a RETURN, it will be as though,

(+ 2 5 3)

had been entered. In figure 2.6 we have rewritten the program of figure 2.5 using the READ procedure. The new procedure is called AVERAGE-FOUR. Now the program prompts for the data to be entered from the keyboard. The first PRINC procedure causes the prompt,

Enter four grades

to be output. The TERPRI procedure is included so that the data entered by the person running the program appears on a new line. The READ procedure is called four times. The person running the program enters four numbers, each terminated by a RETURN. The value of AVERAGE is then computed. The next two PRINC procedures cause the average to be printed with the appropriate text.

```
(DEFUN AVERAGE-FOUR()
   (TERPRI)
   (PRINC "Enter four grades")
   (TERPRI)
   (SETQ AVERAGE (/ (+ (READ) (READ) (READ) (READ)) 4.0))
   (TERPRI)
   (PRINC "The average of four grades is ")
   (PRINC AVERAGE)
   (TERPRI)
   '(PROGRAM OVER)
)
```

Figure 2.6. A procedure that calls for data to be entered from the keyboard

The last line of the program consists of:

'(PROGRAM OVER)   (2-45)

The apostrophe (single quote) causes this to be interpreted literally. Because this is the last line of the procedure, its value is returned by the procedure, thus this literal list is output. The text that appears on the screen during a typical run of AVERAGE-FOUR is shown below:

```
(AVERAGE-FOUR)
Enter four grades
100 90 90 100
The average of four grades is 95.0

(PROGRAM OVER)
```

Note that the first line and the third line, containing the four grades, is typed by the person running the program. All other output is the result of the evaluation of the procedure AVERAGE-FOUR.

2-8. Formatted Output

Output text can be formatted in a variety of ways using the FORMAT primitive of Common Lisp. FORMAT allows data to be easily intermixed with text and, in addition, the form of the data can be specified. The FORMAT procedure is supplied with a string of text to be output. Special character sequences called *format directives* can be embedded within the text of that string. The format directives control the appearance of the output. Let us illustrate the use of the FORMAT procedure. Consider the following:

```
(SETQ X 3)
(SETQ Y 7)
(FORMAT "First is ~D second is ~D" X Y)
```

This sequence will result in the output:

"First is 3 second is 7"

Notice the quotation marks in the output. Let us consider how the FORMAT procedure is used. The atom FORMAT is followed by the letter T (indicating terminal) and a string enclosed in double quotation marks. This is followed by a sequence of values, variables, or expressions that evaluate to values, X and

Y in the example. These are called the *arguments of the format directives*, and there must be a format directive for each argument. A format directive always starts with the *tilde* character (~) and is followed by one or more characters. The format directive ~D stands for decimal. The FORMAT procedure will print the text within the quotation marks. When a format directive is encountered the output will use the argument of that format directive and output the value of the argument. The first format directive corresponds to the first argument, the second format directive corresponds to the second argument, etc. We shall see that there are some particular format directives that do not use arguments. These directives are ignored when relating the format directives to the arguments. Some of these format directives will be discussed later in this section. The atom T following FORMAT refers to the terminal. It shall be discussed in sec. 9-5. Just include it when FORMAT is used.

Table 2.1. Some common format directives.

Some Format Directives
~A Argument printed as though PRINC were used
~S Argument printed as though PRIN1 were used
~D Argument, which must be an integer, printed in decimal
~B Argument, which must be an integer, printed in binary
~O Argument, which must be an integer, printed in octal
~X Argument, which must be an integer, printed in hexadecimal
~F Argument, which must be a floating-point number, printed as floating point number
~E Argument, which must be a floating-point number, printed using exponential notation
~G Argument, which must be a floating-point number, printed using appropriate notation
~C Character output
~% Newline
~& Freshline - Newline unless at beginning of line
~~ Tilde

The arguments for the ~A and ~S format directives must be strings or variables storing strings. As we have seen, the ~D format directive causes integers to be output in the usual way. The ~B, ~O, and ~X format directives are similar to ~D except that the integer is converted into binary, octal, or hexadecimal respectively. If you do not know the binary, octal, or hexadecimal number systems, then ignore these three format directives.

Other optional specifications may be included in the format directives. Let us consider some of them. It is often desirable, especially when tabular data is to be printed, for all numerical data to be printed within a specified field, that is, a particular number of spaces. For instance, it might be desirable for all the rightmost digits in a column to be aligned when a column is printed. The *field width* can be specified as part of the format directive. Let us start by considering the ~D format directive. The field width can be specified by including an integer before the D. For instance,

~7D   (2-46)

will specify a field width of seven spaces for a decimal integer. For instance, if the integer to be output were 346, then the output would appear as,

bbbb346

where the bbbb represents four blank spaces. The number is said to be *padded* with blanks and the blank spaces are said to be *pad characters*. The 7 in (2-46) can be changed to specify a different field width. It is possible that the specified field width is not wide enough for the integer to be printed. For instance, 2345 will not fit into a field that is three characters wide. In this case, the field width will be increased automatically. The default pad character is a blank. A different pad character can be specified by indicating it after the field width. The form of the format directive is,

~w,padcharD   (2-47)

where w is an integer specifying the field width, and padchar is a character that will be used as the pad character. Note the comma in (2-47). It is used to separate the specifications.

There are other specifications that can be included with the ~D format directive. Consult your Lisp manual to determine which ones are applicable to your system. The discussions of the specifications that can be used with the ~D format directive also are applicable to the ~B, ~O, and ~X format directives.

The ~F, ~E and ~G format directives relate to floating-point numbers. They can also be used in conjunction with other optional specifications. The ~F format directive is used to prevent the output from being displayed in exponential form.

For instance, a typical use of the ~F format specifier is:

~7,3F

This indicates that the floating-point number is to be printed in a field of seven spaces and there are to be three digits following the decimal point. The first number, 7 in this case, specifies the field width and the second number, 3 in this case, specifies the number of digits that follow the decimal point. Note that a number such as -121.325 occupies a field of eight spaces. The decimal point and the minus sign each occupy one space. The output number will be rounded so that only the specified number of decimal digits are printed. The stored value of the number will be unchanged by this process. If the field is not wide enough to print the number, then it will be expanded automatically to accommodate it. If the field is wider than than the number of columns required to display the number, then blank spaces will be added to the left of the number as pad characters. In general we can write:

~w,dF   (2-48)

where w is to be an integer that represents the field width and d is an integer that represents the number of decimal digits. Remember that the inclusion of values for w and d is optional. If these parameters are omitted, then the field will be chosen exactly wide enough to output the number with all of the decimal digits that it contains.

There are two other optional field specifiers. Their general form is:

~w,d,overchar,padchar   (2-49)

Padchar plays the same role that it does in the ~D format directive. If padchar is omitted, the pad character defaults to a blank space. If overchar, which should be a character, is included then if the field width is too small it will *not* be expanded. In fact, no number will be output; instead the field will be filled with the specified overchar. For instance, if the overchar is an asterisk and the field width is 7, then seven asterisks will be output if the number is eight or more characters in length.

The ~E specifier is used when floating point numbers are to be output using exponential notation. The general form of its use is:

~w,d,e,k,overchar,Padchar,expcharE   (2-50)

Each of the w, d, e, and k are optional but, if present, each should be an integer. Each of the overchar, padchar, and expchar also is optional but, if present, should be a character. The k is called a scale factor. For most applications it should be omitted, or be set to 0. When either is done, the field will be w characters wide; there will be a single digit followed by a decimal point and d digits; these will be followed by the single expchar and the numerical exponent. If, for the exponent letter, you want to use a character other than the standard ones (S, F, D, or L), then specify an expchar. Remember that the field must provide room for a leading minus sign, to allow for negative numbers, for a minus sign in the exponent, to allow for negative exponents and for the exponent character. The overchar and padchar play the same role as they do for integer output.

If an optional specification is omitted from the list of specifications, then its default value will be used. When a value is omitted, the separating commas should be written adjacent to each other. That is, no commas may be omitted from the specifications. The only exception to this is that a sequence of adjacent commas at the end of the list can be omitted. For instance, ~15,3,,,,,E can be written as ~15,3E.

We shall discuss how characters can be used as data in a subsequent chapter. The ~C format directive is used to output such data.

The ~G specifier acts as a ~F specifier if the number can be output without using exponential notation. If exponential notation is required then the ~G specifier acts as a ~E specifier.

The ~% format directive incorporates a newline character into the string. For instance,

(FORMAT T "First = ~E~%Second = ~D" 3.2E5 26)   (2-51)

will result in the output:

"First = 3.2E5
Second = 26"

The ~& format directive functions in a manner that is similar to that of the ~% directive except that a newline will not occur if the system can detect that the output will be at the start of a new line in any event. For instance, a ~& immediately following a ~% will be ignored. The ~& format directive is called a *freshline*. The ~& is a conditional directive. It generates a newline only when the particular data being output has not just produced a newline.

If you want to incorporate a tilde into your text, then enter two tildes in the string with no space between them (~~). This signifies that the tilde is not being used used to start a format directive.

There are other format directives specified in the Common Lisp standards. Study your Lisp system manual to determine which are applicable for your system. Not all Lisp systems will implement the format directives exactly as specified in the standards. Some Lisp systems do not incorporate them at all.

Exercises

Check any procedures that you write by running them on your computer.

1. Write a function that evaluates the following expression

$$x = [a^3 - 2bc^2 + (a - 2b^2)(c - 4)]/(c + d)$$

If the following integer values are passed to the function,

a=24   c=11
b=14   d=9

the result is 393. Use these values to check your function.

2. Discuss the difference between the MOD and REM functions.

3. Write two functions, one that returns the result of integer division and one that returns the remainder of that division.

4. Check your Lisp system to determine how the / function operates on integers some of which may be negative.

5. What will be the result of the following operation?

(* (/ 4 5) (REM 4 5) (MOD 4 5))

6. Determine the maximum range of FIXNUM on your system.

7. Repeat exercise 6 for BIGNUM.

8. Determine the precision and allowable exponent range for all floating-point types on your system.

9. Write a procedure that, when passed two integers, outputs their quotient and remainder to the screen. Suitable explanatory text should also be output. Do not use FORMAT.

10. Repeat exercise 9 but now have the data input from the keyboard. There should be suitable prompts.

11. Write a procedure that is passed an integer representing seconds, and outputs the corresponding time in hours, minutes, and seconds.

12. Repeat exercise 11, but now have the data entered from the keyboard. There should be suitable prompts and labels on the output.

13. Repeat exercise 9 but now use the FORMAT procedure to output data and text.

14. Repeat exercise 12 but now use the FORMAT procedure to output data and text.

15. Write a procedure that averages seven floating point numbers, ranging between 0.0 and 100.0, that are passed to the procedure. The average should be output in a field that will accommodate three digits after the decimal point.

16. Repeat exercise 15 but now use the exponential form of output.

3

Lists

We shall now discuss lists in a more formal way. Lisp has many procedures designed specifically to manipulate lists and we shall consider some of them in this chapter. In order to fully understand these operations we shall discuss how the Lisp system stores lists. This will provide the basis for our study of more complex Lisp operations.

3-1. Lists and s-expressions

We have discussed the some of ideas relating to lists and Lisp expressions already. Let us now extend some of these ideas. A list is a collection of elements. For instance, the list,

(A B C D)   (3-1)

consists of the elements A, B, C, and D. Of course A, B, C, and D are also atoms. Thus, all the elements of the list of (3-1) are atoms. Now consider the list:

(BOOK (THE TABLE) ON OFF)   (3-2)

This is a list that has four elements: BOOK, (THE TABLE), ON, and OFF. Three of the elements are atoms and the fourth is a list. An element of a list must be either an atom or another list. The elements of a list all are at the same *level*. For instance, BOOK, ON, OFF, and the list (THE TABLE) are not embedded in any other lists, thus they are elements of the list of (3-2). They are said to be at the top-level of the list. On the other hand, THE and TABLE are embedded in the list (THE TABLE) which is an element of the list of (3-2). Thus, THE and TABLE are one level down from the top level and are elements of the list (THE TABLE). THE and TABLE are said to be at the second level of the list of (3-2).

Let us consider another example:

$$(SETQ \ X \ '(+ 3 \ 4 \ (* \ 5 \ (+ \ 6 \ 7)))) \tag{3-3}$$

After this expression is evaluated, X will represent a list with four elements. (Note the single quote.) They are +, 3, 4, and (* 5(+ 6 7)). At the second level, the elements of the embedded list are: *, 5, and (+ 6 7). Finally, at the third (lowest) level there is a list containing three elements which are +, 6, and 7.

The number of elements in a list can be determined using the primitive LENGTH. For instance, if X is bound using (3-3),

(LENGTH X)

will return 4.

Valid Lisp expressions are called *s-expressions*. The s stands for symbolic. Sometimes, they are called Lisp expressions. For instance, (3-3) is an s-expression. The name s-expression emphasizes the symbolic nature of Lisp. An atom is an s-expression also. Note that any valid Lisp expression is an s-expression.

Thus far, we have not concerned ourselves with the actual details of how data is stored in a computer. However, a superficial knowledge of this topic will increase our understanding of Lisp.

The memory of a computer can be considered to be a large collection of bits. Each bit can store only one of the binary digits, 0 or 1. (Normally seven or eight bits are used to store a single character.) Consecutive groups of bits are combined to form a *memory word*, or simply a *word*. For example, a group of eight bits could be a word. Each word has an *address*, which is a number that represents its location in memory. Addresses are numbered in sequence. Thus, address 0 would refer to the first word in memory, address 1 would refer to the second word in memory, and so forth. The central processor can direct operations so that the data stored in a word can be read or can be written. The only way that the central processor can identify a word is by its address. When a word is written the old data that was stored previously is lost. Note that many computers often use words that are longer than 8 bits. However, we shall use eight bits, because it will simplify the discussion. The ideas are similar if more than eight bits are used.

Most programming languages maintain a table called a *symbol table*. For instance, suppose that you enter

(SETQ X 4)   (3-4a)

The name X would be stored in the symbol table along with the address where the data would be stored. In other words there is a certain memory location (address) where the value of X is stored. The programmer does not have to keep track of the address; all that has to be remembered is the name given to the variable, in this case X. The interpreter or compiler will refer to the symbol table to find the address. We have oversimplified somewhat. Usually numbers are stored in more than one address. For instance, if memory uses eight-bit words, then two consecutive words will probably be used to store a FIXNUM. A floating-point number of type LONG might be stored in four words. The interpreter (or compiler) keeps track of the number of words used by various data types. The address of a variable is the address of the first word used to store that variable. The symbol table stores this address which is called a *pointer* to the variable. Variables can also store lists and other types of data that we shall discuss. The length of the stored data for each variable must be known to the system.

In most programming languages, other than Lisp, you must declare the type of data that each variable represents. For instance, prior to entering (3-4a) you would have had to declare that X was of type integer (in a language other than Lisp). In those programming languages, if the following was entered subsequently,

(SETQ X 3.2L3)   (3-4b)

an error would result, because this would represent an attempt to bind a variable, that was declared to represent an integer, to a floating-point number. However no error would result with Lisp. If (3-4b) were entered after (3-4a), X would automatically be changed from a variable representing an integer to a variable representing a floating-point number.

This discussion has been oversimplified. We shall discuss these ideas in greater detail later in this chapter. (Note that we have used the syntax of Lisp here to describe other programming languages.)

Let us consider the SETQ procedure. It causes an atom (variable) to be bound to a value. (Note that the value can be a number, a list, or other data types that we will discuss.) When an atom is bound, its name is stored by the Lisp system in a symbol table. Every time that SETQ is evaluated, using a new variable name, a new entry is made in the symbol table for the name of the atom (variable). Now let us consider what occurs when the data for an existing variable is changed. Remember that the type of data that is stored can be changed. Thus, the amount of memory required for data storage can change also.

Suppose that an atom named X is bound using (3-4a) and subsequently an atom, also named X, is bound using (3-4b). The data for the new X may be stored in new memory locations. The pointer to the data will be changed in the symbol table. When you want to use the variable X at a later time, the Lisp system searches the symbol table for the name X. The value of the new pointer will be the one that is used. Thus, for the example we are considering the value of X will be 3.2L3 and the old value of X will be lost. Note that even if the pointer was not changed the old value would be lost since the old data would be written over by the new data. The functioning of SETQ is different than the assignment statements of other programming languages, as far as the Lisp system is concerned. However, in most applications the programmer can use SETQ just as an assignment statement would be used in another programming language. We shall expand upon these comments throughout the chapter.

In many programming languages other than Lisp, the amount of memory required for a string would have to be specified before that string could be stored. This means that it would not be possible to add data to that string (i. e., make it longer) once it was set up. This is not the case in Lisp. The size of lists can be increased without limit; at least until all the available memory of your computer has been used. Moreover, data can be inserted into the "middle" of a list. One of Lisp's great advantages is the freedom to modify data in ways such as these. (Some other programming languages have some of Lisp's freedom.) This great freedom does provide many advantages as we shall see throughout this book. This freedom is, in part, responsible for Lisp's great power.

It should be noted that many modern programming languages have been constructed so as to deliberately restrict some of this kind of freedom. One drawback of having such freedom in a programming language is that certain errors will not be detected by the system, resulting in programs with bugs that are hard to find. For instance, consider (3-4a) and (3-4b). It is possible for the programmer to become confused as to whether X stores an integer or a floating-point number. This can lead to logical bugs, wherein the program outputs incorrect data. Such bugs are often extremely hard to find. Strongly-typed languages, where the data type must be specified, restrict the programmer's freedom to some extent, but they will detect errors of the type discussed and they often result in almost error free programming. In the interest of reducing the number of bugs and making these errors easier to correct, some of the Common Lisp standards tend to restrict Lisp slightly.

Now let us consider the mechanism that Lisp uses to store lists. If all lists were of fixed length and were never modified, then only the starting address of each list would have to be stored in a symbol table. When you wanted to "read" the list, its name would be supplied to the system, its address would be located in the symbol table, and the required data would be read. This procedure has the advantage of being both fast and simple.

However, it is not versatile enough for Lisp, which permits the programmer a great deal of freedom to manipulate data. Therefore, Lisp uses an indirect procedure. Each element of a list is represented by two memory locations. These are both stored by the system. This pair of memory locations is called a *cons* cell. Each cons cell stores exactly two addresses. The first address is the address at which the element is stored and the second address is the address of the next cons cell. The first address is called the *car* and the second address is called the *cdr*. Let us clarify this. When a memory location, or set of memory locations, stores an address, then the memory location is said to *point* to that address. For instance, if memory location number 3 stores a 7 and memory location number 7 stores the value of the variable X, then memory location number 3 is said to point to memory location 7, or to point to X.

An example is in order here. Suppose that we have the list:

(THE SKY IS BLUE)   (3-5)

This list is composed of four elements, each of which is an atom. Since there are four elements, there will be four cons cells. Remember that each cons cell stores two addresses. The first address (car) of the first cons cell is the address where the atom THE is stored; the second address (cdr) of the first cons cell is the address of the second cons cell. That is, the car of the first cons cell points to THE and the cdr of the first cons cell points to the second cons cell. The car of the second cons cell is the address of the atom BOOK and the cdr of the second cons cell is the address of the third cons cell. This is repeated with each cons cell.

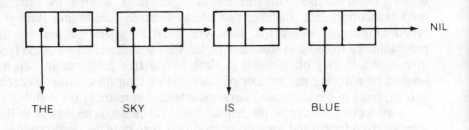

Figure 3.1. An illustration of the cons cell diagram for the list (THE SKY IS BLUE). The dots represent memory addresses.

The second address of the last cons cell points to NIL. NIL represents an empty list and is a recognized address in the Lisp system. This is important, *if the second address of the last cons cell does not point to NIL then the structure does not represent a true list.* There are structures, that will be considered subsequently, where the cdr of the last cons cell does not point to NIL but these structures are not true lists. A diagram, called a *cons cell diagram*, can clarify this discussion. In figure 3.1 we have illustrated the cons cells for the list (3-5). Note that the car of each cons cell points at an element while the cdr of each cons cell but the last points at the next cons cell. The cdr of the last cons cell points at NIL.

Let us consider a more complex example. Suppose that one of the elements of the list is itself a list. For instance, once the expression,

(SETQ ALIST '(THE BOOK (AND PENCIL) ARE BLUE))   (3-6)

is evaluated, the list ALIST will have five elements, one of which is another list.

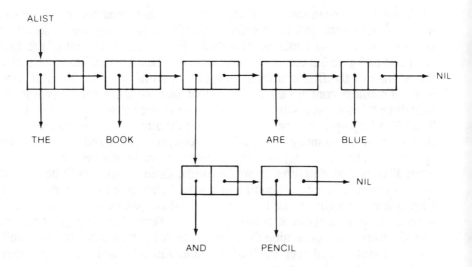

Figure 3.2. The cons cell diagram for ALIST. The list is (THE BOOK (AND PENCIL) ARE BLUE). This list contains four atoms and a list.

The diagrammatic representation of the cons cells for this list is shown in figure 3.2. Note that we indicate the name of the list at the top of the diagram. This indicates that the Lisp system stores the address of the first cons cell under the name ALIST. The car of the first cons cell points at THE and its cdr points at the next cons cell. The car of the second cons cell points at BOOK and its cdr points at the next cons cell. The next element in the list ALIST is itself a list, (AND PENCIL). The car of the third cons cell points not at an atom, but at another cons cell. (The car of the third cons cell points at the third element which is a list.) The car of the first cons cell in this sublist points at AND its cdr points at the second cons cell for the sublist. The car of this second cons cell points at PENCIL and its cdr points at NIL. Remember that the cdr of the last cons cell of *any* true list must point at NIL. Note that the third cons cell of the first row of figure 3.2 points, not at an atom, but at another cons cell, indicating that the next element of the list is itself a list. The cdr of this third cons cell points at the cons cell for the next element in the list. The car of this next cons cell points at ARE and its cdr points at the last cons cell, see figure 3.2. The car of the last cons cell points at BLUE and its cdr points at NIL. Note that each cons cell in the top row of figure 3.2 points to an element (top-level member) of the list. One of these elements happens to be another list. We could continue this type of construction, with lists embedded within other lists.

There are some mechanics of the operation which need not be considered in detail, but which will be mentioned briefly to provide some background information. The car contains an address. For example, the car of the first cons cell of figure 3.2 contains the address of THE. That address is actually the address of the first word that stores any part of the atom THE. If each word of memory contains eight bits, so that each word can store a character, then three memory words are needed to store the three characters that make up THE. The Lisp system must know how long the atom is in order to read all of it. Note that all memory looks alike, a sequence of 0's and 1's. Thus, the system must know exactly how much data to read. In this case, because the atom THE is stored in three memory words, three words should be read. If the atom were a variable, then that fact would also have to be known by the Lisp system. In addition, the Lisp system must keep track of whether the car is pointing at an atom or at another cons cell. Thus, there is a great deal of stored information concerning the address pointed at by the car of a cons cell. The Lisp system will keep track of this automatically, and the programmer need not be concerned with it.

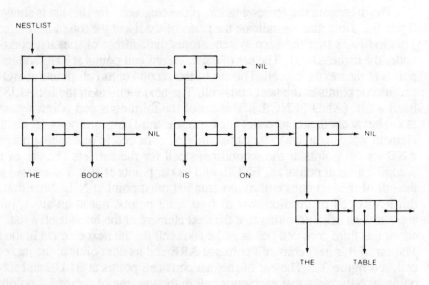

Figure 3.3. A cons cell diagram for the list NESTLIST which is ((THE BOOK (IS ON (THE TABLE)))

Let us consider an example of the cons cells for the list established when the following expression is evaluated,

(SETQ NESTLIST '((THE BOOK) (IS ON (THE TABLE))))   (3-7)

The list NESTLIST contains two elements, each of which is a list. They are (THE BOOK) and (IS ON (THE TABLE)). The second list has three elements, one of which is a list. The cons cell diagram for NESTLIST is shown in figure 3.3. We have drawn the diagram so that each row corresponds to a level of NESTLIST. The top level has two cons cells, corresponding to each of the two elements in the list. The technique of drawing a cons cell diagram so that each row corresponds to a level of the original list helps to illustrate the list structure. When the diagram is complex however, there may not be enough room to do this. Note that cons cell diagrams are not usually drawn in the course of Lisp programming. However, they help us to understand the underlying structure of Lisp.

3-2. Extracting Parts of Lists - CAR and CDR

Lisp provides several primitives that can return parts of a list, without changing the original list. In sec. 3-4 we shall see how to actually modify a list. In this section we shall introduce several procedures, including two called CAR and CDR. These are somewhat related to the car and cdr introduced in sec. 3.1. However, while CAR and CDR are Lisp primitive functions, car and cdr describe the two halves of the cons cell. Note that although the words are spelled in the same way, the notation of this book distinguishes between them by capitalizing one set but not the other.

The CAR function returns the first element in a list. For instance,

(CAR '(THE BOOK IS HERE))   (3-8a)

will return,

THE

and,

(CAR '((THE BOOK) IS HERE))   (3-8b)

will return:

(THE BOOK)

The CDR function returns a *list* that contains the remainder of its argument, which must be a list, after the first element of that list has been extracted. Note that whereas CAR returns an element, which may be an atom or a list, CDR always returns a list. Hence,

(CDR '(THE BOOK IS BLUE))   (3-9a)

will return:

(BOOK IS BLUE)

Note that CDR *always* returns a list, while CAR will only return a list if the first element of the list that is its argument is itself a list.

Let us consider another example. Suppose that,

(SETQ X '((THE BOOK) (IS ON (THE TABLE))))   (3-10)

is evaluated. Then,

(CAR X)   (3-11)

will return:

(THE BOOK)   (3-12)

Note that the first element of the list X is the list (THE BOOK). In addition,

(CDR X)   (3-13)

will return:

((IS ON (THE TABLE)))   (3-14)

Note that the CDR returns a list that is the remainder of the original list after its first element has been removed. Thus, if the remainder of the original list is itself a list, then CDR will return a list that has one element, and that element will be a list. For instance, (3-14) represents a one element list, and that element is the list: (IS ON (THE TABLE)).

The following operation will return the second element of a list:

(CAR (CDR '(THE BOOK IS ON THE TABLE)))   (3-15)

The CDR returns (BOOK IS ON THE TABLE) and the CAR of this list is BOOK. Thus, the desired value is returned. In the course of Lisp programming, we commonly want to extract different parts of lists. By successively applying the CAR and CDR functions, the desired part of the list can be obtained. For instance, suppose that we want to extract the word BOOK from the list X established when (3-10) is evaluated. (We assume that the programmer knows that the first element of the list X is itself a list.) Then, the following operation will return BOOK:

(CAR (CDR (CAR X)))   (3-16)

Note that (CDR (CAR X)) returns the list (BOOK), and that the CAR of a single element list is the element itself.

These type of operations (combinations of CAR and CDR) occur so often that primitives have been written to perform them. For instance, the operation of (3-16) is performed by the primitive CADAR. In a similar way,

(CDDAR X)   (3-17a)

is a primitive function that is equivalent to

(CDR (CDR (CAR X)))   (3-17b)

There are many such primitive functions. Their names all start with a C and end with an R. The intervening letters are either A or D, where A and D indicate CAR and CDR, respectively. Note that the appearance of the A or D in the function name corresponds to the appearance of CAR of CDR in the Lisp expression that performs the same operation. Consult your Lisp manual to see how many of the C---R functions are available on your Lisp system.

```
(DEFUN CDDAR (LST)
    (CDR (CDR (CAR LST)))
)
```

Figure 3.4. The function CDDAR

If your Lisp system does not include these useful C--R functions, they can be written easily. For instance, a definition for the CDDAR function is shown in figure 3.4. The expressions CAR and CDR were established in the early days of Lisp and referred to the contents of various registers in the hardware of the computer. The names have remained, although the Lisp programmer does not have to know anything about registers to use them. Some Lisp systems use other names that reflect the operation of the functions. For instance, some systems will recognize FIRST as CAR, SECOND as CADR, and REST as CDR. Such Lisp systems will, however recognize CAR, CADR, and CDR as well.

3-3. List Construction - Dot Notation

In this section we shall discuss some additional primitives that allow us to build up lists from other lists and atoms. These procedures do not directly modify the lists that are their arguments; instead they return new lists. Let us start by discussing the primitive LIST that is used to build a list. The form of the use of LIST is:

$$\text{(LIST 'THE 'BOOK 'IS 'BLUE)} \qquad \text{(3-18)}$$

This will return the list (THE BOOK IS BLUE). In (3-18) the arguments of LIST were four literal atoms. These arguments became the elements of the returned list. The arguments of LIST can be other lists, literal atoms, atoms that evaluate to lists, or values. Consider the following sequence:

$$\text{(SETQ X '(THE BOOK IS BLUE))} \qquad \text{(3-19a)}$$
$$\text{(SETQ Y 7)} \qquad \text{(3-19b)}$$
$$\text{(SETQ Z (LIST 'HOUSE X Y))} \qquad \text{(3-19c)}$$

After the evaluation of this sequence, Z will be bound to the list:

$$\text{(HOUSE (THE BOOK IS BLUE) 7)} \qquad \text{(3-20)}$$

Another example of LIST is,

$$\text{(LIST '(ONE LIST) '(ANOTHER LIST))} \qquad \text{(3-21)}$$

This will return,

$$\text{((ONE LIST) (ANOTHER LIST))} \qquad \text{(3-22)}$$

Sometimes we want to construct a single list from the *elements* of two or more lists. When a list is used as an argument to LIST, that *list* becomes an element of the resulting list, see (3-21) and (3-22). If we start with the lists (ONE LIST) and (ANOTHER LIST), and we want to obtain the list (ONE LIST ANOTHER LIST), the primitive APPEND should be used. For instance,

    (APPEND '(ONE LIST) '(ANOTHER LIST))   (3-23)

will return:

    (ONE LIST ANOTHER LIST)   (3-24)

For the time being, assume that all of APPEND's arguments are lists. Note that LIST and APPEND *do not change* the original lists.

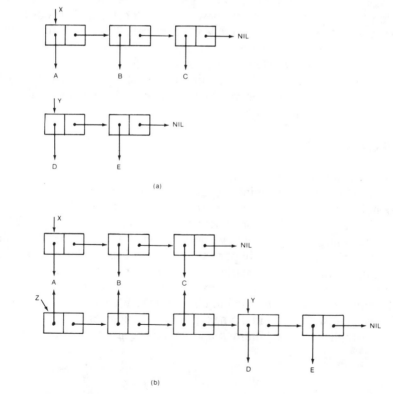

Figure 3.5. (a) Cons cells after evaluation of (3-25a) and (3-25b); (b) Cons cells after evaluation of (3-25c)

Let us consider the relevant cons cell diagram. Suppose that the following sequence is evaluated:

(SETQ X '(A B C))   (3-25a)
(SETQ Y '(D E))   (3-25b)
(SETQ Z (APPEND X Y))   (3-25c)

After this sequence is evaluated, Z will be bound to the list (A B C D E). The cons cell diagram is shown in Fig. 3-5. Figure 3-5a represents the cons cells after (3-25a) and (3-25b) are evaluated. Figure 3-5b represents the cons cells after (3-25c) is also evaluated. Note that after (3-25c) is evaluated the list Y has become part of the list Z. List X has three elements. Three additional cons cells are used by the Lisp system after (3-25c) is evaluated. There is one new cons cell for each element in X. These three new cons cells are the first three cons cells of Z. The cars of these new cons cells point to the corresponding elements of X. (Memory is saved by this procedure because the atoms A, B, and C do not have to be copied into new memory locations.) The cdr of the first new cons cell points at the second new cons cell. The cdr of this second cons cell points at the third new cons cell. The cdr of the third (last) new cons cell *points at the first cons cell of Y*. Because of the structure of the cons cells the Y list is part of the Z list. In particular, if the list Y is actually changed, then the list Z will also be changed. For instance, if the Y list becomes (A NEW LIST), then Z will become:

(A B C A NEW LIST)

On the other hand, if X is changed, Z will *not* be changed. The diagram may not seem confusing on this point because the cars of X's cons cells and the corresponding cars of Z's cons cells point at the same atoms. However, if X is changed then the cars of its cons cells will be changed and point at different memory locations. Thus, X will have been changed. On the other hand, the cars of Z will not be changed. In particular, they will still point at A, B, and C. Operations of this type will be illustrated in the next section.

We must clarify what is meant by actually changing a list. There are special primitives that can be used to change lists. We have not considered any of these, but shall do so in the next section. Remember that, (see sec. 3-1) SETQ establishes new bindings and cannot be used to *change* a list.

Let us illustrate this. Suppose that after the sequence (3-25) is evaluated we enter:

(SETQ Y '(THIS IS A NEW LIST))   (3-26)

The binding of Z will be unchanged by this operation. That is Z will still be equivalent to (A B C D E). This seems to contradict the previous discussion. However, we have actually not changed Y, a new Y has been set up and bound. Each time that a SETQ expression is evaluated, new memory locations are set up to store the data for that variable. The old data becomes inaccessible. For instance, after the structure of figure 3.5b was set up, and (3-26) was evaluated, you could no longer access the list (D E) using the name Y, or any other name for that matter. (It would still be accessible as part of the list Z.) There would be a new list called Y and it would be unrelated to the previous one. We shall discuss this in greater detail later in this chapter.

There is another primitive named CONS that is used to add a new cons cell to the *beginning* of a list. That is, it adds an element to the beginning of the list. For instance, consider the following sequence:

(SETQ X '(IS ON THE TABLE))   (3-27a)
(SETQ Y (CONS 'BOOK X))   (3-27b)

The value of Y will now be:

(BOOK IS ON THE TABLE)   (3-28)

In this case a new cons cell has been established, its car points to BOOK and its cdr points to the start of the X list. Again, if the X list is actually changed (not rebound using SETQ), then the Y list will also be changed.

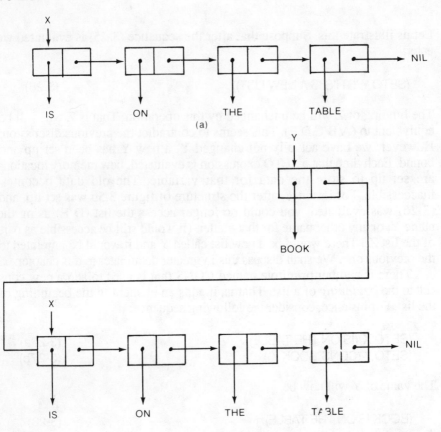

Figure 3.6. Cons cell diagrams (a) for the list x after evaluation of (3-27a); (b) for the lists X and Y after the evaluation of (3-27b)

A cons cell diagram for the operations of (3-27) is illustrated in figure 3.6. Note that if the Y in (3-27b) had been replaced by an X, then the old X would have been lost and the new value of X would be given by (3-28). As an additional example, consider:

(SETQ WW (CONS '(THE BOOK) (ON THE TABLE)))   (3-29)

after evaluation the value of WW will be:

((THE BOOK) ON THE TABLE)   (3-30)

Note that a new cons cell is set up; its car points to the *list* (THE BOOK) and its cdr points to the first cons cell of the list (ON THE TABLE). Thus, the list WW includes the list (THE BOOK) as its first element. The cons cell diagram for this structure is shown in figure 3.7.

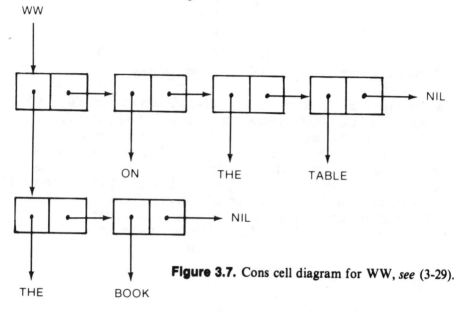

Figure 3.7. Cons cell diagram for WW, *see* (3-29).

DOT NOTATION

Let us consider the operation of the CONS procedure in greater detail. When (3-27b) is evaluated, a new cons cell is set up such that its car points at the atom BOOK and its cdr points at the list X. Suppose, however, that the second argument of CONS is not a list, but an atom. For example,

(SETQ Z (CONS 'BOOK 'TABLE))   (3-31)

A cons cell diagram for z is shown in Fig. 3-8. In this case, the value returned by the CONS procedure, or, equivalently, the value to which Z is bound is

(BOOK . TABLE)   (3-32)

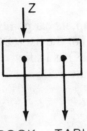

BOOK   TABLE

Figure 3.8. Cons cell diagram for thr dotted pair (BOOK.TABLE) to which Z is bound

We have not seen this notation before. It is called *dot notation* and (3-32) is called a *dotted pair*. (Note the space on either side of the period.) Z has not been set to a true list. Remember that the last cons cell in a true list must point to NIL. Dot notation is a way of representing list-like structures in which the last cdr does not point to NIL. The cons cell set up by (3-31) has its car pointing at BOOK and its cdr pointing at TABLE. In (3-31), CONS is applied to two atoms. A similar result is achieved whenever the second argument of CONS is an atom. (Note that this is not the usual application of the CONS primitive.) If the first argument of CONS is a list, but the second is not a list the result will be a dotted pair. For instance, if,

(SETQ W (CONS '(THE BOOK) 'TABLE)   (3-33)

is evaluated the resulting value of W will be:

((THE BOOK) . TABLE)   (3-34)

A cons cell diagram for the dotted pair W is shown in figure 3.9.

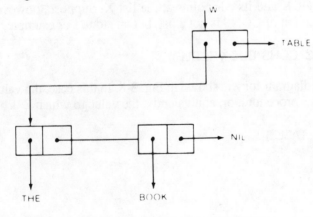

Figure 3.9. The cons cell diagram for W given by (3-34)

When,

(SETQ AA (CONS '(THE BOOK) NIL)   (3-35)

is evaluated, AA will be bound to the list:

((THE BOOK))   (3-36)

Because the cdr of the new cons cell points to NIL a true list has been established. AA is a single-element list. It is, in fact, a list because the car of the new cons cell points at the list (THE BOOK) and the cdt of that cons cell points at NIL.

Dotted pairs can also result when the APPEND procedure is used. For example,

(APPEND '(THE BOOK) TABLE)   (3-37)

will return:

(THE BOOK . TABLE)   (3-38)

The cons cell diagram for (3-38) is shown in figure 3.10. Note that the car of the second cons cell points at the atom BOOK while its cdr points at the atom TABLE. This is not a true list, because the cdr of the last cons cell does not point at NIL, and (3-38) must be represented as a dotted pair. The name to the right of the period will be that which is pointed at by the cdr of the last cons cell.

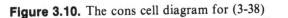

TABLE

THE   BOOK

Figure 3.10. The cons cell diagram for (3-38)

3-4. List Modification - Garbage Collection

We shall now discuss some primitives that can be used to modify existing lists. As we discussed in secs. 3-1 and 3-3, SETQ does not modify the memory used to store the value of an already bound variable but may use additional memory for this storage. That value may be a list. For instance, let us repeat expressions (3-25) here:

(SETQ X '(A B C))	(3-39a)
(SETQ Y '(D E))	(3-39b)
(SETQ Z (APPEND X Y))	(3-39c)

The cons diagram for this operation is shown in figure 3.5. Remember that the list Z does not contain the cons cells of X, but it does contain those of Y. If X is changed Z will not be changed. On the other hand, if Y is changed then Z will be changed.

Now we shall discuss some primitives that do change the cons cells of a list. Rather than set up a new list, these primitives change an existing one. In some sense these primitives are dangerous to use and, therefore their use should be avoided unless you are very sure of their effects. The procedure RPLACA changes the pointer of the car of the first cons cell of a list. RPLACA also sets up the entity to which that that car points. For instance if, after evaluating (3-39), we evaluate,

(RPLACA Y 'NEW)   (3-40)

then the list Y becomes,

(NEW E)   (3-41a)

and, consequently the list Z becomes:

(A B C NEW E)   (3-41b)

If we had used RPLACA to change X (the first argument of APPEND in (3-39c)), we would not have changed Z. Suppose that,

(RPLACA X 'FIRST)   (3-42)

is evaluated. The cons cell diagram after the evaluation of (3-42) is shown in figure 3.11. The car of the first cons cell of X no longer points at the atom A, the atom that was shared by both lists, but now points instead at the atom

FIRST. The car of the first cons cell of Z still points at A. The car of the first cons cell of Y now points at the atom NEW because of (3-40).

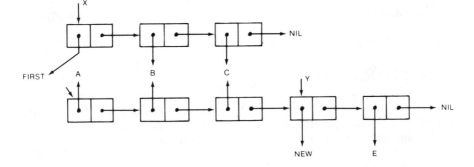

Figure 3.11. The modification of the cons cell diagram of figure 3.5. After (RPLACA Y 'NEW) and (RPLACA X 'FIRST) have been evaluated

The first argument of RPLACA must be a list; the second argument can be either an atom or a list. For instance, after the following sequence is evaluated,

(SETQ W '(A B C D))   (3-43a)

(RPLACA W '(THE BOOK))   (3-43b)

W will be bound to:

((THE BOOK) B C D)   (3-44)

The procedure RPLACD replaces an entire list, except for its first element. For instance, suppose that the sequence (3-39) has been evaluated. Then Y will be bound to (D E). If we now evaluate,

(RPLACD Y '(A NEW END))   (3-45)

the list Y will be bound to:

(D A NEW END)   (3-46)

In addition, Z will now be bound to:

(A B C D A NEW END)   (3-47)

The procedure NCONC takes two lists and causes the last cdr of the first list, which originally pointed at NIL to point at the first cons cell of the second list. For instance suppose that the following are evaluated:

(SETQ X '(A B C))   (3-48a)
(SETQ Y '(D E))   (3-48b)
(SETQ Z (NCONC X Y))   (3-48c)

After (3-48a) and (3-48b) are evaluated, the atoms X and Y will be bound to the lists (A B C) and (D E), respectively. After (3-48c) is evaluated, X and Z both will be bound to (A B C D E) while Y will be bound to (D E). A cons cell diagram for these operations is shown in figure 3.12.

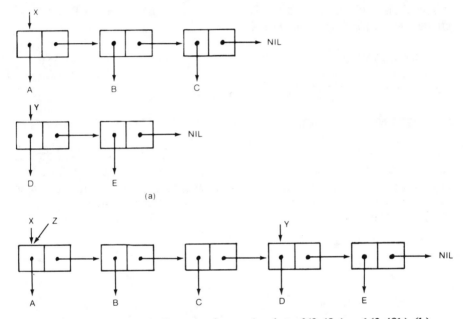

Figure 3.12. (a) Cons cell diagram after evaluation of (3-48a) and (3-48b); (b) Cons cell diagram after evaluation of (3-48c)

The NCONC operation concatenates Y and X. Thus, unlike the case of APPEND, the X list is modified by the NCONC operation. Now suppose that we use RPLACA to modify the first element of X as shown below:

    (RPLACA X 'FIRST)   (3-49)

Now X and Z both will be bound to,

    (FIRST B C D E)   (3-50)

while Y still will be bound to (D E). Now suppose we use RPLACD to change all but the first element of X.

    (RPLACD X '(NEW LIST END))   (3-51)

Now X and Z will both be bound to,

    (FIRST NEW LIST END)   (3-52)

while Y will still be bound to (D E). When (3-51) was evaluated, all of the list X except its first element (the atom FIRST) was replaced by a new list. The last cdr of this new list points to NIL, thus there no longer is a link between this list and Y. A cons cell diagram that illustrates this is shown in figures 3-13a and 3-13b.

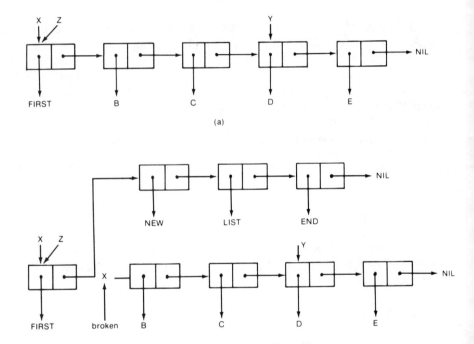

Figure 3.13. (a) Cons cell diagram before the evaluation of (3-51); (b) Cons cell diagram after the evaluation of (3-51)

Note that after (3-51) is evaluated the last cdr of the list that X and Z are bound to points at NIL. Thus, the cells whose cars point to B, C, D, and E, no longer are part of the X or Z lists. The Y list is unchanged by this operation. In figure 3-13b, note the cons cells whose cars point to B and C. They now represent wasted memory. That is, these cons cells never can be accessed. The memory locations that store the atoms B and C are also wasted. Although B and C represent atoms in this example; they could represent long lists. Thus, a great deal of memory could be wasted. Later in this section we shall discuss how these memory locations can be reclaimed for subsequent use.

It is possible to set up structures where the car of one cons cell points back at a previous cell so that a loop is set up. Printing of such structures will never terminate, but instead becomes stuck "in a loop." Once this happens the system will "hang up" and further operations cannot be performed. Some Lisp systems have procedures for interrupting such operations, but often the computer must be stopped and restarted before the user can gain control.

There is a primitive named SETF that is more general than SETQ. For instance, if all the uses of SETQ in this chapter were replaced by SETF, there would be no change in any of the results.

Let us consider some of the more general aspects of SETF. When SETQ is used, its form is:

$$(\text{SETQ A B}) \tag{3-53}$$

A is called the *destination*. The destination can be only an atom when SETQ is used. On the other hand, the destination of SETF may be either an atom or a call to a function. For instance,

$$(\text{SETF (CAR A) 'NEW}) \tag{3-54a}$$

When (3-54a) is evaluated, the first element of the list A will be replaced by the atom NEW. That is (3-54a) is equivalent to:

$$(\text{RPLACA A 'NEW}) \tag{3-54b}$$

When (3-54a) is evaluated, the list A will be changed, as it would be if (3-54b) was evaluated. (Of course, in this discussion we assume that A has been previously bound to a list.)

Another use of SETF is,

$$(\text{SETF (CDR A) '(A NEW END)}) \tag{3-55a}$$

This is equivalent to:

(RPLACD A '(A NEW END))   (3-55b)

Again the evaluation of either (3-55a) or (3-55b) causes the list A to be changed rather than simply establishing a new variable (symbol table entry).

There are many functions that can be used with SETF. Consult your Lisp manual to determine which can be used with your system.

```
(DEFUN RPLACELIST(OLDLST LST)
   (RPLACA OLDLST (CAR LST))
   (RPLACD OLDLST (CDR LST))
)
```

Figure 3.14. A function that changes a complete list.

Sometimes you want to replace one list with another one. figure 3.14 lists a procedure called RPLACELIST that can be used for this purpose. Observe that this procedure simply uses RPLACA and RPLACD successively.

GARBAGE COLLECTION

When SETQ is used to bind a variable whose name is the same as one that has been previously bound, the memory locations that store the "old" data are no longer needed because they can no longer be accessed. There are other situations that cause memory locations to become inaccessible. For instance, consider figure 3.13b. The cons cells that point to atoms B and C cannot be accessed. Therefore, the memory locations that store A and B are also inaccessible. During the running of a typical Lisp program, a great deal of memory may become inaccessible. In the next chapter we shall discuss procedures whereby operations may be made to loop so that the same procedures are repeated many times. If some memory is made inaccessible for each pass through the loop then, after many loops, there may be a large area of inaccessible memory.

Inaccessible memory is wasted memory. Large Lisp programs may use a great deal of memory. It is possible that the program may run out of memory and not be able to run. This situation would be alleviated if the inaccessible memory could be reused. After all, if the memory cannot be accessed, then the data stored in it is useless. Such memory is sometimes referred to as *garbage*. Lisp systems keep track of the memory that is free to be used for data storage. Those memory locations are maintained in a list called a *free storage list*. The inaccessible memory is not available for such storage. Periodically, however, the system performs an operation called a *garbage collection*. The system studies the data storage and determines those memory locations that can never be accessed. Those memory locations are then placed back on the free storage list, thus becoming available for reuse.

A garbage collection is not a simple operation. For instance, suppose that X is bound to a list and then:

(SETQ X '(A NEW LIST))   (3-56)

Now the memory locations that stored the data for the "old" X are no longer accessible under the name X, but they may be accessible under some other name. For instance, in figure 3.13a the entire list can be accessed under the name X and under the name Z. Thus, even if (3-56) were evaluated, the memory locations of figure 3.13a would not become inaccessible because Z is bound to them. Thus, the determination of whether memory is in fact, inaccessible involves a considerable amount of checking and may take some time. As a further example of the problems involved in garbage collection, again consider figure 3.13a. Even if SETQ were used to bind both X and Z, all of the memory locations do not become inaccessible, because some of the memory locations are accessible under the name Y.

When a garbage collection takes place all other operations cease. Thus, garbage collection slows the operation of the system. If garbage collection takes place while a program is running, the computer may appear to pause for no reason. Thus, garbage collection has it advantages and disadvantages. However, all Lisp systems use garbage collection to make the best use of memory. If garbage collection were not used many Lisp programs could be run only on computers whose memory was impractically large.

Exercises

Test any exercises that contain Lisp expressions by running them on your computer.

1. What are the elements of the list:

   (+ (* 2 4) 5 (/ 6 (+ 3 5)))

2. Repeat exercise 1 for the list:

   (THE BOOK (ON THE (TABLE IS) A) (LONG BOOK))

3. What is meant by an s-expression?

4. Describe the levels in the list of exercise 2.

5. Describe the operation of the SETQ procedure. Does SETQ always set up a new variable?

6. Draw a cons cell diagram for the list of exercise 2.

7. Write an expression that extracts the first element of the list of exercise 2.

8. Write an expression that extracts the list:

   (BOOK (ON THE (TABLE IS) A) (LONG BOOK))

   from the list of exercise 2.

9. Write an expression that extracts the first atom BOOK from the list of exercise 2.

10. Write an expression that extracts the second atom BOOK from the list of exercise 2.

11. Write a function that acts as the primitive CDADR.

12. Write a function that sets up a list from four elements (atoms or lists) that are passed to it.

13. Draw the cons cell diagram for the structure that results after the first two of the following expressions are evaluated. Then draw the cons cell diagram for the structure that results after all three expressions are evaluated.

```
(SETQ X '(THE BALL (AND THE BAT))
(SETQ Y '(ARE ON THE GROUND))
(SETQ Z (APPEND X Y))
```

14. If, after the expressions of exercise 13 are evaluated, the following is evaluated:

```
(SETQ X '(NEW LIST))
```

what will be the values of Y and Z.

15. Draw the cons cell diagram for the lists of exercise 14.

16. If, after the expressions of exercise 13 are evaluated, the following is evaluated,

```
SETQ Y '(AN ADDITIONAL LIST))
```

what will be the values of X, Y, and Z?

17. Draw the cons cell diagram for the lists of exercise 16.

18. Draw the cons cell diagram for the structure that results after the first two of the following expressions are evaluated. Then draw the cons cell diagram for the structure that results after all three expressions are evaluated.

(SETQ X '(THE BALL (AND THE BAT))
(SETQ Y '(ARE ON THE GROUND))
(SETQ Z (CONS X Y))

19. If, after the expressions of exercise 18 are evaluated, the expression,

(SETQ X '(A NEW LIST))

is evaluated, what will be the values of X, Y, and Z?

20. Draw the cons cell diagrams for the lists of exercise 19.

21. If, after the lists of exercise 18 are evaluated, the expression,

(SETQ Y '(AN ADDITIONAL LIST))

is evaluated, what will be the values of X, Y, and Z.

22. Draw the cons cell diagrams for the lists of exercise 21.

23. Why is dot notation used?

24. What is the result of the evaluation of the following expression:

(CONS '(A LIST) 'WORD)

25. Why do Lisp systems incorporate a garbage collection routine?

26. Discuss the problems encountered in garbage collection.

27. Draw the cons cell diagram for the structure that results after all four of the following expressions are evaluated:

        (SETQ X '(THE BALL (AND THE BAT))
        (SETQ Y '(ARE ON THE GROUND))
        (SETQ Z (CONS X Y))
        (RPLACA X 'FIRSTX)

What are the values of X, Y, and Z?

28. Draw the cons cell diagram for the structure that results after all four of the following expressions are evaluated:

        (SETQ X '(THE BALL (AND THE BAT))
        (SETQ Y '(ARE ON THE GROUND))
        (SETQ Z (CONS X Y))
        (RPLACA Y 'FIRSTY)

What are the values of X, Y, and Z?

29. Draw the cons cell diagram for the structure that results after all four of the following expressions are evaluated:

        (SETQ X '(THE BALL (AND THE BAT))
        (SETQ Y '(ARE ON THE GROUND))
        (SETQ Z (CONS X Y))
        (RPLACD X 'FIRSTX)

What are the values of X, Y, and Z?

30. Draw the cons cell diagram for the structure that results after all four of the following expressions are evaluated:

```
(SETQ X '(THE BALL (AND THE BAT))
(SETQ Y '(ARE ON THE GROUND))
(SETQ Z (CONS X Y))
(RPLACD Y 'FIRSTY)
```

What are the values of X, Y, and Z?

31. Draw the cons cell diagram for the structure that results after all four of the following expressions are evaluated.

```
(SETQ X '(THE BALL (AND THE BAT))
(SETQ Y '(ARE ON THE GROUND))
(SETQ Z (NCONC X Y))
(RPLACA X 'FIRSTX)
```

What are the values of X, Y, and Z?

32. If, after the expressions of exercise 31 are evaluated, the expression,

```
(SETQ X '(NEW LIST))
```

is evaluated, what will be the values of X, Y, and Z? Draw the cons cell diagram for the lists.

33. Repeat exercise 32 using the expression:

```
(SETF X '(NEW LIST))
```

34. Repeat exercise 32 using the expression:

```
(SETF (CAR X) '(NEW START))
```

35. Repeat exercise 32 using the expression

   (SETF (CDR X) '(A NEW END))

4

Control Structures

Thus far we have written procedures in which the expressions were evaluated in order, one after the other. Such procedures are of limited utility. Programs that can take one of several *paths* or *branches*, based on some decision-making process, can be very powerful. The choice of a particular branch is dictated by things such as input data and/or values calculated earlier in the program. For instance, one branch might be chosen if the name TOM were input, while another branch would be chosen if the name BILL were input. In this chapter we shall discuss procedures for incorporating branching into programs.

There are many circumstances in which a program must perform a particular operation many times in succession. It would be impractical to have to repeat the expressions that control such an operation over and over again in the program. In this chapter, we shall also discuss procedures whereby programs can be made to *loop* back over a particular set of expressions.

Branching and looping are very powerful and versatile tools that allow the programmer to write complex programs. Such programs are prone to errors. There are programming techniques that can be used to write programs that tend to be relatively error free. If such programs do contain errors, they are relatively easy to debug. We shall discuss these programming techniques in this chapter.

4-1. Predicates

We shall now consider some Lisp primitives called *predicates*; these primitives return values that represent true or false. These procedures are used to test if their arguments have certain properties. Branching and/or looping can be controlled by the results of these tests. In Lisp, false is symbolized by the value NIL while true is often symbolized by the special Lisp variable T. Actually any value that is not NIL is considered by the Lisp system to represent true.

The first predicate that we shall consider is called EQUAL. This tests to see if its arguments are equal. For instance,

(EQUAL '(BOOK) '(BOOK))   (4-1)

will return the value T. Let us consider some additional examples. Suppose that the following sequence is evaluated:

(SETQ X 4)   (4-2a)
(EQUAL X (+ 2 1 1))   (4-2b)

The EQUAL expression will return the value T because (+ 2 1 1) returns 4. Also consider:

(SETQ A '(A B C))   (4-3a)
(SETQ B '(A B C))   (4-3b)
(EQUAL A B)   (4-3c)

The equal expression will return the value T. In general, the EQUAL expression will return the value T if its arguments evaluate to the same value. This usually means that the returned values will print in an identical way. Note that the value could be a list, a number, or one of the other data types that we shall subsequently discuss.

The predicate EQ compares its arguments and returns NIL if they are not actually identical. That is they must represent the *same* stored data. This is a more stringent test than that performed by EQUAL. Whereas EQUAL tests only if its arguments evaluate to the same thing, EQ will test to see if they are stored in the same memory location(s). For instance, if (4-3a) and (4-3b) were evaluated, and then the following was evaluated,

(EQ A B)   (4-4)

the returned value will be NIL. Although A and B both evaluate to (A B C), the two lists are not stored in the same memory locations, hence, they are not identical and EQ returns NIL. (Note that if two entities are identical and one is changed, then the other will be changed also. (*See* chapter 3 for a discussion of changing versus rebinding.) If the arguments of EQ are the lists X and Z whose cons cell diagrams are given in figure 3.12, then the returned value will be T because X and Z are identical; they are different names for the same list.

If, after (4-3a) and (4-3b) are evaluated, we then evaluate the following sequence,

(SETQ C A)	(4-5a)
(EQ C A)	(4-5b)

the value T will be returned. When SETQ is used to bind one atom to another atom, the first atom becomes identical to the second one. That is, after (4-5a) is evaluated, C and A will not only evaluate to the same result, but their data will occupy identical memory locations.

If the arguments of EQ are numbers, then the operation may be somewhat different. If both arguments represent numbers of the same type, and those numbers are equal (i. e., the arguments evaluate to the same number) then EQ will evaluate to T, even if the two arguments are not identical objects. The operation of EQ with numbers is very system dependent. Thus, in one system T may be returned while with another system NIL will be returned. There is another data type called character, it is used to represent single characters. (We shall discuss characters in chapter 8.) The comments about numbers when used as arguments to EQ apply to characters also. You should perform several examples using numbers with EQ to determine how your system performs.

There is another predicate named EQL that resolves the ambiguity that we have just discussed. If the arguments of EQL are neither numbers nor characters, then EQL functions just as does EQ. On the other hand, if the arguments of EQ represent numbers or characters, then EQ will return T if both arguments evaluate to equal numbers of the same type, or if they both evaluate to the same character. For example consider,

(SETQ X 7)	(4-6a)
(SETQ Y (+ 3 4))	(4-6b)
(EQL X Y)	(4-6c)

The EQL expression (4-6c) will return T since both X and Y evaluate to the FIXNUM 7. On the other hand, if the expressions,

(SETQ X 7)	(4-7a)
(SETQ Y 7.0)	(4-7b)
(EQL X Y)	(4-7c)

are evaluated, the EQL expression (4-7c) will return NIL, because X and Y are of different types. Note that EQUAL will also return NIL if its arguments represent numbers of different types, even if they are numerically equal. For instance, after (4-7a) and (4-7b) are evaluated,

(EQUAL X Y)   (4-8)

will return NIL.

The predicate ATOM tests to see if its argument is an ATOM. For instance, if the following expressions are evaluated,

(SETQ X 7)	(4-9a)
(ATOM X)	(4-9b)

the value returned by the last expression will be T. Note that X evaluates to a number and numbers are atoms. On the other hand, after:

(SETQ Y '(THE BOOK IS HERE))	(4-10a)
(ATOM Y)	(4-10b)

are evaluated, the last expression will return NIL since Y evaluates to a list. The following expression will also return T when evaluated:

(ATOM 'HOUSE)   (4-11)

The predicate LISTP returns T if its argument is a list. If X and Y are bound using (4-9a) and (4-10a), respectively, then,

(LISTP X)   (4-12)

will return NIL, while,

(LISTP Y)   (4-13)

will return T.

The predicate NULL tests to see if a list is empty. For instance,

(NULL ())   (4-14)

will return T. NIL represents an empty list. Thus,

(NULL NIL)

will return T.

The predicate MEMBER tests if an *atom* is a member of a list. For instance, consider that the following is evaluated:

(SETQ BB '(THE BOOK IS (ON THE) TABLE)   (4-15)

If we then evaluate,

(MEMBER 'CAT BB)   (4-16)

NIL will be returned, because CAT is not a member of the list BB. Note that the atom is the first argument of MEMBER and the list, or the name of the atom to which the list is bound, is the second argument of MEMBER.

If the atom that is the first argument of MEMBER occurs in the list that is the second argument, MEMBER does not return T. Instead, the sublist from the specified atom to the end of the list is returned. For instance,

(MEMBER 'IS BB)   (4-17)

will return (IS (ON THE) TABLE).

If the first argument of member is not an atom, then NIL will be returned even if that argument is an element of the list. For instance,

(MEMBER '(ON THE) BB)   (4-18)

will return NIL even though (ON THE) is an element of BB. On the other hand, consider the evaluation of the following sequence,

(SETQ AA '(ON THE))   (4-19a)
(SETQ CC (LIST 'THE 'BOOK 'IS AA 'TABLE)   (4-19b)
(MEMBER AA CC)   (4-19c)

Expression (4-19c) will return ((ON THE) TABLE). Note that the first argument of MEMBER is the atom AA and the atom AA *actually is* part of the list CC. That is, the cars of the appropriate cons cells of CC and AA each point to the same entity. The reason why MEMBER behaves as it does is that it uses EQL, rather than EQUAL to compare the atom to the elements of the list. In sec. 5-3, we shall discuss this in greater detail.

Some Lisp systems implement MEMBER in a somewhat different manner. If the atom is a member of the list then, instead of returning the sublist, an integer will be returned. The integer will be equal to the position of the atom in the list. For example, in those systems (4-19c) would return 4, because AA is the fourth element in the list CC. Some Lisp systems, such as TLC Lisp, implement a function named MEMQ, that is equivalent to MEMBER. That is, when the atom is a member of the list, MEMQ returns the sublist.

There are some predicates that take numerical arguments. We shall consider some of them here. The predicate NUMBERP returns T if its argument is a number. For instance,

        (SETQ X 3.4)   (4-20a)
        (NUMBERP X)   (4-20b)

will return T. The number can be of any type. In addition, the predicates INTEGERP, FLOATP, and RATIONALP return T if their (single) argument is an integer, a floating-point number, and a ratio, respectively.

There are predicates that test the relative size of numbers. The predicate > tests if each of its numerical arguments is greater than (not equal to) the argument to its right. For instance,

        (> 5 4 -1 -100)   (4-21)

will return T. On the other hand,

        (> 5 -1 0 -10)

will return NIL, because -1 is not greater than zero. Some Lisp systems allow only two arguments to >. All the arguments of > must be numbers or an error will result. Most Lisp systems will allow mixed numerical types as arguments of >.

The predicate < tests if each of its numerical arguments is less than the argument to its right. The general ideas concerning > apply to < as well.

The predicates >= and <= function in essentially the same way as do > and < respectively except that they will return T if adjacent arguments are equal.

The predicate = returns T if all of its numerical arguments are equal (i. e., evaluate to the same number). Otherwise it returns NIL. The predicate /= returns T if all of its numerical arguments are different. It returns NIL if any of its arguments are equal.

The predicate ZEROP tests if its (single) argument is zero. It returns T if the argument is zero and NIL otherwise. The predicates PLUSP and MINUSP tests whether their single argument is positive or negative, respectively. They return T if the result of the test is true and NIL otherwise. The predicates EVENP and ODDP test whether their (single) argument is even or odd, respectively.

LOGICAL PREDICATES

There is a set of predicates that perform the operations of mathematical logic. The arguments to these predicates are values that are either true or false or expressions that evaluate to true or false. These are called *Boolean variables*. The arguments are usually, but not always, obtained from the results of the evaluation of other predicates. The AND predicate returns the value NIL if any of its arguments is NIL, or if any of its arguments evaluates to NIL. Let us consider an example of this operation. Suppose that we have:

$$(AND\ (>5\ 4)\ (=4\ 3)\ (<5\ 9)) \tag{4-22}$$

The second argument is false, and returns the value NIL. Thus, (4-22) will return NIL. The operation of AND is somewhat different than the other procedures that we have discussed previously. When most Lisp procedures are evaluated, all the arguments are evaluated, as long as there is no syntax error. When AND is evaluated, its arguments are evaluated from left to right. If a NIL results then no further arguments are evaluated and the result NIL is returned. If none of the arguments evaluate to NIL, then AND returns the value of the last argument. For example,

$$(AND\ (>5\ 4)\ (=4\ 4)) \tag{4-23}$$

will return the value T, while,

$$(AND\ (>5\ 4)\ (*\ 2\ 3)) \tag{4-24}$$

will return the value 6. Remember that any nonNIL value is considered to be true.

The OR predicate returns NIL only if *all* of its arguments are NIL. The arguments of OR are evaluated from left to right. The first nonNIL value that is obtained is returned. The remaining arguments are not evaluated. For example,

$$(OR (= 3\ 3) (> 6\ 9)) \tag{4-25}$$

will return T, because (= 3 3) returns T. In addition,

$$(OR (= 3\ 4) (*\ 2\ 3) (= 5\ 6)) \tag{4-26}$$

will return 6 and,

$$(OR (= 3\ 4) (= 4\ 7) (> 5\ 9)) \tag{4-27}$$

will return NIL.

The predicate NOT takes a single argument. It returns NIL if the argument is not NIL and returns T if the argument is NIL. Therefore, the NOT predicate changes true to false and vice versa.

We have considered the most useful predicates in this section. However, many Lisp systems implement additional predicates. Check your Lisp manual to determine these predicates that are available for your system.

4-2. The COND Operation

The predicates of the last section returned values that represented either true or false. Remember that false is represented by NIL, while true is represented either by the variable T or any other nonNIL value. In this section we shall discuss the COND operation that utilizes predicates to obtain programs that branch. The basic construction of a COND operation is:

$$(COND (B1\ E1)) \tag{4-28}$$

B1 and E1 both represent s-expressions, i. e., Lisp expressions. If B1 is nonNIL, then E1 will be evaluated, and the value returned by (4-28) will be the value returned by E1. If B1 is NIL, or if it returns NIL after it is evaluated, then E1 will be ignored and (4-28) returns NIL. Thus, the value of B1 determines whether E1 is evaluated or not. The value of B1 is tested to determine if E1 is evaluated. To distinguish between B1 and E1, we shall call the s-expression, B1, a *test expression*.

The COND operation is more versatile than we have indicated, there can be a sequence of pairs of test expressions and Lisp expressions. For instance, we could have:

```
(COND (B1 E1)
(B2 E2)
(B3 E3)                                                    (4-29)
(B4 E4)
)
```

In (4-29) there are four pairs of expressions of the form (Bn En) (n = 1, 2, 3, 4). Each test expression, Bn, is evaluated in turn. When the *first* nonNIL value is found, the corresponding Lisp expression, En, is evaluated and the COND operation then terminates. Only *one* of the several Lisp expressions will be evaluated. For instance, if B1 and B2 are NIL while B3 and B4 are nonNIL, then E3 will be the only expression that is evaluated. Of course, BI, B2, and B3 will also be evaluated. Note that although (4-29) has four branches, the branch that is actually taken is determined by the values returned by the test expressions. If all the test expressions in (4-29) evaluate to NIL then none of the Lisp expressions will be evaluated and NIL will be returned.

At times, it is undesirable for the COND to return NIL. That is, at least one branch of the COND construction should be evaluated. You can ensure that at least one Lisp expression is evaluated by adding a last pair to the COND construction. The test expression for this last pair should always evaluate to true. For instance,

```
(COND (B1 E1)
(B2 E2)
(B3 E3)                                                    (4-30)
(B4 E4)
(T  E5)
```

If any of B1, B2, B3, or B4 are nonNIL then (4-30) will function in the same way as (4-29). However if all of B1, B2, B3, and B4 are NIL then E5 will be evaluated because its test expression is T, which is always nonNIL. We have illustrated the COND operation with four, or five, pairs of test expressions and Lisp expressions. Actually, any number of pairs can be used.

```
(DEFUN IS-BILL(A)
   (COND ((EQUAL A 'BILL)  (PRINT '(THE INPUT IS BILL)))
         (T (PRINT '(THE INPUT IS NOT BILL)))
   )
)
```

Figure 4.1. A simple illustration of the COND operation

Let us illustrate the use of the COND operation with several examples. We shall start with a simple procedure whose argument is a single atom. If that atom is BILL then "THE INPUT IS BILL" will be output and returned. If the atom passed to the procedure is not BILL, then "THE INPUT IS NOT BILL" will be output and returned. The procedure IS-BILL is illustrated in figure 4.1. There are two branches in this procedure. The first test expression is:

(EQUAL A 'BILL)   (4-31)

If this evaluates to T, "THE INPUT IS BILL" will be output and the second branch will be ignored. The second test expression of figure 4.1 is T. Therefore, if the value passed to IS-BILL is not the atom BILL, then the first test expression returns NIL, the first branch is ignored, and the Lisp expression of the second branch will be evaluated.

```
(DEFUN MAX-THREE(A B C)
   (COND  ((>= A B)
               (COND ((>= A C) A)
                     (T C )
               )
          )
          (T   (COND ((>= B C) B)
                     (T C)
               )
          )
   )
)
```

Figure 4.2. The function MAX-THREE

A more complex example of the use of COND is illustrated by the function MAX-THREE, *see* figure 4.2. This function has three numerical arguments; it returns the largest argument. This function illustrates *nested* COND operations. That is one, or more, branches of the COND construction contain other COND constructions.

Let us consider how the procedure MAX-THREE works. The first test expression is:

$$(>= A B) \qquad\qquad (4\text{-}32)$$

If A is equal to or greater than B, then the first branch is taken and the second COND expression, which is nested within the first COND statement, will be evaluated. The first test expression of this nested COND statement is:

$$(>= A C) \qquad\qquad (4\text{-}33)$$

If A is equal to or greater than C, then the simple expression A will be evaluated, and evaluation of the function will terminate. Thus, the value of A will be returned. If A is not equal to or greater than C, then (4-33) will return NIL. In this case A will be equal to or greater than B but A will be less than C. Thus, C is the largest argument of MAX-THREE. The second test expression of the first nested COND expression, is the variable T. Thus, C will be evaluated and its value returned.

On the other hand, if B is greater than A, then (4-32) will return NIL, and the first branch of the outer (first) COND statement will be ignored. The second test expression of the outer COND statement will always be true, because it is the variable T. Thus the second nested COND expression will then be evaluated. Its first test expression is:

$$(>= B C) \qquad\qquad (4\text{-}34)$$

If B is equal to or greater than C then B will be returned. On the other hand, if C is greater than B then (4-34) will return NIL and C will be returned because the last test expression is always true (T). Thus, MAX-THREE functions as desired.

```
(SETQ PASS '(TOM ABC BILL DEF JOE GHIJ))

(DEFUN PWD-CHECK(PWF)
    (TERPRI)
    (PRINC "Enter log-in name  ")
    (SETQ NAME (READ))
    (TERPRI)
    (PRINC "Enter password  ")
    (TERPRI)
    (SETQ PWD (READ))
    (COND ((EQUAL PWD (CADR (MEMBER NAME PWF))) (PRINC "System accessed"))
        (T (PRINC "Access denied"))
    )
)
```

Figure 4.3. The procedure PWD-CHECK which checks for proper password entry

Another example of the use of COND is illustrated in figure 4.3. The procedure PASS-CHECK is used to check passwords. Such a procedure could be used to grant or deny access to potential users of a computer system. The user enters his/her name and then is prompted for a password. If the password corresponding to the user's name is entered, "System accessed" is output. If an improper password is entered, "Access denied" is output. In this example, the output of the phrases "System accessed" or "Access denied" replace the operations that would take place in an actual system to grant or deny access.

The user names and passwords are stored in a list. The list PASS, *see* figure 4.3, is such a list. Note that the list consists of a sequence of pairs of names and passwords. Each name is followed by the corresponding password. The procedure PWD-CHECK is called by entering:

(PWD-CHECK PASS)   (4-35)

Note that PASS is the name of the list that stores the data. Within the procedure, that list is assigned to the variable PWF. The prompt "Enter log-in name" is output. The users enter their names, which are assigned to the variable NAME. Then the prompt "Enter password" is output and the user enters his/her password. The variable PWD is bound to the entered password. That password must be compared with the password corresponding to NAME in the list PWF. When the expression,

(MEMBER NAME PWF)   (4-36)

is evaluated, the list starting with the atom bound to NAME will be returned. Thus,

(CADR (MEMBER NAME PWF))   (4-37)

will return the password corresponding to the input name. The evaluation of the COND expression causes the desired output. That is, if the password is correct, "System accessed" will be output whereas if the password is incorrect, "Access denied" will be output. Note that if the atom to which NAME is bound is not an atom in the list PASS, then "Access denied" will be output also.

One of Lisp's great advantages is that programs can modify themselves. Let us consider an example of this. Computer systems are often subject to attack by persons who should not have access to them. Those people try passwords at random until they find one that is correct. In such cases, a single password system often is not adequate; it might be desirable to use a system that requires two passwords. On the other hand, if there is no tampering, then the use of two passwords would be a nuisance to the users. Thus, it would be appropriate for the procedure PWD-CHECK to require only one password when there is no evidence of tampering, but to change itself and require two passwords if there is evidence of tampering.

```
(SETQ PASS '(TOM ABC BILL DEF JOE GHIJ))


(DEFUN PWD-CHECK(PWF)
   (TERPRI)
   (PRINC "Enter log-in name   ")
   (SETQ NAME (READ))
   (TERPRI)
   (PRINC "Enter password   ")
   (TERPRI)
   (SETQ PWD (READ))
   (COND ((EQUAL PWD (CADR (MEMBER NAME PWF))) (PRINC "System accessed"))
         (T (PRINC "Access denied")
            (DEFUN PWD-CHECK(PWF)
               (TERPRI)
               (PRINC "Enter log-in name")
               (TERPRI)
               (SETQ NAME (READ))
               (TERPRI)
               (PRINC "Enter first password")
               (TERPRI)
               (SETQ PWD (READ))
               (COND ((EQUAL PWD (CADR (MEMBER NAME PWF)))
                      (PRINC "Enter second password")
                      (TERPRI)
                      (COND ((EQUAL (READ) 'ZXCVB) (PRINC "System accessed"))
                            (T (PRINC "Access denied"))
                      )
                  ).
                  (T (PRINC "Access denied"))
            )
         )
      )
   )
)
```

Figure 4.4. A modified procedure PWD-CHECK that modifies itself if an improper password has been entered

A procedure that modifies itself is illustrated in figure 4.4 where we have rewritten PWD-CHECK. The first part of figure 4.4 is the same as that of figure 4.3. In fact, if the correct password is entered, the operation will be the same as that of the procedure of figure 4.3. If an improper password is entered the words "Access denied" will be output just as if the procedure of figure 4.3 were being evaluated. However, there are additional expressions in the second branch of figure 4.4. In particular note the second line,

(DEFUN PWD-CHECK(PWF)   (4-38)

This line, and the 19 lines following it, define a new procedure that is also called PWD-CHECK. If an improper password is entered, the lines starting with (4-38) will be evaluated and a new PWD-CHECK procedure will be established. This new procedure is very similar to the original one except that if the correct password is entered, a prompt asking for a second password is output. This second password is the same for all users and is ZXCVB. The second password is input and compared with ZXCVB. If the second password is not correct, access is denied. Note that we have oversimplified the process here. For instance, we assume that a single error is evidence of tampering. Of course, it might be simply a typing mistake on the part of a valid user of the system. You might want to modify the program so that several incorrect passwords have to be input before two passwords are required. However, the procedure of figure 4.4 serves as an illustration of a procedure that can modify itself.

If two functions are defined with the same name, the function that is defined last will be the one that is used. Thus, the procedure of figure 4.4 appears to rewrite itself. When this program is executed, the computer appears to think. That is "it decides that its program is unsatisfactory and rewrites it." Of course, the computer is directed by its program at all times and does not actually think.

Many years ago a program such as this one might have been considered to be an example of artificial intelligence. This no longer is the case and it is considered just to be an example of Lisp programming. One of the advantages of Lisp programming is that it is easy to write programs that modify themselves. If these programs are complex enough, they can be considered to be examples of artificial intelligence. The reader should note that artificial intelligence is a poorly defined term. Typically, tasks that, before they are completely understood, are assumed to be examples of artificial intelligence, are considered to be ordinary programming problems once they have been completed.

Other programming languages could be used to write a procedure that would function in the same way as that of figure 4.4. However, it is more convenient to do so in Lisp.

4-3. Looping

In some programs a sequence of calculations must be repeated many times. It is impractical to repeat the Lisp expressions over and over again. This is not only tedious, but the number of repetitions may depend upon a value passed to a function, or upon a value calculated by the program. In this case, the number of repetitions is a variable and is not known when the program is written. There are several ways that a program can be made to loop over a set of expressions. A simple construction that accomplishes looping is the DO construction. Its basic form is:

```
(DO ((I 1 (+ I 1))   ;start of first part
     (J 2 (* J 3))
    )      ;end of first part
    ((>= I 5) (PRINT I) J) ;second part                    (4-39)

    (Body of loop)  ;third part
)
```

There are three parts of the DO construction. The first part sets up the *parameters of the loop* and binds them to *initial values*. For instance, in (4-39) the loop parameters are the variables I and J, their initial values are 1 and 2 respectively. The loop parameters are commonly changed at the end of each pass through the loop. In this case, this change also is specified in the first part of the DO construction. For instance, (+ I 1), in the first line of (4-39), indicates that I will be incremented by one at the end of each pass through the loop. Similarly J is multiplied by three at the end of each pass through the loop.

The second part of the DO construction contains a test consisting of an s-expression, plus an optional sequence of s-expressions (Lisp expressions). In (4-39) the test is (>=I 5). When the result of that predicate becomes nonNIL, (that is, true) looping terminates. The DO loop of (4-39) will loop for values of I equal to 1, 2, 3, and 4. Once I becomes 5, the test will return true and looping will cease. At this time, but not before, the s-expressions in the second part of the DO construction will be evaluated. The last result of these evaluations will be the one that is returned when looping ceases. This means that when the loop (4-39) terminates, the value of I will be output and the value of J will be returned.

The third part of the DO construction is the body of the loop. This consists of valid Lisp expressions. (Note that (4-39) does not show any explicit expressions.) These expressions are executed on each pass through the loop. Note that the values of the parameters of the loop can be changed in the body of the loop. Whether this occurs or not, the loop parameters will be changed, at the end of each pass through the loop, in accordance with the directions in the first part of the DO construction.

The loop parameters (I and J in (4-39)) are called *local variables*. They exist only while the loop is being executed. For instance, suppose that the body of the DO construction (4-39) contained the following expressions:

(SETQ ABC (* 2 I))   (4-40a)
(SETQ I (* 2 I))   (4-40b)

Both SETQ expressions would be evaluated on each pass through the loop. After the loop terminated, there would be a variable called ABC that would be bound to a number equal to twice the value of I that was used last. This variable (ABC) could be used subsequently. On the other hand, after the loop terminated, the variable I, which was a parameter of the DO loop, would *not* exist and could *not* be used. The variable I is said to be local to the loop. Any variable that is initialized in the first part of the DO construction is local to the loop.

If the DO construction is embedded in a larger procedure, then variables that have been established and bound prior to the running of the loop can be used within the loop. The range over which a variable can be used is called its *scope*. The scope of the local variables is over the DO loop only. Suppose that a DO loop is embedded in a procedure and that prior to the occurrence of the loop in the procedure, the statement,

(SETQ X 3)   (4-41)

is evaluated. In this case, the scope of X will include the DO loop and therefore, X can be accessed both outside and within the DO loop. For instance, there could be an expression,

(SETQ I (+ X 4))   (4-42)

within the body of the DO loop. We shall call this variable X, whose scope includes the DO loop, an external variable. (We shall discuss other names in reference to scoping in the next chapter.)

Although a variable of the outside procedure may have the same name as one of the local variables of the DO construction, these are actually *different* variables. For instance, suppose that the DO loop of (4-39) is embedded in a procedure that has previously bound a value to a variable called I. This would cause two different variables to exist with the same name, i. e., I. One is the external variable I and the other is the local variable I. The external variable I *cannot* be accessed from within the DO loop. This is because there is a local variable that has the *same* name as the external variable. The Lisp system will assume that all references to I within the DO loop refer to the local variable. In this case, the local variable is said to have *shadowed* the external variable. The subject of scoping is a complex one. Scoping is especially important when we consider programs that are composed of many procedures. Although we shall discuss scoping in detail in the next chapter, we shall consider some examples of it in this section.

```
(DEFUN FACTORIAL(N)
   (DO ((FACT 1)
        (I 1 (+ I 1))
        )
       ((> I N) FACT)
       (SETQ FACT (* FACT I))
   )
)
```

Figure 4.5. A function that uses DO looping to compute the factorial

Let us consider some examples of the DO construction. We shall start by writing a procedure that computes the factorial of a number. The factorial of a number, n, is called factorial n and is equal to:

$$n(n-1)(n-2)...(1) \qquad\qquad (4\text{-}43)$$

For instance, factorial 5 is given by:

$$5(4)(3)(2)(1) = 120 \qquad\qquad (4\text{-}44)$$

The procedure FACTORIAL is listed in figure 4.5. In the first part of the the DO construction, the local variables FACT and I are both initialized to 1, and it is established that I will be incremented by 1 at the end of each pass through the loop. (Notice that the first part of the DO construction is written in three lines to improve readability.) The second part of the DO construction establishes that the loop will terminate when I becomes greater than N and that the returned value will be the last computed value of FACT.

The body of the DO construction consists of the single expression,

(SETQ FACT (* FACT I))   (4-45)

The initial value of FACT is 1. In each pass through the loop, FACT is multiplied by a successively larger value of I, and that product is assigned to FACT. Thus, when the looping terminates the value of FACT will be equal to the desired factorial. This value will be returned and looping will terminate.

The variable FACT is local to the DO construction. Any attempt to access FACT from outside the loop would result in an error.

```
(DEFUN FACTORIAL(N)
    (DO ((I 1 (+ I 1))
         (FACT 1 (* FACT I))
         )
        ((> I N) FACT)
    )
)
```

Figure 4.6. A modification of figure 4.5 where the do loop does not contain a body

The DO construction does not have to contain a body. Figure 4.6 is a DO construction, without any body, that also computes the factorial. Note that I and FACT are each initialized to 1 in the first part of the DO construction. In addition, the instructions there cause I to be incremented by 1 and FACT to be replaced by the product of FACT times I at the end of each pass through the loop. Thus, all the necessary calculations are performed and there is no need for a body in the DO construction. Note that all DO constructions must have a first part (parameter specification) and a second part (test), even if these parts are empty lists. We shall see an example of this shortly.

The procedure called RETURN can be used to terminate a DO loop from within its body. As soon as an expression starting with RETURN is evaluated, the DO loop will be immediately terminated. The argument of RETURN is returned when the DO loop terminates. Figure 4.7 is another procedure that evaluates the factorial. The looping is terminated by the RETURN expression within the body of the loop. In addition, there is no instruction to increment I within the first part of the DO construction. I is incremented due to the evaluation of an expression lying within the body of the DO loop. Note that FACT and I still are initialized in the first part of the DO construction.

The second part of the DO construction consists only of:

(NIL)   (4-46)

Of course, this will never become true and the loop will never terminate in the ordinary way. Now consider the body of the loop. The first SETQ expression causes I to be incremented. The next expression is,

(COND ((> I N) (RETURN FACT)))   (4-47)

When I becomes greater than N, the RETURN statement will be evaluated, looping will be terminated, and the last computed value of FACT will be returned. The last line of the body of the DO construction is the same as (4-45). Thus, the factorial is computed.

```
(DEFUN FACTORIAL(N)
   (DO ((FACT 1)
        (I 1)
       )
       (NIL)
       (SETQ I (+ I 1))
       (COND ((> I N)  (RETURN FACT)))
       (SETQ FACT (* FACT I))
   )
)
```

Figure 4.7. A modification of figure 4.5. The form of figure 4.5 is superior to this one.

The procedure of figure 4.7 is relatively awkward and that of figure 4.5, or figure 4.6, ordinarily would be used. Figure 4.7 is included for illustrative purposes. Note that it is permissible to include a test condition in the second part of the DO construction in addition to one or more RETURN expressions in the body of the loop. If a RETURN expression is evaluated, the loop will terminate. It is possible that the second part of the DO construction contains only a test. An example of this is,

((> I 10))

Note the parentheses here. If no value is returned, side effects probably occurred due to looping. It is these side effects that are utilized.

Figure 4.8 lists a simple function that illustrates some ideas of scoping. Note that the variable Y is established before the DO loop is invoked. This means that Y can be used within the DO loop as in the following expression:

(SETQ Z (+ I Y))   (4-48)

This expression both establishes and binds Z. Because Z is established within the body of the DO loop and is not a parameter of the DO loop, its scope extends beyond the loop. In particular, note the expression,

(PRINT Z)   (4-49)

that lies outside of the loop. This will be evaluated without an error. The variable I is, however, local to the loop. This would be true even if there was a SETQ expression that bound I within the loop. The comment in the next to last line of figure 4.8 emphasizes this. For instance, if this comment were replaced by (PRINT I), an error would result because I would be an unbound variable when (PRINT I) was evaluated. The expression (PRINT I) could, however, be included within the body of the DO construction.

```
(DEFUN TEST(X)
    (SETQ Y (* 2 X))
    (DO ((I 1 (+ I 2)))
        ((> I 5) Z)
        (SETQ Z (+ I Y))
    )
    (PRINT Z)
    ;  I cannot be accessed from this point
)
```

Figure 4.8. A procedure used to illustrate some ideas of scoping.

4-4. Mapping

A repeated series of operations, such as that produced by the DO construction is called *iteration*. In this section we shall consider another form of iteration. Sometimes it can be very convenient to be able to perform an operation using each element of a list in turn. For instance, suppose that we have a list of numbers and want to generate a new list that contains the square of each of the numbers in the original list. We could write a procedure using a series of CARs and CDRs that extracts each element of the list. Each of these elements could be squared and, finally all the squares could be combined into a list using the primitive LIST. Because procedures such as this would have to be written often, Lisp programming could become very tedious. Fortunately, there are some primitives that can perform the desired operations with a single expression. This type of processing of successive items in a list is termed a *mapping*. We shall consider mapping procedures in this section.

The primitive MAPCAR is a mapping function. Let us consider an example of its use. Assume that the two expressions,

(SETQ X '(1 2 3 4))   (4-50a)
(SETQ Y '(5 6 7 8 9 10))   (4-50b)

are evaluated, thus binding each of X and Y to different lists of numbers. Suppose that we want to add the first element of X to the first element of Y and then add the second element of X to the second element of Y, until all the elements of the shorter list have been used. The desired result can be obtained by the evaluation of:

(MAPCAR #'+ X Y)   (4-51)

The list (6 8 10 12) will be returned. Before discussing the operation of MAPCAR let us consider some notation. Note that the function name, + in this case, is preceded by a pound sign (#) and an apostrophe. In some Lisp systems, the pound sign is omitted and in other Lisp systems both the pound sign and the apostrophe are omitted. We shall discuss this again when the topic of scope is considered in the next chapter.

When (4-51) is evaluated, the + procedure is applied to the first elements of the X and Y lists, i. e., these elements become the arguments of the + function. Next, the + procedure is again applied to the second elements of the X and Y lists. This procedure is repeated with successive elements of the X and Y lists until *all* the elements of *one* of the lists are exhausted. The results of all the applications of the + procedure are then placed in a list. For the case in question this is the list (6 8 10 12). Note that the X list has four elements while the Y list has six elements. Thus, when (4-51) is evaluated, the + procedure will be applied four times. Expression (4-51) illustrates the use of MAPCAR with a function (+) with two arguments (each being a corresponding element of X and Y). Thus, (in 4-51) MAPCAR has three arguments. In most Lisp systems the allowable number of arguments of MAPCAR depends on the number of arguments allowed to the function that is the first argument of MAPCAR (+ in our example). (Note that some Lisp systems do limit the total number of arguments allowed to MAPCAR.)

In general, MAPCAR's first argument is a procedure. When MAPCAR is evaluated, successive corresponding elements of the lists that are the second and third (or more) arguments are supplied to that procedure as its arguments. The results of each evaluation of the function are combined into a list. That list is returned by MAPCAR.

As an additional example of the use of MAPCAR, let us write a function that takes a single list of numbers as its argument and returns another list, each of whose elements is the square of the corresponding element in the argument list. In addition, one element is to be added to the resulting list; That element is to be the sum of all the preceding elements of the new list. In other words, the resulting list is to contain the squares of the elements of the argument plus one additional number that is the sum of all the squares. The function is called SQUARE-LIST-SUM and it is illustrated in figure 4.9. The function has a single argument, LST. It is assumed that LST represents a list, each of whose elements is a number. The list of squares is obtained using the expression:

(SETQ SQUARED-LIST (MAPCAR #'* LST LST))   (4-52)

```
(DEFUN SQUARE-LIST-SUM(LST)
   (SETQ SQUARED-LIST (MAPCAR #'* LST LST))
   (SETQ SQUARED-LIST (APPEND SQUARED-LIST (LIST (APPLY #'+ SQUARED-LIST)))))
)
```

Figure 4.9. An illustration of the use of MAPCAR and APPLY.

Each of the elements of LST is multiplied by itself and a list of these squares is set up. The variable SQUARED-LIST is bound to the resulting list.
Now we have a problem. We want to sum the elements of a list that has been assigned to a variable. We cannot simply write,

(+ SQUARED-LIST) ;wrong   (4-53)

because the + procedure will treat SQUARED-LIST as an atom which is bound to a number. We must be able to indicate to the procedure that the variable name (SQUARED-LIST), represents a list of arguments rather than an atom. This can be accomplished using the primitive APPLY. For example, to obtain the desired sum we would write,

(APPLY #'+ SQUARED-LIST)   (4-54)

As in the case of MAPCAR, the pound sign and/or the apostrophe may be omitted with some Lisp systems. Expression (4-54) causes the elements of SQUARED-LIST to become the arguments of the + function. Thus, the desired operation has been obtained. APPLY is not a mapping procedure. It simply causes the value to which an atom is bound, which may be a list, to become the arguments of a procedure.

The sum obtained from the evaluation of (4-54) must be appended to the list SQUARED-LIST. This is accomplished using the next to last line of figure 4.9. The LIST primitive returns a single element list that contains the desired sum. This is then APPENDed to the the list SQUARED-LIST.

Note that the procedure SQUARE-LIST-SUM sets up a variable called SQUARED-LIST. This variable can be accessed after the procedure has terminated. (We shall modify this statement somewhat in the discussions of the next chapter.) You must be careful when variables are established inside a procedure. Suppose that the procedure SQUARE-LIST-SUM was called by another procedure. If the calling procedure also had a variable called SQUARED-LIST, then that variable would be modified when SQUARE-LIST-SUM was evaluated. If you did not intend for such a change to occur, then your program would contain a logical error. Such errors are often difficult to detect. In figure 4.10 we illustrate another SQUARE-LIST-SUM procedure that does not establish a new variable within itself. This procedure, however, will take longer to run, and will use more memory than that of figure 4.9 because,

```
(MAPCAR #'* LST LST)
```

must be evaluated twice.

```
(DEFUN SQUARE-LIST-SUM(LST)
    (APPEND (MAPCAR #'* LST LST) (LIST (APPLY #'+ (MAPCAR #'* LST LST)))))
)
```

Figure 4.10. A modification of the function of figure 4.9 that does not bind a variable.

Let us consider some additional examples of the use of MAPCAR. Suppose that the following statements are evaluated:

```
(SETQ AA '(TOM ED WILLIAM BOB))                    (4-55a)
(SETQ BB '(SMITH JONES THOMPSON WILSON))           (4-55b)
```

Assume that AA represents a list of first names and BB represents a list of last names. Now suppose that we want a list of first names followed by corresponding last names. If,

(MAPCAR #'LIST AA BB)   (4-56)

is evaluated, the list that is returned will be:

((TOM SMITH) (ED JONES) (WILLIAM THOMPSON) (BOB WILSON))
(4-57)

The LIST procedure sets up a list each of whose elements is one of the arguments to LIST. Thus, a different list will be set up for each of the elements of AA (or BB). All of the lists will be combined into a single list of lists, see (4-57).

Suppose that, instead of a list of lists, a single list is wanted. For the case in question, that list would be:

(TOM SMITH ED JONES WILLIAM THOMPSON BOB WILSON) (4-58)

Such a list could be generated from the list (4-57) by extracting the sublists using CAR and CDR, repeatedly. The single list could be set up by proper application of NCONC. This is a tedious operation. Fortunately, however, such an operation is not necessary because there is a Lisp primitive named MAPCAN that will do it for you. MAPCAN is equivalent to MAPCAR except that it combines all the output sublists into a single list. (When MAPCON is used, each individual operation should return a list.) For instance,

(MAPCAN #'LIST AA BB)   (4-59)

will return (4-58). The comments concerning the pound sign and the apostrophe that relate to MAPCAR apply to MAPCAN also.

There are several other mapping procedures. MAPLIST is similar to MAPCAR except that it repeatedly supplies entire *lists*, rather than *elements* of lists, as arguments to the procedure that is the first argument of MAPLIST. The lists supplied by MAPLIST as arguments to the specified procedure consists of the original lists and successive CDRs of those lists. For instance,

(MAPLIST #'LIST AA BB)   (4-60)

will return:

  (((TOM ED WILLIAM BOB) (SMITH JONES THOMPSON WILSON))
  ((ED WILLIAM BOB) (JONES THOMPSON WILSON))
  ((WILLIAM BOB) (THOMPSON WILSON)) ((BOB) (WILSON)))

                                             (4-61)

The lists that MAPLIST supplies to the procedure that is its first argument are the original lists that are the second, and additional arguments, of MAPLIST; the original lists with the first element removed, the original lists with the first two elements removed, etc.

    The procedure MAPCON is similar to MAPCAN except that it works with lists in the same manner as does MAPLIST. For instance,

  (MAPCON #'LIST AA BB)   (4-62)

will return,

  ((TOM ED WILLIAM BOB) (SMITH JONES THOMPSON WILSON)
  (ED WILLIAM BOB) (JONES THOMPSON WILSON) (WILLIAM BOB)
  (THOMPSON WILSON) (BOB) (WILSON))

                                             (4-63)

Note that each of MAPCAR and MAPCAN provides arguments that are elements of lists to the function that is their first argument while MAPLIST and MAPCON provide arguments that are lists to the function that is their first argument.

    When mapping procedures are evaluated, there may be side effects. What these side effects are will depend on the procedure that is used as the first argument of the mapping procedure. Sometimes it is these side effects that are of prime importance to the program while the entity returned by the mapping procedure is not used at all. In such cases the operation would be faster if the mapping procedure simply returned NIL, or one of its arguments. Such mapping procedures are provided in many Lisp systems. For instance MAPC acts in the same way as does MAPCAR except that it returns its first argument. (MAPC returns NIL in some Lisp systems.)

    We have considered several mapping procedures in this section. Some Lisp systems provide additional mapping procedures. However, they are similar to those that we have considered here. Consult your Lisp manual to determine all the mapping procedures that are available for your system.

4-5. Local Variables - LET - LET* - DO*

In the last section we discussed that the procedure of figure 4.9 might be prone to logical errors because SETQ was used inside the procedure to bind a variable called SQUARED-LIST. Remember that if the procedure SQUARE-SUM-LIST were called by another procedure, that also happened to include a variable called SQUARED-LIST, that variable might be changed inadvertently. (We shall discuss these ideas in greater detail in the next chapter.) The DO construction, *see* sec. 4-3, set up local variables that were parameters of the loop. These local variables did not exist outside of the loop. The above discussed problems do not occur when local variables are used. That is, a change in a local variable will not change an external one, and vice versa. It would be desirable to be able to set up and bind local variables that are not parameters of a DO loop.

Lisp provides the LET construction to establish local variables that exist only within that construction. In addition, these local variables can be bound to initial values. The initial values can be computed and these computations can include branching. The techniques that are used to set up the initial values for the local variables of the LET construction also can be used to establish the initial values for the parameters of a DO loop. Thus, the discussions of this section apply to the parameters of a DO loop as well. In fact, we shall extend the discussion of DO looping in this section.

Let us consider a specific use of the LET construction.

```
(LET ((VAR1 3)
      (VAR2 5)
      ) ;end of variable definition and initial binding
   (Body of LET construction)
)                                                            (4-64)
```

The first part of the LET construction consists of variable definition and initial binding. It is exactly the same as the first part of the DO construction. Local variables are established and optionally can be given initial values. In (4-64) there are two variables, VAR1 and VAR2, with initial values of 3 and 5, respectively. The body of the LET construction contains valid Lisp expressions. These can use VAR1 and VAR2. In fact, VAR1 and/or VAR2 can be rebound using SETQ within the body of the LET construction. After the expressions in the body of the LET construction have been executed, the LET operation terminates. The variables VAR1 and VAR2 are local to the LET construction. They cannot be accessed from outside that construction. If the LET construction were embedded within a procedure that used variables that happened also to be called VAR1 and VAR2, those variables would not be changed by operations on VAR1 and VAR2 within the body of the LET construction. Observe that the LET construction is very similar to the DO construction, except that the second part of the DO construction is missing from the LET construction. The LET construction can be thought of as a DO construction that loops only once.

```
(DEFUN SQUARE-LIST-SUM(LST)
   (LET ((SQUARED-LIST))        ;start of LET construction
     (SETQ SQUARED-LIST (MAPCAR #'* LST LST))
       (APPEND SQUARED-LIST (LIST (APPLY #'+ SQUARED-LIST)))
   )        ;End of LET construction
)
```

Figure 4.11. A modification of the procedure of figure 4.9 that binds local variables only.

As an example of the LET construction, we have rewritten the procedure SQUARE-LIST-SUM of figure 4.9. The new procedure is listed in figure 4.11. We now have used the LET construction to make SQUARED-LIST a local variable. Note that we have not assigned an initial value to SQUARED-LIST. Such assignment is optional in the LET (and DO) construction. Thus, the first part of the LET construction has the form:

((SQUARED-LIST))   (4-65)

Note that the list which contains the sum of the squares is returned by the procedure SQUARE_LIST_SUM. However, we did not bind the variable SQUARED_LIST to this list. There is no reason to do so because SQUARED_LIST cannot be accessed outside the procedure SQUARE_LIST_SUM.

```
(DEFUN TEST(N)
   (LET ((A (COND ((> N 3) 6)
                  (T 1)
            )
         )
         (B (* 2 A))        ;Error A not yet bound
     )
       (PRINT A)
       (PRINT B)
   )
)
```

Figure 4.12. A LET construction which contains an error because A is not bound at the time that the initial value of B is established

The initial values can be obtained from the result of a calculation. For instance, consider the procedure TEST of figure 4.12. There are two local variables, A and B. The initial value assigned to A depends upon N, the parameter of TEST. If N is greater than three, the initial value of A will be 6. On the other hand, if N is equal to or less than three, then the initial value of A will be 1. The initial value of B will be two times the initial value of A. *All of the initial values are established before any one of them is bound.* This means that A is not bound to a value until after the value of B is calculated. There is an error in figure 4.12 because the initial value of B depends upon the value of A. However, at the time that the initial value of B is being calculated, A has not yet been bound. Thus, an unbound error will result. When LET is evaluated, we say that the initial values are *assigned in parallel.*

```
(DEFUN TEST(N)
   (LET* ((A (COND ((> N 3) 6)
                   (T 1)
           )
         )
         (B (* 2 A))
      )
         (PRINT A)
         (PRINT B)
   )
)
```

Figure 4.13. A LET* construction without the problem of figure 4.12

There are times when we want to assign initial values *sequentially*. Fortunately Lisp provides an alternative primitive LET*, pronounced LET star, that operates in the same way as does LET, except that the initial values are assigned sequentially. That is, the first initial value is computed and bound and then the second initial value is computed and bound, etc. For example, consider figure 4.13, which is essentially the same as figure 4.12 except that the asterisk (*) is written after LET. In the procedure of figure 4.13, the value of A is computed and A is bound to that value; *next* the value of B is computed and B is bound to it. Now the procedure works, because a value has been assigned to A before the value of B is calculated.

It may seem as though LET* always should be used. Of course, there are occasions when it makes no difference. However, there are instances when it is desirable to use LET. Suppose that when the procedure TEST of figure 4.12 is evaluated, a variable called A has already been bound to a numerical value. Let us call this the external A. When LET is evaluated, the value of the external A will be used when the initial values are calculated. Let us consider this in detail. When LET is used, the initial values of its local variables are computed and temporarily stored in memory. After *all* the initial values are computed, the values are retrieved from memory and bound to the local variables. Before this takes place, the local variables are unbound. Thus, if a local variable has the same name as an external variable, the local variable will not shadow the external variable, *see* sec. 4-3, until *after* all the initial values have been calculated. For example, suppose that procedure TEST of figure 4.12 is part of an external procedure that has bound A to 8. Now the evaluation of TEST will not result in an error because the external A will be used to compute the initial value of B. (This may not be what was intended, however.) In this case the initial value of A will depend upon the parameter of TEST, e. g., A will be assigned the value 6 if N is greater than 3. However the initial value of B will always be 16, because B's initial value is twice the value of the *external* A, the only A that exists when B's initial value is computed. Once the initial values are assigned the local A will shadow the external A during the evaluation of the LET construction.

The assignment of the DO loop parameters in a DO construction follows the same rules as those for the LET construction. That is, all the initial values are calculated before any of them are assigned. Thus, the previous discussion also applies to the initial values of the DO loop parameters of the DO construction. In addition, the DO loop parameters of the DO construction are updated at the end of each pass through the DO loop. This is also done in parallel. That is, all the updated values are calculated and *then* the new values are assigned. If one DO loop parameter's updated value depends upon another parameter, the old value of that local variable is used in the calculation. Note that both the initial values and the updated values are assigned in parallel.

There is a construction called DO* that has the same relation to DO that LET* has to LET. That is, when DO* is used, each initial value is computed and immediately bound. In addition, each updated value of the parameters of the DO* loop are bound immediately after they are computed. The variables are calculated and bound in the order that they are written in the first part of the DO* construction. Note that this order may effect the computed updated values of some of the parameters of the DO* construction. For instance, assume that the updated value of one of the DO* loop parameters, say J, depends on the value of a another DO* loop parameter, say I. The updated value of J will be a function of the *updated* value of I only if J is defined *after* I in the first part of the DO* construction.

4-6. Some Additional Operations

In this section we shall discuss some additional kinds of control operations. We shall start by considering some operations that sometimes can be used as an alternative to COND.

THE IF CONSTRUCTION

The COND construction can set up any number of branches in a program. However, there are occasions when only two branches have to be established and the choice of branching depends on only a single condition. If that condition is true, then one branch is taken; otherwise the other branch is taken. Of course, the COND construction could be used for such branching, as figure 4.3 illustrates. However, there is a somewhat simpler construction, called IF, that directly implements this situation. The advantage of IF is that it is somewhat simpler than COND and, furthermore, it relates to similar constructions that are used in other programming languages.

A very simple example of the use of the IF construction is:

$$\text{(IF T (PRINT "YES") (PRINT "NO"))} \qquad \text{(4-66a)}$$

When this is evaluated "YES" will be output. On the other hand, if,

$$\text{(IF NIL (PRINT "YES") (PRINT "NO"))} \qquad \text{(4-66b)}$$

is evaluated, "NO" will be output. The general form of the IF construction is the word IF followed by a test and two s-expressions. If the test evaluates to true, then the first s-expression will be evaluated and the second will be ignored. If the test evaluates to false, then the first s-expression will be ignored and the second one will be evaluated.

```
(SETQ PASS  (TOM ABC BILL DEF JOE GHIJ))

(DEFUN PWD-CHECK(PWF)
   (TERPRI)
   (PRINC "Enter log-in name   ")
   (SETQ NAME (READ))
   (TERPRI)
   (PRINC "Enter password   ")
   (TERPRI)
   (SETQ PWD (READ))
   (IF (EQUAL PWD (CADR (MEMBER NAME PWF))) (PRINC "System accessed")
                  (PRINC "Access denied")
   )
)
```

Figure 4.14. A modification of the program of figure 4.3 that uses the IF construction

A more realistic example of the IF construction is shown in figure 4.14 which is a modification of the password check program of figure 4.3. The COND construction of figure 4.3 has been replaced by the IF construction of figure 4.14.

THE CASE CONSTRUCTION

Often, computer programs present the person running the program with a menu of options. The user then enters a letter, a number, or sequence of letters and/or numbers to pick the desired option. Each option usually represents a branch of the program and such branching could be obtained using the COND construction. The test in each case would have to verify if the proper sequence of characters had been entered. The CASE construction is similar to the COND construction but it avoids the necessity of writing the tests. The general form of the CASE construction is

```
(CASE KEYFORM
    (KEYLIST1 s-expressions1)
    (KEYLIST2 s-expressions2)
    (KEYLIST3 s-expressions3)                    (4-67)
    (...)
)
```

In general, KEYFORM represents a variable while KEYLIST1, KEYLIST2, ... each represent a string of alphanumeric characters. If KEYFORM is assigned the same value as KEYLIST1, then s-expressions1 will be evaluated; if KEYFORM is assigned the same value as KEYLIST2, then s-expressions2 will be evaluated, etc. The value returned by the CASE construction will be the value returned by the last evaluated s-expression. Of course the evaluation of the s-expressions can introduce side effects. If KEYFORM does not match any of the KEYLISTs, then no s-expressions will be evaluated and NIL will be returned. A KEYLIST and its corresponding s-expressions are called a *clause* of the CASE construction.

```
(DEFUN ARITH(A B)
   (TERPRI)
   (PRINC "MENU")
   (TERPRI)
   (PRINC "ADD TO ADD")
   (TERPRI)
   (PRINC "MULT TO MULTIPLY")
   (TERPRI)
   (CASE (READ)
      (ADD (+ A B))
      (MULT ( * A B))
    )
)
```

Figure 4.15. An example of a menu operation using the CASE construction

Figure 4.15 contains a listing of a procedure that uses the CASE construction. The procedure ARITH has two arguments which are numbers. When the procedure is run the following menu appears on the screen:

```
MENU
ADD TO ADD
MULT TO MULTIPLY
```

The person running the program then enters either ADD or MULT. If ADD is entered, then the sum of the two arguments is returned. If MULT is entered, then the product of the two arguments is returned. Note that the KEYFORM variable of (4-67) does not appear explicitly in figure 4.15. The READ procedure is put in place of the KEYFORM variable. Thus, the value entered from the keyboard assumes the function of the KEYFORM variable.

The program of figure 4.15 has a potential problem. If the person running the program makes a mistake and enters something other than ADD or MULT in response to the menu, NIL will be returned and no operation will be performed. In this simple case, the program could be run again without much loss of time. On the other hand, the menu might be output near the end of a program that has been running for a long time. If a typographical error causes that program to terminate, much time would have been wasted. Programs with menus often are written by experienced programmers, but are designed to be run by people who have little or no programming experience. Programs that are designed to be run by such people should provide for *error trapping*. That is there should be some provision to handle errors so that a simple mistake in keyboard entry does not prevent the program from running. (Note that this is true even if the program is to be run by experienced programmers.) The program of figure 4.15 should be modified so that if something other than ADD or MULT is entered in response to the prompt of the menu, an error message is printed allowing the person running the program has a chance to try again.

```
(DEFUN ARITH(A B)
  (TERPRI)
  (PRINC "MENU")
  (TERPRI)
  (PRINC "ADD TO ADD")
  (TERPRI)
  (PRINC "MULT TO MULTIPLY")
  (TERPRI)
  (DO () (NIL)
    (CASE (READ)
        (ADD   (RETURN (+ A B)))
        (MULT (RETURN (* A B)))
        (OTHERWISE (PRINC "WRONG ENTRY TRY AGAIN") (TERPRI))
    )
  )
)
```

Figure 4.16 An improved version of the program of figure 4.15 that properly handles input errors

The CASE construction does provide for error trapping. If the *last* KEYLIST is either T or OTHERWISE, then that clause will be evaluated if the KEYFORM does *not match* any of the KEYLIST terms. In this case the last clause is called a *default*. Let us illustrate the use of the default by modifying the program of figure 4.15 to incorporate error trapping. The program is shown in figure 4.16. Note that there is a DO loop whose second part is NIL. Thus, the DO loop will cycle indefinitely unless a RETURN is evaluated. The body of the DO loop consists of a CASE construction. If the response to the menu is ADD or MULT, a RETURN expression will be evaluated and the looping will terminate. The value returned will be either the sum or the product depending upon the response to the menu. If the response to the menu is something other than ADD or MULT, then the OTHERWISE clause of the CASE construction will be evaluated, "WRONG ENTRY TRY AGAIN" will be output and the loop will cycle again. The menu will be redisplayed and the person running the program will have an opportunity to try again. The loop will keep cycling until a proper response is entered.

We have used examples of the CASE construction where the KEYLISTs were strings of letters. Actually numbers and/or other types can be used. The order of the clauses does not matter except that, if a default clause is present, it must be the last clause in the CASE construction. Our examples of the CASE construction involved menus. Of course, the CASE construction is used for other applications.

Remember that the clauses of the CASE construction can contain more than one s-expression. For instance, the first clause of the CASE construction of figure 4.16 could be:

(ADD (PRINT (+ A B)) (RETURN '(PROGRAM FINISHED)))

THE PROG CONSTRUCTION

We shall now consider another control procedure that can produces looping. Indeed, this procedure can be used to cause control to jump about in a procedure. Actually this is an undesirable form to use because it can result in programs that are very error prone and that are hard to debug. This form should be avoided in most cases. However, there are rare occasions when it may be useful and, because of that, we include it here.

Early Lisp systems introduced the *programming feature* that allowed programmers to write programs that incorporated features that were similar to those found in other programming languages. Since Lisp has been expanded these features are seldom needed. The general form for the PROG construction is:

```
(PROG (Optional list of local variables)
    (Body of PROG)                                    (4-68)

)
```

The optional list of local variables consists of a list of variable names. These will be local to the body of PROG. They function in the same way as do the local variables in the LET construction. Note that there is no provision for initialization of the local variables when PROG is used. The body of the PROG construction contains s-expressions. The execution of a RETURN will terminate the evaluation of PROG.

The PROG construction allows the use of the GO expression and for the use of *labels*. The general form of the GO expression is,

(GO SOMEPLACE)   (4-69)

where SOMEPLACE is an arbitrary name. When (4-69) is evaluated, operation will jump to the point in the program marked SOMEPLACE. Such a marker is called a *label*. For instance, we could have,

```
(PROG (ABC)
    s-expressions1
    SOMEPLACE
    s-expressions2                                               (4-70)
    (GO SOMEPLACE)
)
```

When (4-70) is evaluated, s-expressions1, which represents a sequence of s-expressions, will be evaluated; then s-expressions2 will be evaluated. When (GO SOMEPLACE) is evaluated, operation will jump to the label SOMEPLACE. Thus, s-expressions2 will be evaluated again. This process will continue indefinitely until a RETURN expression is evaluated. If the program is not to be trapped in an endless loop, then s-expressions2 must contain a RETURN statement, usually as part of a COND operation.

```
(DEFUN FACTORIAL(N)
    (PROG(FACT I)          ;This form should not be used
        (SETQ FACT 1)
        (SETQ I 1)
    BAD-FORM
        (SETQ I (+ I 1))
        (COND ((> I N)    (RETURN FACT)))
        (SETQ FACT (* FACT I))
        (GO BAD-FORM)
    )
)
```

Figure 4.17. An example of the use of PROG and GO. This form of programming should be avoided

Figure 4.17 is an illustration of the use of PROG and GO. It is a modification of the FACTORIAL function of figure 4.5. In this example, GO is used to obtain looping.

The operation will loop from the,

(GO BAD-FORM)

expression to the BAD-FORM label. Note that the value of I is incremented by a SETQ expression and the COND statement is used to terminate looping.

If the PROG construction does not incorporate looping, there is no need for a RETURN expression. In this case NIL will be returned after the last s-expression has been evaluated.

There are some variants of PROG, that are only vaguely related to it. These constructions do not allow looping to be used and cannot be used to set up local variables, but they do allow sequences to s-expressions to be grouped. They now are rarely used, but were used in the early days of Lisp when sequences of s-expressions were not allowed in the branches of a COND construction. They are still used with the IF construction. When a PROG1 construction is evaluated, each of its s-expressions is evaluated in order, but the value returned by PROG1 is the value of the first s-expression. Note that local variables cannot be set up with PROG1 and a RETURN cannot be evaluated to terminate the operations of PROG1. In addition, PROG1 can not be used with looping. All the s-expressions in the body of PROG1 will be evaluated in order. The value of the first evaluated s-expression will be that returned by PROG1. For instance, when,

```
(PROG1 (SETQ X 3)
       (SETQ Y 4)
       (PRINT (* X Y))                                        (4-71)
 )
```

is evaluated, the value returned will be 3. However, as a side effect, the value of 12 will be printed. PROG2 functions in the same way as PROG1 except that the value returned by PROG2 will be the value returned by the second s-expression in the body. PROGN functions in the same way as PROG1 except that it returns the value of the last s-expression in the body of the PROGN construction. Note that the IF construction allows only single Lisp expressions to be evaluated. However, several Lisp expressions can be grouped into one "compound expression" using PROG1 or PROGN. For example (4-71) could be used to replace either Lisp expression in (4-66a) or (4-66b).

The use of the GO expression is called incorporating a *goto* into the program. Modern programming techniques teach us to avoid the use of goto's. It is possible to use GO expressions and labels in such a way that the program loops back on itself like a pretzel. Such programs can contain subtle logical bugs, and debugging can become extremely difficult. Modern programming techniques involve writing programs in a form that is called *structured programming*. One of the prime rules of structured programming is that the programs should not use GO constructions.

Another rule of structured programs is that they should be *self documenting*. That is, the program should be understandable not only to the programmer who wrote it, but also to other programmers who read it. A program can be made self documenting by choosing meaningful variable names. For instance a variable in a program that calculates interest should be called INTEREST rather than I. In addition, comments should be distributed throughout a complex program to explain its operation.

Documentation is also supplied in the form of text that tells users of the program how to run it. Often, these users are not programmers. The documentation should very clearly state how to run the program. The program itself should include additional information that helps the people to run it. For instance, menus can be included when the person running the program has to make a choice. Prompts should be provided whenever data is to be entered. Note that menus can be overdone. Once the person running the program becomes familiar with its operations, menus can become cumbersome. Thus, there should be some provision for making the menus optional. Documentation for users is important. Many good programs have been ruined by poor documentation. If people do not understand how to run your program, then it will not be used, no matter how good it is!

Exercises

Test any procedures that you write by running them on your computer.

1. What is a predicate? How does the Lisp system represent true and false?

2. Discuss the similarities and differences among the predicates EQUAL, EQ, and EQL.

3. Write an expression that determines if two atoms are bound to two lists each of which prints the same.

4. Write a function that determines if two atoms are bound to an identical list. (That is, there is only one list stored in memory).

5. Write a function that has four numbers as arguments. The function is to return true if the first argument is equal to the second argument and the second argument is greater than the third argument, and the third argument is greater than the fourth argument. The function is to return false otherwise.

6. Write a function that returns a student's letter grade. The arguments of the function are to be four individual test grades. The letter grade is to be based on the student's average. If the average is 90 or more, the grade is to be A; if the average is 80 or more, but less than 90, the grade is to be B; if the average is 70 or more, but less than 80, the grade is to be C; if the grade is 60 or more, but less than 70, the grade is to be D; if the average is less than 60 the grade is F.

7. Write a function that has four numerical arguments and returns the smallest of them.

8. Write a function that has four numerical arguments and returns the one that has the smallest absolute value.

9. A list contains the names of people. They are listed in the order: first name last name. For instance:

(JOHN SMITH WALTER ANDERSON EDWARD BAKER)

Write a function that is passed the name of the list and a first name. The function is to return the corresponding last name. Assume that no first name is duplicated.

10. Repeat exercise 9, but now assume that the function is passed the last name and is to return the first name. Assume that no last name is duplicated. Hint: use LENGTH and looping.

11. Repeat exercise 9 but now assume that several people may have identical first names. All the last names that correspond to the input first name should be output to the screen.

12. Repeat exercise 10 but now assume that several people may have identical last names. All the first names that correspond to the input last name should be output to the screen.

13. Modify the password check program of figure 4.3 so that the person running the program has two chances to input the proper password. That is, if the improper password is input,

Try again

is output to the screen and the user can try again. Only two attempts should be allowed.

14. Modify the password check program of Fig. 4-4 so that the person running the program has three chances to enter the proper password. If, after three tries, the proper password is not entered, the program should rewrite itself so that two separate passwords are required.

15. Write a function that reads five numbers entered from the keyboard and returns their average. Use looping to obtain the sum.

16. Write a function that is passed a list of numbers and returns their average. Hint: The number of numbers in the list can be obtained using LENGTH. The individual numbers can be extracted by successively applying CAR and CDR. Do not use APPLY.

17. Write a function that is passed a list of names and returns the number of times that SMITH appears in the list. Do not use mapping in your function.

18. What is meant by a local variable.

19. Use your Lisp system to demonstrate that the DO loop parameters are local variables.

20. What is meant by a mapping?

21. Repeat exercise 17 but now use mapping. Hint: write a procedure that sets up a dummy list and then use MAPCAR.

22. Write a function that checks to see if each element of a list is an atom.

23. Repeat exercise 22, but now check if each element is a list.

24. There are four lists, each of which contains the grades for 10 students in a test. (There are four tests. Student number one's grade is listed first; student number two's grade is listed second, etc.) Write a function that outputs a list that contains each student's average.

25. Repeat exercise 16, but now use APPLY.

26. Write a procedure that takes the first atom in a list of numbers and increments a variable called SUM by the numerical value of that first atom. The procedure is to return the number read from the list if the list is not empty, and NIL if the list is empty. Then use this function and MAPLIST to obtain the sum of all the numbers in a list of arbitrary length.

27. Write a function that computes the value of the following expression.

$$f = 2x + 3y + x^2$$

Then use that function to obtain f for all integral values of x between -5 and 5 and all values of y between 0 and 10.

28. Write a function which, when input two lists of names, outputs to the screen any name that appears on both lists. Use LET to make any internal variables local. Assume that no duplicate names appear on either list.

29. Discuss the differences between LET and LET*. Write procedures to check your discussion.

30. Discuss the differences between DO and DO*. Write procedures to check your discussion.

31. Write a procedure that is passed a list and returns the number of numerical atoms in the list. Use the IF construction in your function.

32. Write a program which, depending on the choice of the person running the program either: (1) Outputs the average of an arbitrary number of positive grades entered by the person running the program. Entry stops when a negative number is entered. (2) Supplies a letter grade when an average is entered by the person running the program. The grading standards of exercise 6 are to be used here. (3) Returns the highest and lowest of four grades entered by the person running the program.

A menu of the three possible operations is to be provided. If the response to the menu is in error, a message is to be output and the person running the program is to be given another chance. The user is to be prompted for all input data.

33. Why should the use of GO expressions be avoided?

34. Why is it important to have proper documentation?

5

Procedures

Some basic concepts relating to procedures were introduced in chapter 1. Using these ideas we were able to write simple procedures. However, a fuller discussion of procedures is necessary. A thorough understanding of procedures and their use is of great importance to Lisp programming. We shall consider additional topics that relate to procedures in this chapter. The subject of scoping shall be considered in detail here.

A very powerful feature of Lisp, and other modern programming languages, is the ability of procedures to call themselves. We shall discuss such recursive procedure calls in this chapter. The subject of lambda definitions, which is related to procedures, shall also be considered here.

5-1. Additional Features of Procedures

All of the procedures that we have written thus far had a list (perhaps empty) of arguments. The values of these arguments were passed to the procedure. (Remember that the list of arguments is called a formal parameter list.) These values were, presumably, manipulated by the procedure. The variables in the formal parameter list were local variables of the procedure. The formal parameter list is more versatile than we have indicated. Let us discuss some useful extensions to operations with parameters and then see how they can be implemented.

Up to this point, a fixed number of arguments has been specified for each procedure. For instance, suppose that we wrote a procedure that averaged four numbers. The expression that calls the procedure must have exactly four arguments. However, we might want to average more than four numbers. In fact, the total number might be arbitrary. There should be a way of designating an arbitrary number of arguments for the averaging procedure.

There are times when a parameter of a procedure is fixed most of the time, but may vary only on rare occasions. For instance, suppose that a procedure calculates the profit of a store based upon costs, sales and a fixed markup rate. Most of the time the markup rate is fixed. However, occasionally you might want to run the program using a different markup rate. It should not be necessary to enter the markup rate unless it differs from the standard value. The standard value should be the *default*. There should be provision for having optional arguments of a procedure. If no parameter is entered for an optional argument, the parameter should take on a specified default value. On the other hand, if a value is specified for that parameter, then the default value should be replaced by the specified value.

In sec. 4-5 we discussed that local variables could be established using LET* (as well as LET). At times, it would be more convenient if the local variables could be specified in the formal parameter list. The programmer should be able to specify the initial values of these local variables in the same way as he or she could with LET*.

We shall now see how these ideas can be implemented when procedures are written. Let us start by discussing how to write a procedure with an arbitrary number of arguments. If the word &REST, followed by a name is included after the normal list of formal parameters, then any "extra" arguments will be placed into the named list. For example if a first line in a procedure definition is,

(DEFUN TEST(A B C &REST STORE)   (5-1)

the procedure test will have three arguments A, B, and C. (Note the unmatched parentheses in (5-1). Of course the closing parenthesis occurs at the end of the listing of the function TEST.) If TEST is passed *more* than three arguments, then the additional arguments will be stored in a list named STORE. Note that the name STORE has no significance. If there are exactly three arguments passed to TEST, STORE will evaluate to NIL (i. e., the empty list). If less than three arguments are passed to TEST, an error will result. For example, if the calling expression is,

TEST(4 5 6 7 8)   (5-2a)

then the variables A, B, and C will be assigned 4, 5, and 6, respectively. STORE will be assigned the list:

(7 8)

However, if the calling expression is,

(TEST 4 5 6)   (5-2b)

then the variables A, B, and C will be assigned 4, 5, and 6, respectively, while STORE will be assigned NIL.

```
(DEFUN ARB-AVERAGE(A B C &REST LST)
    (COND (LST (SETQ SUM (APPLY #'+ LST))
               (SETQ NUMBER (+ 3 (LENGTH LST)))
          )
               (T (SETQ SUM 0)
                  (SETQ NUMBER 3)
               )
    )
    (SETQ SUM (+ SUM A B C))
    (/ SUM NUMBER)
)
```

Figure 5.1. A procedure that uses &REST so that it can pass three or more arguments

As an illustration of the use of &REST let us write a procedure that returns the average of its arguments. We shall assume that there will be a minimum of three arguments. The procedure ARB-AVERAGE is shown in figure 5.1. Note that a minimum of three arguments are required, they are assigned to A, B, and C. Any additional arguments will be assigned to the list

LST. If there are only three arguments in the calling statement then LST will be empty, that is it will evaluate to NIL.

The sum of all the arguments must be obtained and that sum must be divided by the number of arguments. Consider the COND procedure. If LST is nonNIL then a variable called SUM will be bound to the sum of all the variables in the list bound to LST. Remember that any non-NIL value is considered to be true. Note that we use APPLY to obtain the desired sum. In addition, NUMBER will be bound to three plus the length of LST. Thus, NUMBER will be assigned the total number of arguments of ARB-AVERAGE. On the other hand, if LST evaluates to NIL, then SUM will be bound to 0 and NUMBER will be bound to 3.

Next, the sum of the first three arguments will be added to the value assigned to SUM. Thus, SUM will finally be assigned the sum of all the arguments. The desired average is computed in the next-to-last line.

The variables SUM and NUMBER in the procedure of figure 5.1 are not local to it. In general, it would be desirable to make these local variables. The LET or LET* constructions could be used to accomplish this. However, it may help a reader to better understand the operation of the procedure if the local variables are defined in the first line of the procedure. If the word &AUX followed by a list of variables is included in the formal parameter list of the procedure defining statement, those variables become local variables. If &REST is included, the &AUX should follow (i. e., be to the right of) &REST and its variable name. The list of variables has the same form as the variable list when LET* is used, *see* sec. 4-5. Initial values can be declared and computed. The initial values are assigned sequentially, as in the case of LET*. If an initial value is not included for a variable, then that variable will be bound to NIL. For example, the following first line of a procedure,

(DEFUN TEST1(A B &AUX R S T) (5-3)

establishes that R, S, and T will be local variables. They will be bound to NIL, because initial values have not been declared for them. The following first line of a procedure,

(DEFUN TEST2(A B &AUX (R 3) (S (+ 2 R)) (T (* R S))) (5-4)

establishes R, S, and T as local variables. R, S, and T will be bound to 3, 5, and 15 respectively. As is the case with LET*, R is computed and bound before S is computed and bound, etc. In general, the variables in the formal parameter list are bound sequentially, from left to right.

```
(DEFUN ARB-AVERAGE(A B C &REST LST &AUX (SUM 0) (NUMBER 3))
    (COND (LST (SETQ SUM (APPLY #'+ LST))
               (SETQ NUMBER (+ 3 (LENGTH LST))))
        )
    )
    (SETQ SUM (+ SUM A B C))
    (/ SUM NUMBER)
)
```

Figure 5.2. A procedure that uses &AUX to set up local variables and bind them to enclosed values.

Figure 5.2 contains an improved version of the procedure of figure 5.1. The variables SUM and NUMBER have been made local variables and have been assigned the initial values 0 and 3, respectively. Because these variables have been assigned initial values, it is not necessarily to include the second part of the COND expression. Thus, the procedure of figure 5.2 is shorter than that of figure 5.1.

Optional arguments are written following the word &OPTIONAL. The optional arguments should precede (be to the left of) &REST, if it is used. Remember that &REST should be to the left of &AUX, if it is used. The variables following &OPTIONAL have the same form as those following &AUX. If optional variables are not assigned default values then their default values will be NIL. For example, consider the following first line of a procedure:

(DEFUN TESTB(A B &OPTIONAL (C 3) (D (* A C)) (E 5))

$$(5-5)$$

The procedure TESTB has five arguments, three of which are optional. If TESTB is called using,

(TESTB 9 7)   (5-6)

then A and B will be assigned 9 and 7 respectively. No values have been passed to the optional parameters; therefore C, D, and E will be assigned the values 3, 27, and 5 respectively. Note that the optional arguments in the formal parameter list are bound sequentially, from left to right. Thus, A, B, and C will be bound before D is calculated. Hence, the default value of D can depend upon A, B, and C.

```
(DEFUN FINDER(LST &OPTIONAL (LNAME 'SMITH) (TRIES (/ (LENGTH LST) 2))
                  &AUX X POSITION)
   (DO ((I 1 (+ I 1)))
       ((> I TRIES) (RETURN LNAME))
       (SETQ X (MEMBER LNAME LST))
       (COND (X (SETQ POSITION (- (LENGTH LST) (LENGTH X) 1))
              (DO ((J 1 (+ J 1)))
                  ((> J POSITION))
                  (SETQ LST (CDR LST))
              )
              (PRINT (CAR LST))
              (SETQ LST (CDDR LST))
           )
           (T (RETURN LNAME))
       )
   )
)
```

Figure 5.3. The procedure FINDER that has optional arguments

An example of the use of optional arguments is the procedure FINDER, *see* figure 5.3. This procedure searches a list containing a sequence of pairs of first and last names and outputs, to the screen, the first names that correspond to a specified last name. For instance, if the following list,

    (BILL JONES ED SMITH WILLIAM THOMPSON JOHN SMITH
      TOM JONES DON SMITH)   (5-7)

were bound to LL and FINDER was to determine the first names corresponding to the last name SMITH, the following would be output:

    ED
    JOHN
    DON

Let us consider the details of the procedure FINDER. The first line of figure 5.3 is:

    (DEFUN FINDER(LST &OPTIONAL (LNAME 'SMITH)
      (TRIES (/ (LENGTH LST) 2)) &AUX X)

                                      (5-8)

The first parameter, LST, is the name of the list that stores the names. There are two optional parameters. LNAME, which stores the specified last name. The default value bound to LNAME is the atom SMITH. If no last name is specified, SMITH is the one that will be used. The second optional parameter is TRIES. This represents the number of searches that will be made. For instance, the list LL, see (5-7) has three SMITHs. If TRIES is specified as 1, only the initial first name, ED, will be found; if TRIES is specified as 2, the first two first names, ED and JOHN, will be found, etc. The default value for TRIES is:

(/ (LENGTH LST) 2)   (5-9)

That is, TRIES defaults to half the number of elements in the list that is supplied as a parameter; thus it is equal to the number of pairs of first and last names. If the default value is used, the complete list will be searched. Note that we have used the first formal parameter in the computation of the default value of TRIES. Remember that the arguments are bound sequentially starting with the leftmost argument. Finally, note that X is declared to be a local variable.

Let us consider the operation of the procedure. There is a pair of nested DO loops. The outer DO loop has a parameter I, that cycles from 1 to TRIES. This DO loop returns LNAME. In the body of the DO loop, X is bound to the result of the evaluation of:

(MEMBER LNAME LST)   (5-10)

If LNAME is in LST, then the list starting with the atom bound to LNAME will be returned and bound to X. Otherwise NIL will be returned and bound to X. The position of the last name in the list is the difference between the length of LST and the length of X. Thus, the position of the first name is one less than this. If X is nonNIL, then this number will be assigned to POSITION.

The inner DO loop will then be cycled POSITION times. Each time that,

(SETQ LST (CDR LST))

is evaluated, the first element will be removed from LST. Thus, after the inner DO loop has completed its cycle, the first element of LST will be the desired first name, which then will be output to the screen.

When,

(SETQ LST (CDDR LST))

is evaluated, the first two elements will be removed from (the reduced) LST. These elements are the first occurrences of the matching first and last names. The operation then cycles again.

If the last name is not found in LST, then (5-10) will cause X to be bound to NIL. The expression,

(RETURN LNAME)

will be evaluated, and the procedure will terminate. Note that the list of first names is output to the screen and the specified last name is returned. Of course, if FINDER is not called from another procedure, but is entered directly into the READ-EVAL-PRINT loop, then the last name will be output after all the first names are output.

If any optional arguments is to be specified in the calling expression, then all of the optional arguments to the left of the desired argument must be specified as well. For instance, if the list LL is to be searched for all matches for a last name of JONES, then the calling expression would be:

(FINDER LL 'JONES)

If only the first occurrence of SMITH were desired, the calling expression would be:

(FINDER LL 'SMITH 1)

Note that even though SMITH is a default value, it must be included in the calling expression because the TRIES argument is to the right of the LNAME argument. Thus, if the TRIES argument is to be specified, the LNAME argument must be specified also.

If &OPTIONAL, &REST, and &AUX are all used in the formal parameter list, they should be used exactly in that order as in the following:

(DEFUN TEST(A B C &OPTIONAL (X 1) (Y 2)
          &REST L & AUX (Z 3))

If, in this case, additional parameters are specified to be assigned to the list L, then the optional parameters must be explicitly included in the calling statement, even if their values are the same as their default values. For instance, if 1, 2, 3, and (4 5) are to be passed to A, B, C, and L respectively, the calling statement would be:

(TEST 1 2 3 1 2 4 5)

Note that the default values of the optional parameters are included in the arguments. Of course, values other than the default values could be used in the place of the defaults.

There is another specification &KEY, that can also be used in the formal parameter list. This specification is used in many primitive procedures although it can be used with user defined procedures. In its simplest form parameters called *keywords* are set up that are used in the same way as optional parameters. The form used to pass keyword values in the list of arguments is different from the form used to pass optional variables. Let us illustrate its use. Suppose that the first line in a procedure definition is:

(DEFUN TEST(A B &KEY (C 3) (D 4))   (5-11)

A and B are simple arguments while C and D are keywords. Within the body of the procedure, the keywords can be used in the same way as any other parameters. The default value of C is 3 and the default value of D is 4. If the keyword values are not specified when the procedure is called, the keywords assume their default values. The value for akeyword can be specified in the list of arguments. This is done by listing the keyword, preceded by a colon, and followed by its specified value in the list of arguments. For instance if,

(TEST 2 4 :C 7 :D 9)   (5-12)

is used to invoke the procedure TEST, then the value of the C keyword would be 7 and the value of the D keyword would be 9. Note that, in contrast to optional parameters, the keywords themselves are included in the list of arguments. Because of this the arguments of the keywords do not have to be identified by the order in which they appear in the list of arguments. Thus, keywords need not be specified in any particular order. In addition, all the keywords need not be specified. For instance, the D keyword could be specified without specifying the C keyword. The &KEY should follow any other specifications in the formal parameter list except for &AUX, and the keywords should be specified after all other arguments when the procedure is invoked.

When keywords are used as arguments, the name of the keyword must be known. This is an inconvenience. However, there are occasions when the advantage gained by using keywords offsets the disadvantage. Suppose that optional variables rather than keywords are used and that there are very many optional variables which usually take on their default values. Assume that, on one occasion, the procedure is to be run with the value of the last optional variable different from its default value. A value would have to be entered for each of the optional variables. Of course, they would have to be entered in the proper order. Thus, a long list of variables would have to be specified even though only one of them was to be changed. On the other hand, if the optional parameters were replaced by keywords then, only the one argument would have to be specified.

Procedures can be passed as parameters. For instance, consider the following:

```
(DEFUN COMPARE(A B &KEY (C 'EQUAL))
   (COND ((FUNCALL C A B) (PRINT 'TRUE)))
)                                                    (5-13)
```

The procedure FUNCALL used (5-13) has not been discussed. It will be considered in detail in sec. 5-6. For the time being consider that,

```
(FUNCALL C A B)                                      (5-14a)
```

is equivalent to evaluating the function specified by C with arguments A and B. That is, if C has its default value, then (5-14a) is equivalent to:

```
(EQUAL A B)                                          (5-14b)
```

If (COMPARE 2 2) is evaluated, TRUE will be output because the test of the COND is true. That is A and B are EQUAL and the PRINT expression will be evaluated. (Note that the PRINT expression can be replaced by and valid sequence of Lisp expressions.) The test of the COND construction can be passed as an argument. For instance,

```
(COMPARE 3 2 :C '>)                                  (5-14c)
```

will result in the output of TRUE because the test condition of the COND construction now is >.

Many Lisp primitives use the &KEY form of option. There are certain *standard keywords* that are used for this purpose. For example, TEST is such a keyword. It is used to vary a test condition. For instance, the keyword in (5-

13) was C. In standard Lisp usage we would have called it TEST. There are many primitive procedures that use keywords. Consult your Lisp manual to determine the keywords that are used with the primitives that are supplied with your system. The procedure MEMBER, *see* sec. 4.2, often is supplied so that its first condition can be changed using the keyword :TEST. The default value is EQL. For instance (4-18) could be written as:

(MEMBER '(ON THE) BB :TEST 'EQUAL)

Now EQUAL would be the test condition.

5-2. Recursive Procedure Calls

A Lisp procedure can call itself. This is called a *recursive procedure call*. Recursive operation is very powerful and can simplify procedures greatly. In addition, many mathematical operations, including those of mathematical logic, are based upon recursive operations. Thus, the ability to implement recursive operations simplifies the Lisp procedures that perform these kinds of logical operations.

Let us start by considering an example of a recursive operation. Suppose that we want to compute factorial n. This was accomplished with nonrecursive procedures that used DO looping in the procedures of figures 4.5 to 4.7. Now let us consider how it can be accomplished recursively. Remember that the definition of factorial n is:

$$n(n-1)(n-2)...1 \qquad\qquad (5-15)$$

We can also state that factorial n is n times factorial n-1. Now suppose that we want to compute factorial 5. We could multiply 5 by factorial 4. This requires that we know factorial 4. However, it can be computed by multiplying 4 by factorial 3. Again we do not know factorial 3, but it can be computed by multiplying 3 by factorial 2. Again factorial 2 could be computed by multiplying 2 by factorial 1. Factorial 1 could be obtained by multiplying 1 by factorial 0. It seems as though we must continue indefinitely in this vein. If this were the case, a solution could never be obtained. If this recursive procedure is to work, we must know the value of the factorial for one particular value of n. The other values can be built up from this one. In this case, we define factorial 0 as being equal to 1. Note that this is equivalent to saying that factorial 1 is equal to 1. (Factorial 0 is used in some mathematical operations and is defined as 1.) It has taken a great many words to explain how recursion can be used to obtain the factorial. However, we shall see that it can be expressed very simply by a recursive Lisp procedure.

Before considering an actual example of a recursive procedure, let us outline the steps to be taken. 1) The procedure is defined in terms of a reduced form of itself plus some simple operation. In the case of factorial n, the reduced form is factorial (n-1) and the simple operation is the product of the reduced form and n. 2) Keep repeating the basic procedure until the reduced form is so simple that its value is known. In the case of factorial n, the known value is factorial 0. 3) The result is then built from this known form. Note that the form whose result is known is the stopping point of the recursion. It is necessary to have a stopping point; otherwise the recursion will continue indefinitely.

```
(DEFUN FACTORIAL(N)
    (COND ((= N 0) 1)
          (T (* N (FACTORIAL(- N 1))))
    )
)
```

Figure 5.4. A function that uses recursion to compute the factorial.

Figure 5.4 is a listing of the function FACTORIAL that is used to recursively calculate the factorial. Consider the COND operation. It states that if N is zero then 1 is returned and the procedure terminates. If N is greater than zero, then N times factorial (N-1) is returned. Note that when N is greater than zero, there is a recursive call to the function FACTORIAL. As far the operation is concerned, this could be a call to any other procedure. The calling function does not terminate until the evaluation of,

$$(* N (FACTORIAL (- N 1))))$$ (5-16)

has been completed. This in turn depends upon the result being returned by FACTORIAL.

Now let us trace the operation when factorial 3 is evaluated. The following construction will illustrate the operation:

```
Enter FACTORIAL - Arguments (3)
  Enter FACTORIAL -Argument (2)
    Enter FACTORIAL - Argument (1)
      Enter FACTORIAL - Argument (0)                    (5-17)
      Exit FACTORIAL - Return 1
    Exit FACTORIAL - Return 1
  Exit FACTORIAL - Return 2
Exit FACTORIAL - Return 6
```

The level of indentation indicates the level of the procedure call. This form indicates that (FACTORIAL 3) is called, this in turn calls (FACTORIAL 2), which in turn calls (FACTORIAL 1), which calls (FACTORIAL 0). Because the argument is 0, this last call returns 1. Now the control returns to the third (next level up) call to FACTORIAL. Now the evaluation of (5-16) within this function can be completed because N is known and the evaluation of FACTORIAL (- N 1) is also known. The third call to FACTORIAL returns 1. Control now returns to the second call to FACTORIAL. Now the evaluation of (5-16) can be completed and the second call to FACTORIAL returns 2. Control then returns to the first call to FACTORIAL, (5-16) is evaluated and 6 is returned. The procedure then terminates.

Note that the value of N in each successive call to FACTORIAL is shadowed from the previous one. In addition, each N is local to its particular call. In the previous example there were four calls of the function FACTORIAL. Thus, there were four *different* variables called N.

Most Lisp systems have a procedure called TRACE that will output a form such as that of (5-17). Consult your Lisp manual to determine how to invoke TRACE. There usually is a procedure called UNTRACE that can be used to turn off the tracing. Tracing is invaluable as a debugging tool when many procedure calls are made. The calls need not necessarily be recursive. Various intermediate results are output when trace is invoked.

The recursive procedure FACTORIAL of figure 5.4 is much shorter than the nonrecursive FACTORIAL procedures of figures 4.5 to 4.7. One of the advantages of writing recursive procedures is that short, elegant programs can be written. Short recursive procedures do not necessarily execute in less time than longer nonrecursive procedures. Actually, the nonrecursive procedures may execute faster. However, the shorter programs are often easier to write, saving the programmer time.

As a second example of recursive procedures we shall calculate the *Fibonacci numbers*. These numbers show up in a variety of mathematical calculations. The Fibonacci numbers consist of an infinite sequence of numbers. The first part of the sequence is:

1, 1, 2, 3, 5, 8, 13, 21, 34, 55, ...

The first two Fibonacci numbers are both 1. Each successive Fibonacci number is obtained by adding the two previous Fibonacci numbers. If we designate f_n to be the nth Fibonacci number, then f_0 and f_1 are both equal to 1. The other Fibonacci numbers can be obtained using the formula:

$$f_n = f_{n-1} + f_{n-2} \quad n = 2, 3, ... \tag{5-18}$$

A procedure named FIB that can be used to calculate the Fibonacci numbers is shown in figure 5.5. If N is is either 0 or 1, then FIB returns 1. If N is neither 0 nor 1, then FIB is called recursively with arguments of N-1 and N-2. The returned values are then added. Thus, the desired Fibonacci numbers are obtained.

```
(DEFUN FIB(N)
   (COND ((= N 1) 1)
         ((= N 0) 1)
         (T (+ (FIB (- N 1)) (FIB (- N 2))))
   )
)
```

Figure 5.5. The function FIB that calculates the FIBONACCI numbers

Suppose that (FIB 3) is evaluated. There will be calls to (FIB 2) and (FIB 1). The call to (FIB 1) immediately returns 1. However, the call to (FIB 2) results in calls to (FIB 1) and (FIB 0). Each of these return 1, then the call to (FIB 2) returns 2. Finally, the original procedure call returns 3.

```
(DEFUN RTEST(N)
   (PRINC 'START)
   (PRINC N)
   (TERPRI)
   (COND ((> N 1) (RTEST (- N 1))))
   (PRINC 'END)
   (PRINC N)
   (TERPRI)
)
```

Figure 5.6. A function illustrating recursive function calls

The procedure RTEST of figure 5.6 can be used to illustrate some aspects of recursive calls. The procedure RTEST is called using the expression,

(RTEST n)   (5-19)

where n is an integer. The atom START followed by the number n will be output. If n is greater than one, RTEST will be called recursively using an argument of n-1. After the return from the recursive call of RTEST, the atom END followed by the number n will be printed. If RTEST is called using the expression,

(RTEST 3)

the output will be:

        START3
        START2
        START1
        END1   (5-20)
        END2
        END3

In this case RTEST will be called three times. To differentiate among the three calls to RTEST, the first-called RTEST shall be designated the outer RTEST, the second-called RTEST shall be dsignated the middle RTEST and the last-called RTEST shall be designated the inner RTEST. When the procedure is originally called, START3 is output and then the middle RTEST is called. Next START2 is output and then the inner RTEST is called. Now START1 is output. In this case the parameter passed to the inner RTEST is 1. Thus, the condition (> N 1) is false and there are no subsequent calls to RTEST. Then END1 is output and the inner RTEST terminates. Now control returns to the middle RTEST. The expression after the one that called the inner RTEST is now evaluated. Thus, END2 is output and then the middle RTEST terminates. Now control returns to the outer RTEST, END3 is output and the procedure terminates. Remember that a recursive procedure call can be considered as calls to different procedures, all of which perform the same operation.

```
(DEFUN FINDER(LST &OPTIONAL (LNAME 'SMITH) (TRIES (/ (LENGTH LST) 2))
                   &AUX X POSITION)
   (SETQ X (MEMBER LNAME LST))
   (COND ((AND X (> TRIES 0))(SETQ POSITION (- (LENGTH LST) (LENGTH X) 1))
         (DO ((J 1 (+ J 1)))
             ((> J POSITION))
               (SETQ LST (CDR LST))
            )
            (PRINT (CAR LST))
            (SETQ LST (CDDR LST))
            (SETQ TRIES (- TRIES 1))
            (COND ((> TRIES 0) (FINDER LST LNAME TRIES)))
         )
    )
    LNAME
)
```

Figure 5.7. A modification of the procedure FINDER *(see Fig. 5-3)* that uses recursive procedure calls. Note that the next to last line causes the name to be returned.

Another example of a recursive procedure call is shown in figure 5.7. There we have rewritten the procedure FINDER of figure 5.3. (We assume that you are familiar with that procedure.) The outer DO loop of figure 5.3 has been removed in the procedure of figure 5.7. If LNAME stores a MEMBER of the list LST, then the appropriate first name is output and all the elements up to and including the first occurrence of the specified first and last name will be stripped from the first part of the list LST, and the value assigned to TRIES is reduced by 1. If this value is greater than 0, FINDER is called recursively. Note that the optional arguments are explicitly specified in this recursive call. This is necessary to avoid having the default values used for the optional arguments whenever recursive calls are made to the procedure.

The test of the first COND condition has been changed from that of figure 5.3. The test now is:

(AND X (> TRIES 0))   (5-21)

If the test were not written in this way, a first name could be output even if the specified value of TRIES was 0. Usually a person running the procedure FINDER would not enter 0 for TRIES. However, the procedure could be called from another procedure that calculated a value of TRIES, in which case it is possible that the value of the parameter TRIES could be 0. The inclusion of the test of (5-21) ensures that no undesired output will be obtained. Note that the test of (5-21) does not have to be included in the FINDER procedure of figure 5.3 because the outer DO loop would not cycle if the value assigned to TRIES was zero.

The procedure of figure 5.7 does call FINDER recursively. However, its form is different than those that we have considered earlier. Each call to FINDER obtains a result, i.e., a first name. In this case recursion is used simply to obtain many results. In the previous examples recursion was used to perform many calculations that yielded a single result.

5-3. Some Special Recursive Forms

There are some special recursive forms that can be very helpful on occasion. We shall discuss them here. It is often useful to write a recursive procedure in two parts (i.e. as two procedures.) An example of such *two-part recursion* is shown in figure 5.8, where we have calculated the factorial in yet another manner. Let us consider the operation of this procedure. The first procedure is called TAIL-FACT. (The reason for the choice of this name will become clear later in this section.) It is called to obtain the factorial. For instance,

(TAIL-FACT 6)   (5-22)

will return 120. The only thing that the procedure TAIL-FACT does is call another procedure named FFACT and pass it n and (n-1).

Now consider the procedure FFACT. The values passed to it as n and (n - 1) are assigned to X and Y respectively. If Y is equal to -1 (x=0) then FFACT returns 1. If Y is equal to 0 then FFACT returns X, which is the value that was passed to it. If the second argument, Y, is greater than 0, X is replaced by the product of X and Y, the value of Y is reduced by one, and FFACT is called again. Its arguments are the new values of X and Y.

If N is greater than one then, after the first evaluation of FFACT, the value of X will equal the product of N and (N - 1). (These are currently represented as X and Y.) The recursive calls terminate when the evaluation of (- Y 1) becomes zero. At this time the last computed value of X will then be returned back through all the recursive calls of FFACT. This value will be unchanged and finally it will be returned to TAIL-FACT, which will, in turn, return it. Thus, the desired factorial will be computed. The expression starting with the test (= Y -1) will return true only if factorial 0 is to be computed. This expression is included so that factorial 0 does return a value of one.

The general idea of two-part recursion is that the second procedure is passed an additional parameter(s) that can then be utilized in the computation. This additional parameter(s) may contain information as to whether recursion is to proceed. The use of two separate procedures provides the programmer with additional versatility.

```
(DEFUN TAIL-FACT(N)
    (FFACT N (- N 1))
)

(DEFUN FFACT(X Y)
    (COND ((= Y -1) 1)
          ((= Y 0) X)
          (T (SETQ X (* X Y))
             (SETQ Y (- Y 1))
             (FFACT X Y)
          )
    )
)
```

Figure 5.8. A two-stage, tail recursive procedure

The procedure of figure 5.8 is such that data is passed to the function FFACT, computations are performed, and FFACT is called recursively. This process repeats until the recursion terminates. After this time *no further calculations are performed*. A value is returned from one procedure to the one that called it recursively. However, nothing is done with that value, it is simply returned. Such an operation is called a *tail recursion*. To reiterate, a tail recursion is one in which no computations are performed after the innermost recursive function terminates. The value computed at that point is simply handed back unchanged up the chain of recursion calls until it reaches the highest level and is returned.

The tail recursive factorial procedure is certainly longer than the recursive procedure of figure 5.4. This is often the case with tail recursive procedures. A question that could be asked is why bother to give such operations a special name. Every procedure call carries a certain amount of overhead. The execution of the program does not proceed in a orderly way, evaluating one expression after the other when a procedure is called. The state of operations prior to the procedure call must be retained so that the evaluation of the statements can resume after the operation of the procedure has terminated. This involves the storage and retrieval of extra data. All of this takes time. In a recursive operation, there may be many procedure calls. In general, a single recursive call of a procedure takes as much overhead as any other procedure. Thus, although recursive procedure calls may be shorter, and faster, for programmers to write, they often take longer to run than the corresponding nonrecursive operations. We shall not consider the details here, but it is always possible to rework a tail recursive procedure into a nonrecursive one.

Optimizing Lisp interpreters and compilers can be written to perform such conversions automatically. If such an interpreter or compiler is available it is desirable to use tail-recursive procedures rather than ordinary recursive procedures for those applications where speed is important. In many cases, such optimizing Lisp systems are not used; in which instances much of the advantage of the tail-recursive procedures is lost.

In sec. 4-1 we discussed the primitive named MEMBER that determined if an atom was a member of a list. For instance, if the list LLL is bound to,

$$(A B (C D) (E (F (G H))) I J) \qquad (5\text{-}23)$$

then,

$$(MEMBER \text{ 'B LLL}) \qquad (5\text{-}24a)$$

will return (B (C D) (E (F (G H))) I J) while,

$$(MEMBER \text{ '(C D) LLL}) \qquad (5\text{-}24b)$$

will return NIL. The reason that (5-24b) returns NIL is because MEMBER utilizes the predicate EQL to compare its first argument with the each of the elements of its second argument. If the arguments of EQL are lists, then if true is to be returned, the two arguments must actually represent the same list. Remember that not only must the two entities be equal, they must also be stored in the same memory location(s). The first argument of (5-24b) is not stored in the same memory locations as is (C D) of the list LLL. Thus, (5-24b) will return NIL.

We shall rewrite MEMBER using EQUAL to compare entities. (Note, the test in MEMBER can, at times, be specified using the keyword :TEST, see sec. 5-1.) This version of the function will not have the above discussed restriction. We shall call our new version SP-MEMBER. For example,

$$(SP\text{-}MEMBER \text{ '(C D) LLL}) \qquad (5\text{-}25)$$

will return ((C D) (E (F (G H))) I J).

```
(DEFUN SP-MEMBER(ITEM LST)
   (COND ((NULL LST) NIL)
         ((EQUAL ITEM (CAR LST)) LST)
         (T (SP-MEMBER ITEM (CDR LST))))
   )
)
```

Figure 5.9. The function SP-MEMBER that is a special version of MEMBER. EQUAL rather than EQL is used for comparison. Note that EQUAL can also be used with MEMBER if the keyword :TEST and 'EQUAL are used as the last two items in the list of arguments.

SP-MEMBER is listed in figure 5.9. If LST is empty NIL will be returned. If ITEM is equal to (CAR LST), that is, if ITEM and the first element of the list LST are the same, then LST is returned. If neither of these are true then there is a recursive call to SP-MEMBER. The list that is passed in each recursive call is (CDR LST), that is, the original list with the first element removed. The procedure terminates either when ITEM is found or when (CDR LST) returns an empty list.

Let us consider the philosophy underlying this type of procedure. Every list is composed of cons cells. The car points at an element of the list and the cdr points at the next cons cell, i. e., the rest of the list. Thus, the entity pointed at by the first car is examined to see if it is equal to ITEM. If this is not the case, the car of the list pointed at by the cdr of the first cons cell is examined. This procedure is repeated. A test is applied to the car of the list; if it returns NIL the operation is repeated with the cdr of the list. This is repeated successively. The procedure is based on the cons cell structure of lists. The procedure repeats itself recursively until a match is found, or until the remaining list becomes empty. Such recursive procedures are called *structurally recursive* procedures, because they utilize the structure of lists.

As an additional example of a structurally recursive procedure, we shall modify SP-MEMBER so that it will find a match for ITEM at any level of the list. That is, ITEM need not match a top level element of the list; it need only match an element of any of the elements or subelements of the list, no matter how deep in the list structure it is. The new function will be called TOTAL-MEMBER. The following examples will illustrate its use:

(TOTAL-MEMBER '(C D) LLL)   (5-26a)

will return ((C D) (E (F (G H))) I J), where LLL is defined in (5-23). In addition,

(TOTAL-MEMBER 'G LLL)   (5-26b)

will return ((E (F (G H))) I J). Note that if the entity being searched for is one or more levels down in a top level element of the original list; the entire top level element and all succeeding elements, of the original list, will be returned.

```
(DEFUN TOTAL-MEMBER(ITEM LST)
    (COND ((NULL LST) NIL)
          ((EQUAL ITEM (CAR LST)) LST)
          ((AND (LISTP (CAR LST)) (TOTAL-MEMBER ITEM (CAR LST))) LST)
          (T (TOTAL-MEMBER ITEM (GDR LST)))
    )
)
```

Figure 5.10. The function TOTAL-MEMBER that will find list components at any level

The function TOTAL-MEMBER is listed in figure 5.10. It is a structurally recursive procedure. Note that TOTAL-MEMBER is very similar to SP-MEMBER. There is one extra branch in the COND construction. It is:

((AND (LISTP (CAR LST)) (TOTAL-MEMBER ITEM (CAR LST)))
     LST)

(5-27)

Note that the test part of this is:

(AND (LISTP (CAR LST)) (TOTAL-MEMBER ITEM (CAR LST)))

(5-28)

This condition will be true if (CAR LST) is a list and if ITEM is equal to any element, or a subelement, of (CAR LST). That is, if the first element of LST does not match ITEM and the list LST is not empty then test (5-28) will be evaluated. That test will return true only if the first element of LST is itself a list and if,

(TOTAL-MEMBER ITEM (CAR LST))

(5-29)

returns true. (Remember that any nonNIL value is considered to be true.) Note that if (CAR LST) is not a list, then,

(LISTP (CAR LST))

(5-30)

will return NIL and (5-29) will *not* be evaluated. On the other hand if (5-30) returns true, then (5-29) will be evaluated. This order is important. If LST were not a list (e.g., an atom), then, with some Lisp systems, the evaluation of (CAR LST) would result in an error, the operation would stop, and the procedure would not function properly.

We do not have to concern ourselves with the depth of the search for ITEM. Each call to TOTAL-MEMBER works with the same kind of cons cell structure until a match is found or an empty list is encountered. For instance, suppose that the first element in the list is a list containing deeply nested sublists. There will be a series of recursions through the sublists until a match is found or until NIL is returned from the last evaluation of (5-28). This will propagate back through the recursive calls. If no match is found, the first evaluation of (5-27) will return NIL. In this case the first three tests of the COND construction will have returned false, the fourth line of the COND construction will then be evaluated, and the operation will proceed with the second element of the original list.

Note that the procedure starts with the first cons cell. Its car is considered. If it points at a list, then that list is analyzed. After this analysis is complete, if the procedure has not terminated, the operation is repeated with the second cons cell of the original list, etc. The original list and any potential lists pointed at by cars of any cons cell are treated in essentially the same way. We have used structural recursion to write a relatively short procedure that analyzes a general list structure.

5-4. Anonymous Procedures - LAMBDA Expressions

When a procedure is established using DEFUN, that procedure is stored by the Lisp system. Because the procedure is called by its name, both that name and the location (address) of the procedure also must be stored in a symbol table. If a procedure is used in only one place in the program, then the storage of the name and location represents extra overhead. Not only does this take up extra memory, but extra time is required to find the procedure name and look up its storage location. Lisp allows the definition of procedures that do not have names and that are written at the point at which they are to evaluated. Of course, it makes sense to only do this if the procedure is called from no more than one point in the program. A procedure without a name is called a LAMBDA procedure or an *anonymous* procedure.

It might appear as though a procedure need not be written, and that the required sequence of expressions could simply be written and executed. Remember that some procedures such as APPLY and MAPCAR take only procedures as arguments. Thus, these procedures could not be used on a sequence of expressions. The inability to use such procedures could result in tedious additional programming. Suppose that you want to square each element of a list of numbers and obtain a list of all the squares. If a function that squares a single number were available, then it could be used in conjunction with MAPCAR to obtain the desired list of squares. This technique will work even if the length of the list is unknown at the time that the program is written. On the other hand, if the steps are written into the program as a sequence of expressions, then the length of the input list must be found using LENGTH and a list of squares must be set up using LIST to obtain the output list, etc. It is much less tedious to use MAPCAR and a procedure. An anonymous procedure that squares a number could be used in this kind of construction.

An anonymous procedure is set up in almost the same way as is a named procedure. The only differences are that the DEFUN is replaced by LAMBDA and that no procedure name is written. All the other features are the same. For instance, &LIST, &OPTIONAL, and &AUX can be used in the formal parameter list. An unnamed procedure cannot be called recursively, simply because it does not have a name.

```
(MAPCAR #'(LAMBDA(X) (* X X)) W)
```

Figure 5.11. The use of a LAMBDA definition to find a list of squares.

Figure 5.11 includes a LAMBDA definition of a function that squares a number. Its form is:

$$(LAMBDA(X) \atop (*XX) \atop) \tag{5-31}$$

This is written on one line in figure 5.11. Now suppose that W is bound to the list:

(1 2 3 4 5 6)

When the expression in figure 5.11 is evaluated,

(1 4 9 16 25 36)

will be returned. Note that the LAMBDA-defined function is used in the same way as is a DEFUN-defined function. Remember that some Lisp systems allow the # and/or the ' to be omitted when MAPCAR is used. In common Lisp the use of the # and/or ' are related to scoping, a concept we will discuss in the next section.

```
(APPLY #'(LAMBDA(LST &OPTIONAL (LNAME  SMITH) (TRIES (/ (LENGTH LST) 2))
          &AUX X POSITION)
         (DO ((I 1 (+ I 1)))
            ((> I TRIES) (RETURN LNAME))
             (SETQ X (MEMBER LNAME LST))
             (COND (X (SETQ POSITION (- (LENGTH LST) (LENGTH X) 1))
                      (DO ((J 1 (+ J 1)))
                         ((> J POSITION))
                          (SETQ LST (CDR LST))
                      )
                      (PRINT (CAR LST))
                      (SETQ LST (CDDR LST))
                   )
               (T (RETURN LNAME))
          )
      )
   )
Z)
```

Figure 5.12. A LAMBDA definition applied to the procedure of figure 5.3. The data is supplied in a list.

Figure 5.12 contains another example of a LAMBDA function. Here we have written the procedure called FINDER, *see* figure 5.3, as an anonymous procedure. The procedure is the same as that of figure 5.3 except that DEFUN has been replaced by LAMBDA and the name FINDER is not written. The expressions of figure 5.12 are written assuming that the data is supplied in a list named Z. Suppose that the following expressions have been evaluated prior to the evaluation of the expressions of figure 5.12:

(SETQ N1 '(BILL JONES ED SMITH WILLIAM THOMPSON
JOHN SMITH TOM JONES DON SMITH))

(SETQ Z (LIST N1 'JONES))

The output to the screen will be:

    BILL
    TOM
    JONES

(Note that JONES will only appear on the screen if the procedure of figure 5.12 is evaluated as part of the READ-EVAL-PRINT loop.) Let us consider the output. APPLY is used in figure 5.12. Thus, the list that is assigned to Z is used as the supplied data for the procedure. That list consists of the list N1 and the atom JONES. Thus, in the anonymous procedure the list N1 will be assigned to LST and JONES will be assigned to LNAME. A third argument is not supplied; thus the default value is used for TRIES. If the Z list had been set up using,

    (SETQ Z (LIST N1 'SMITH 2))

the first names ED and JOHN would be output. Now both optional arguments have been provided. Note that &OPTIONAL and &AUX are used just as they are with named procedures. The same statement applies to the use of &REST.

```
(APPLY #'+  (MAPCAR   #'(LAMBDA(LST)
            (APPLY #'+ LST)
) Z))
```

Figure 5.13. An application of a LAMBDA definition that will sum a list of lists.

Let us consider another application of anonymous procedures. Suppose that we have a list that is composed of lists of numbers. For example, if Z were bound to,

    ((1 2 3) (4 5 6 7) (8 9))   (5-32)

then Z would represent such a list. In general, the number of lists and the length of each list is arbitrary. Now suppose that we want the sum of all the numbers in such a list. For example, the sum of all the numbers in (5-32) is

45. The construction of figure 5.13 accomplishes this. To explain its operation let us break it into subparts. Evaluation of,

(APPLY #'+ LST)   (5-33)

will sum all the elements in the list LST. A single number will be returned. Now,

    (MAPCAR #'(LAMDA(LST)
        (APPLY #'+ LST)   (5-34)
) Z)

will cause (5-33) to be successively applied to each of the sublists in the list that is assigned to Z with the results being put into a list. For instance, if the list assigned to Z is given by (5-32), then evaluation of (5-34) will return:

(6 22 17)   (5-35)

Finally the outermost APPLY of figure 5.13 will cause all the numbers in the list of (5-35) to be added so that the desired result is obtained.

LAMBDA had to be used in (5-34) because MAPCAR can be applied only to a procedure. Thus, a procedure was set up using LAMBDA. This assumed that we did not want to use DEFUN to set up a named procedure to perform this kind of addition.

5-5. Scope and Extent

The subject of *scope* was introduced in conjunction with looping and procedures. For instance, the scope of the parameters of a DO loop existed only over that DO loop. If I were the parameter of a DO loop, then that I could not be accessed from a point outside of the loop. In addition, if there were a variable called I that was defined outside of the DO loop, then a change in the DO loop parameter I would not change the value of I outside of the loop. In this section we shall formalize and extend the ideas related to scope.

Before starting this discussion a word of warning is in order. There is no general Lisp convention for scoping. The scoping conventions of Common Lisp differ from those of other Lisps. We shall consider the Common Lisp standard and we shall also consider other standards of scoping here. It is hoped that the various ideas of scoping will be made clear. In many cases it is possible to write Lisp programs that will work on different systems, even if the rules of scoping are different on each. We shall consider how this can be done. Lisp is a language that has grown up without rigid standards.

Consequently, there are many different versions or dialects. Common Lisp attempts to set up standards for Lisp. As Lisp becomes more widely used, the concept of *portability* becomes increasingly important. A portable Lisp program is one that although written on one system will run on other systems. In this section we shall consider some principles which, if followed, will help to make programs portable. Remember, however, that the rules of scoping may differ from one system to another, so that programs that utilize the scoping rules of one Lisp system may not run without modification on another system.

We shall now discuss some terminology that relates to scope. *Lexical scoping* means that the scope is determined by position of the particular object in the *program*. By program, we refer to a collection of procedures and expressions that performs some specific operation. A variable is said to be a *free variable* with respect to a procedure if that variable is used in the procedure, but does not appear in the formal parameter list of the procedure. For instance, a variable that is not included in a procedure's formal parameter list, but is established by a SETQ is a free variable.

```
(DEFUN OUTER(X Y &AUX A B C V)
    (DEFUN INNER(Z T &AUX W)
        (SETQ W (+ A Z T))
        (DO ((I 1 (+ I 1)))
            ((> I W) (RETURN I))
            (PRINT I)
            (SETQ V (* 2 I))
        )
    )
    (SETQ A 3)
    (SETQ B (* A X Y))
    (SETQ C (INNER A B))
    (PRINT V)
    ; Cannot evaluate (PRINT W) from here
    (PRINT C)
)
```

Figure 5.14. Procedures used to illustrate scoping

When variables are lexically scoped, then those variables exist only within the body of the construction that defines them. In this case a construction refers to something like a procedure or a DO loop. We shall illustrate these ideas with examples. In figure 5.14 we have listed a procedure called OUTER. The second through nineth lines of this procedure defines a procedure called INNER. The procedure INNER is lexically within OUTER. That is, the text of INNER lies within the text of OUTER.

Consider the DO loop parameter I. It is lexically within the DO loop. Because lexical scoping is used for DO loop parameters, I can be accessed from only within the DO loop. Note that essentially every Lisp system does use lexical scoping for DO loop parameters. The same is true for variables that are defined as parameters of a procedure. For instance, in Fig. 5-14, the variables Z and T can be accessed only from within the procedure INNER.

The procedure INNER lies within the procedure OUTER, thus the the scope of the variables X and Y includes the procedure INNER. Thus, X and Y could be referenced and/or changed from within INNER. Note that variables established in OUTER must exist before they are accessed by INNER. For instance, because the variable A is established *before* the call of INNER, it exists when INNER is called. If A was not established before the call to INNER, this would not be the case and A could not be used within INNER.

```
(SETQ X 3)

(DEFUN TEST(&AUX (X 5))
   (DEFUN OUTER-1()
      (TERPRI)
      (PRINC 'OUTER)
      (PRINC X)
      (INNER-1)
      (TERPRI)
      (PRINC 'OUTER)
      (PRINC X)
      (SETQ X 9)
      (TERPRI)
      (PRINC 'OUTER)
      (PRINC X)
   )
   (OUTER-1)
)


(DEFUN INNER-1()
   (TERPRI)
   (PRINC 'INNER)
   (PRINC X)
   (SETQ X 17)
   (TERPRI)
   (PRINC 'INNER)
   (PRINC X)
)
```

Figure 5.15. Additional procedures used to illustrate scoping

Another form of scoping is called *indefinite scope.* In this case, once an identity is established, it can be accessed from anywhere in the program. For instance, if there is a indefinite scope and we enter,

(SETQ X 5)   (5-36)

at the *listener* or *top* level, that is into the READ-EVAL-PRINT loop, then X can be referenced and possibly changed in any procedure. (Note that X can be shadowed by a variable in a formal parameter list. We shall discuss this in detail later in this section.)

Let us consider some other differences between lexical and indefinite scope. Consider the program sequence shown in figure 5.15. The procedure

TEST binds X to 5 and then calls OUTER-1. Procedure OUTER-1 is established as part of TEST. Thus, OUTER-1 is lexically contained in TEST. The procedure INNER-1 is not defined within TEST. Note that the expression,

(SETQ X 3)

and the two procedures are established at the top level.

Now let us assume that lexical scoping is being used. All references to X in TEST and OUTER-1 refer to the same variable. The references to X in INNER-1 refer to a different variable, that happens to have the same name. The X in OUTER-1 is local to test, while the X in INNER-1 is a free variable. When TEST is evaluated the following output will be obtained:

    OUTER5
    INNER3
    INNER17   (5-37)
    OUTER5
    OUTER9

The first value of X that is output is from a call to OUTER-1, the value of 5 is output. Next INNER-1 is called. If no value was bound to a variable called X as part of the construction that contained INNER-1 when it was established, then an error would result at this point and the operation might cease. However, in this case X has been bound to 3 at the top level so that this number is output. The next value of X that is output is again due to the evaluation of INNER-1, which occurs after the evaluation of the SETQ expression in that procedure. Hence, the value of 17 is output for X. Now the operation returns to OUTER-1. The value of X is then output. This value is 5. The evaluation of INNER-1 did not affect the value of X in OUTER-1. The last output of X occurs after the SETQ expression in OUTER-1. Hence the value of 9 is output.

Now let us consider what the output would be if indefinite scoping is used. In this case assume that &AUX X 5 is removed from the formal parameter list of TEST. Now the output will be of the form:

    OUTER3
    INNER3
    INNER17   (5-38)
    OUTER17
    OUTER9

Now all the references to X refer to the same variable. Thus, the SETQ expression in INNER-1 changes the value of X in OUTER-1 as well.

EXTENT

Entities such as variables or procedures may exist only for a certain time. The time that a variable does exist is called its *extent*. There are two types of extent, *dynamic extent* and *indefinite extent*. We shall again provide examples in terms of variables. If a variable has dynamic extent, then that variable can be referred to only between the time that it is established and the time that it is disestablished. When the construct that establishes the variable terminates, that variable no longer exists. On the other hand if a variable has indefinite extent, then the variable remains in existence as long as it is possible to reference it.

Suppose that we are working with dynamic extent and the procedure TEST of figure 5.15 is being evaluated. In addition suppose that X had not been established at the top level. The variable X, of TEST, could not be referenced after TEST terminated, since it would no longer exist. On the other hand, if there were indefinite extent, then X could be referenced after TEST terminated. We shall modify this statement when we combine the discussion of scope and extent.

There are times when a programmer specifically wants to terminate the binding of a variable. The procedure MAKUNBOUND can be used to unbind a variable. For instance, suppose that Y has been bound to the list (A B C). Then, the evaluation of,

(MAKUNBOUND 'Y)   (5-39)

will cause Y to become unbound. (Note the use of the apostrophe.) There are times when a reference to an unbound variable will result in an error and operation will terminate. There is a predicate named BOUNDP that can be used to test if a name has been bound. For example,

(BOUNDP 'ABC)   (5-40)

can be used to test if the atom ABC has been bound to a value.

When we discussed scoping we did not consider extent and when we discussed extent, we did not consider scoping. This simplified the discussions because we did not have to consider scope and extent at the same time. To fully understand a program's operation scope and extent must be considered simultaneously. In Common Lisp, the usual variables have lexical scope and indefinite extent; on the other hand, there are *special variables* that have indefinite scope and dynamic extent. Unfortunately, the confusing term *dynamic scope* is applied to these variables. That is, the term dynamic scope refers to those variables that have indefinite scope and dynamic extent. In many versions of Lisp, other than Common Lisp, nonlocal variables have dynamic scope. Common Lisp provides two different types of variables.

```
(DEFUN EX(&OPTIONAL (B NIL))
   (COND (B (SETQ AA 3)))
   (PRINT AA)
)
```

Figure 5.16. A procedure used to illustrate extent

Now let us consider an example of lexical scope and indefinite extent. Consider the procedure EX of figure 5.16. It has an optional parameter B, whose default value is NIL. If B is nonNIL then the expression,

$$(SETQ\ AA\ 3) \tag{5-41}$$

will be evaluated. If B is NIL, then expression (5-41) will not be evaluated. Now consider that AA is initially unbound. If,

$$(PRINT\ AA) \tag{5-42}$$

is evaluated without (5-41) being executed, an error will result. Now suppose that,

$$(EX\ T)$$

is evaluated. Because B is now true AA will be bound and the evaluation of (5-42) will result in the output of 3. Now suppose that there is a subsequent evaluation of (EX). Because B is set to its default of Nil, (5-41) will not be evaluated. Although lexical scoping implies that AA will exist only within the body of (EX), the extent of AA is indefinite. Thus, the evaluation of (EX) will again result in the output of 3; the binding of AA caused by the previous call (EXT) has remained in effect.

Now let us assume that there is indefinite scope with dynamic extent and that AA is initially unbound. Now the execution of (EX T) will result in an output of 3 as before. Now suppose that there is a subsequent call to (EX). The dynamic extent seems to imply that an error would result because the bound value of AA no longer exists. However, the scope must also be considered. The first time that EX was evaluated, expression (5-41) was evaluated. The scope is indefinite. Thus, this variable is considered to belong to all parts of the program and is not restricted to the construction that established it. For this reason, that variable does not become unbound when EX terminates. If the variable AA had been local to the procedure, then it would have become unbound when the procedure terminated. Note that the results for the lexically scoped, indefinite extent variable and for the indefinitely scoped, dynamic extent variables were the same for this particular example. However, the reasons for the results were different in the two cases.

```
(DEFUN EXX(I)
    (COND ((BOUNDP 'A) (PRINT 'BOUND))
          (T (PRINT 'UNBOUND))
    )
    (SETQ A 3)
    (SETQ I (- I 1))
    (COND ((> I 1) (EXX 0)))
)
```

Figure 5.17. A recursive procedure used to illustrate extent

An additional example of dynamic extent is illustrated in figure 5.17. The procedure EXX calls itself recursively, exactly once (because the argument of the recursive call is 0.) If we assume that A is initially unbound, then the initial execution of the COND expression will cause UNBOUND to be output. Next the SETQ expression will be evaluated and A will become bound. Next EXX will be called recursively. The "first" EXX will still exist during this recursive call. Thus the variable A will exist and can be used by the "second" EXX.

To clarify the ideas concerning scope and extent, it may help to think of fictitious symbol tables that store variable names. Symbol tables are used by the Lisp system to access the variables. When lexical scoping is used, each construction, such as a procedure, has its own symbol table associated with it. If one construction is lexically embedded within another one, then the inner construction can use the symbol table of the outer construction. Suppose that a variable called A is referenced in the inner construction. During evaluation of the inner construction, the Lisp system will search the inner symbol table for A. If it does *not* find A there, then the outer symbol table will be searched. This procedure will be searched through all levels of the constructions. Thus, the scope of the variables of the outer construction will extend over the inner construction. However, the scope of the variables of the inner construction will not extend over the variables of the outer construction.

If the inner construction and the outer construction both set up variables called XX then, in theory, the scope of the outer XX will extend over the inner construction. Suppose that XX is referenced from the inner construction. That constructions symbol table will be searched, and XX will be found and the search will be ended; thus the inner XX will be used. In this case there will be no way for the outer XX to be referenced from the inner construction. The outer XX is said to be *shadowed* by the inner XX.

When indefinite scoping is used, there is only one symbol table and all variables are stored there. In this case all variables are accessible from all constructions. Although, in general, the scoping is indefinite, there are some special cases that use lexical scoping. For instance, the local variables of DO loops and all the arguments of procedures are always lexically scoped even if the Lisp system uses indefinite scoping for most variables.

When variables have dynamic extent, each symbol table is erased after the construction that sets it up terminates. For instance, if there is lexical scoping and dynamic extent, then the table "belonging to" a procedure will be removed after the procedure terminates. If there is indefinite scope and dynamic extent, then there is one large symbol table. Various constructions can cause entries to be made into this table. That table does not "belong" to any one construction and entries are not removed from that table even if the construction that established those particular entries terminates. Thus, even with dynamic extent, the presence of indefinite scoping means that the termination of a construction does not necessarily mean that all variables established by that construction will become unbound.

If lexical scoping is used and a procedure is established, the symbol table referenced for that procedure will depend upon the environment that was in force when the evaluation of the defining expression of the procedure (i.e. DEFUN) was performed. Let us illustrate what we mean by this somewhat confusing statement. Figure 5.15 will be used in this discussion. The expression,

(SETQ X 3)

and the procedures TEST and INNER-1 are evaluated from the top level. X is a free variable for the procedure INNER-1. Thus, the X of INNER-1 will refer to the symbol table of the top level. This will not change even if, subsequently, INNER-1 is called from within another procedure. The only way that X, in INNER-1 can be changed is if the binding of X is changed at the top level.

Now let us consider that indefinite scope and dynamic extent are used. In this case, which symbol table is referenced by INNER-1 will depend upon the environment that is in force when the procedure is *called*. X is still a free variable of INNER-1. However, the symbol table to be searched for #X is not specified until INNER-1 is called. When INNER-1 is called from within OUTER-1, the system searches for a variable called X in OUTER-1's symbol table. Because there is a variable called X in that symbol table, that symbol table entry is used for the X that is the free variable of INNER-1. Note that when lexical scoping is used the same symbol table entry for the free variable of INNER-1 will always be used while with dynamic scoping, different symbol tables may be used depending on the calling environment.

The procedures SETQ (and SETF) require some special comment. Suppose that lexical scoping is used and there is a set of nested procedures. If,

(SETQ X 5)

is evaluated in the innermost procedure, then the following takes place. The symbol table for the innermost construction is searched. If it contains a variable called X, then that variable's assignment is changed to 5 and the operation terminates. If that symbol table did not contain X, then the symbol table of the next outermost construction would be searched for an entry named X. If that table contains an X, then its value is bound to 5 and operation terminates. If that symbol table does not contain an X, then the operation is repeated with the symbol table of the next level of the construction, etc. If no X is found in the symbol table of the outermost construction, or any of the nested ones, then X will be established in the outermost symbol table and be bound to 5.

We indicated that ordinary variables in Common Lisp were lexically scoped with indefinite extent, but special variables were indefinitely scoped with dynamic extent. Special variables must be declared in a particular way. The DECLARE construction is used to make declarations. There are various types of declarations. We shall discuss some of them subsequently. Currently, we want to declare that certain variables are of type SPECIAL. This is done with the following construction.

(DECLARE (SPECIAL A B C))   (5-43)

Here we have declared the variables A, B, and C to be special variables. The declaration usually follows the first line in the construction. For instance, it follows the DEFUN expression. Remember that in Common Lisp, ordinary (undeclared) variables have lexical scope and indefinite extent while special variables have indefinite scope and dynamic extent and that such special variables are said to have dynamic scope.

A *global variable* is one that can be accessed from all parts of the program. If there is indefinite scope, then the binding of a (non-local) variable using SETQ (or SETF) will establish a global variable. On the other hand, if there is lexical scoping then global variables can be established using SETQ (or SETF) in the outermost procedure of the program only. This assumes that the all of the procedures are lexically contained within the main procedure. Global variables are used to store variables that are accessed by many subprocedures of the program. Care should be taken when global variables are used. A change in a global variable can result in changes in all parts of the program. If you make an error, the resulting error may be very hard to correct, because there may be no indication of where in the program the error has occurred.

There is no one fixed scoping standard used in Lisp. Common Lisp is an attempt to obtain a standardized Lisp. However, there are many Lisp systems that do not follow this standard. If you want to write programs that are portable to such systems, then your procedures should not depend on particular scoping standards. Therefore, all values should be passed to procedures using the formal parameter list and global variables should not be used. LET, LET*, or &AUX should be used to make local variables of all the internal variables used by the procedure. All calculated values should be returned by the procedure in the normal manner. If these rules are followed, then most problems relating to scoping standards will be avoided.

There are times when more than one entity is computed in a procedure. However, only one entity ordinarily can be returned. In such cases, put all the computed entities into a list and return that list. For instance, if the three entities that are bound to A, B, and C are to be returned from the procedure, then make the last evaluated expression of the procedure:

(SETQ LL (LIST A B C))   (5-44)

This will put all the data in a single list LL, that will be returned. After the list is returned, successive application of CAR and CDR can be used to extract the desired data from the list.

5-6. The Use of Procedure Names as Arguments

Sometimes it is desirable to assign a procedure name to a variable and to subsequently use that variable name to invoke the procedure. The procedure FUNCALL can be used to call a procedure when its name has been bound to a variable. For instance, suppose that after the procedure ARB-AVERAGE of figure 5.1 has been established, we evaluate,

(SETQ AA 'ARB-AVERAGE)   (5-45)

We now can pass the variable AA and valid arguments of ARB-AVERAGE to FUNCALL to invoke ARB-AVERAGE. For instance if,

(FUNCALL AA 100 90 90 100)   (5-46)

is evaluated, the value returned will be:

95

When (5-46) is evaluated, the first argument of FUNCALL is evaluated. The result of this evaluation is used as a procedure name, and the remaining arguments of FUNCALL are used as the arguments of the procedure. Thus, the evaluation of (5-46) eventually results in the evaluation of:

(ARB-AVERAGE 100 90 90 100)   (5-47)

The following is equivalent to (5-46):

(FUNCALL 'ARB-AVERAGE 100 90 90 100)   (5-48)

Note that when 'ARB-AVERAGE is evaluated, the result is ARB-AVERAGE.

The first argument of FUNCALL is always evaluated. That argument could be a complex Lisp expression, as long as the result of its evaluation is a procedure name, or a lambda expression. For instance, the evaluation of the following sequence,

(SETQ X '(LAMBDA(A B C) (+ A B C)))   (5-49)
(FUNCALL X 3 4 5)   (5-50)

will return 12. Similarly, a COND expression could be the first argument of FUNCALL. Remember that a procedure name must result when the first argument of FUNCALL is evaluated.

In Lisp a program can be part of the data. In particular, the first argument of FUNCALL could be supplied as data. Thus, the input data can specify the particular procedure to be performed. As an example suppose that,

(FUNCALL (READ) (READ) (READ) (READ))

is executed. Operation will pause until the user enters four items. If they are X, 3, 4, and 5, then the operation will be the same as if (5-50) were executed. The ability to specify procedure names as data is a very powerful feature of Lisp.

5-7. Closures

Sometimes we want a variable used by a procedure to change its value during a call to that procedure. The new binding is to be saved and this changed value is to be used for that variable's value the next time that the procedure is invoked. For example, suppose that we modify the procedure PWD-CHECK of figure 4.3 so that it will keep track of how many times it has been used. This will indicate how many times the system has been accessed. The procedure of figure 5.18 will accomplish this.

```
(DEFUN PWD-CHECK(PWF)
   (TERPRI)
   (PRINC "Enter log-in name   ")
   (SETQ NAME (READ))
   (TERPRI)
   (PRINC "Enter password   ")
   (TERPRI)
   (SETQ PWD (READ))
   (COND ((EQUAL PWD (CADR (MEMBER NAME PWF))) (PRINC "System accessed"))
         (T (PRINC "Access denied"))
   )
   (COND ((BOUNDP 'NUMBER-CALLS) NIL)
         (T (SETQ NUMBER-CALLS 0))
   )
   (SETQ NUMBER-CALLS (+ NUMBER-CALLS 1))
)

(SETQ PASS-CHECK (CLOSURE '(NUMBER-CALLS PWD) #'PWD-CHECK))
```

Figure 5.18. An example of a CLOSURE

(For the time being ignore the last line of the figure, which actually is not part of the procedure PWD-CHECK.) We assume that the variable called NUMBER-CALLS has not been bound before the procedure is called. The first time that the procedure is called, the last COND construction causes NUMBER-CALLS to be bound to zero. Subsequently the condition,

(BOUNDP 'NUMBER-CALLS)   (5-51)

will return true and NUMBER-CALLS will not be further modified by this COND construction. NUMBER-CALLS is a free variable. In the next expression of the procedure, NUMBER-CALLS is incremented, and the new value of NUMBER-CALLS is bound and returned by the procedure. Because NUMBER-CALLS is a free variable, its binding will be unchanged by the termination of the procedure. Thus, its value will be remembered and used the next time that PWD-CHECK is invoked. Thus, the procedure will operate as desired.

There is one potential problem with the procedure PWD-CHECK. As previously stated, NUMBER-CALLS is a free variable. If another procedure also uses a free variable called NUMBER-CALLS, its value could be changed and an error would result. Thus it would be desirable to make the variable NUMBER-CALLS private to the procedure PWD-CHECK. The usual means for setting up local variables would not suffice here. For instance, if we used LET, LET*, or &AUX to make NUMBER-CALLS a local variable, then it would be rebound to its initial value each time that the procedure was called. (If no initial value were specified, it would be bound to NIL each time that the procedure was called.) Thus, appropriate value of NUMBER-CALLS would not be saved.

Lisp allows us to establish procedures that have private free variables; these variables are *hidden* from the rest of the system. This is called a *closure*. A closure is a new entity that is lexically scoped. This entity contains a copy of the procedure. Copies of the specified free variables are also associated with this new lexical region. Thus, these specified free variables will be invisible to the rest of the program. Any unspecified free variables of the new procedure will not be associated with the lexical region and thus will be visible to the rest of the system.

In order to establish a closure, the CLOSURE operation is invoked after the procedure has been written in the ordinary way. This establishes a copy of the original procedure. Certain free variables used in the procedure can be made specified as private to the procedure. The original free variables are unmodified by this operation but, in the copy of the procedure, there are (new) free variables that are invisible to the rest of the program. The following expression will invoke CLOSURE:

```
(SETQ PASS-CHK (CLOSURE '(NUMBER-CALLS) #'PWD-CHECK))
```
(5-52)

The variable PASS-CHK stores the closure. Note the form of the CLOSURE expression.

```
(CLOSURE '(NUMBER-CALLS) #'PWD-CHECK)
```
(5-53)

That is, the atom CLOSURE is followed by a *list* of free variable names that are to be made private to the copy of the procedure, a pound sign and an apostrophe followed by the name of the procedure. The procedure is invoked using FUNCALL. For instance, if the passwords were stored in a file called PASS, then evaluation of the following expression would produce the desired result:

```
(FUNCALL PASS-CHK PASS)
```
(5-54)

Note that if you invoke the original function using,

```
(PWD-CHECK PASS)
```
(5-55)

then the original (unisolated) free variable NUMBER-CALLS will be used. However, when the password checking procedure is invoked using (5-54), the private NUMBER-CALLS will be used. Although they share the same name, these variables are unrelated, except for the fact that the initial value assigned to the private NUMBER-CALLS was equal to the value assigned to the original NUMBER-CALLS at the time when the CLOSURE was invoked. Note that NUMBER-CALLS *must* be bound at the time that (5-52) is evaluated or an error will result.

In the last line of figure 5.18 we illustrate the invoking of CLOSURE with a list of private variables. In this case both NUMBER-CALLS and PWD become private.

```
(DEFUN CL-TEST( )
    (COND ((BOUNDP 'A) NIL)
          (T (SETQ A 1)) 
    )
    (PRINT A)
    (SETQ A (+ A 1))
    (COND ((< A 3) (CL-TEST)))
)
```

Figure 5.19. A recursive procedure

As a further example of CLOSURE, consider figure 5.19. The procedure of figure 5.19 calls itself recursively. Suppose that A is initially unbound; in which case the procedure will call itself recursively one time. If the procedure is invoked again, there will be no recursive call, because the value of A will be equal to 3. If SETQ were used at the top level to bind A then the number of recursive calls of CL-TEST could change. Now suppose that a closure is established. For instance, suppose that,

$$(SETQ \ CLO\text{-}TEST \ (CLOSURE \ '(A) \ \#'CL\text{-}TEST)) \qquad (5\text{-}56)$$

is evaluated at the time that A is bound to 0. When,

$$(FUNCALL \ CLO\text{-}TEST) \qquad (5\text{-}57)$$

is evaluated, the procedure will be called three times (two recursive calls). Remember that the values initially assigned to the private free variables will be equal to the values of their public counterparts. If, after (5-57) is initially evaluated, it is evaluated again, there will be no recursive calls because the private A will be bound to 3 before (5-57) is reevaluated. There is no way to change this private A at the top level. In particular, a SETQ evaluated at the top level, will not change the private A.

There may be circumstances where you want several procedures to "share" the same private free variables. Some Lisp systems provide a mechanism for doing this. Check your Lisp manual to see if your Lisp system has such a mechanism.

The notation used to invoke closures may vary from that shown here. For instance, CLOSURE may be replaced by FCLOSURE. Some Lisp systems do not require the pound sign. Check your Lisp manual to determine the form used to invoke closures on your system.

5-8. Debugging Programs

In the last chapter we mentioned that programs containing GO forms were often hard to understand and difficult to debug. We stressed the fact that modern programming techniques result in programs, called *structured programs* that are easier to understand and debug. One of the definitions of structured programming is that GO forms are not used. Another characteristic of structured programming is that a program is broken into small modules that can be written and tested separately. That is, the program should consist of a main procedure that calls subprocedures. These subprocedures may call other subprocedures in turn. An error in a small module is much simpler to correct than is an error in a large program. An error in a single, long, complex, procedure may be difficult to locate. All complex programs have errors and time must be allocated for debugging. When programs are difficult to debug, then the debugging time can exceed the writing time. Thus, it is desirable to write all programs in a structured form.

Even structured programs have bugs. In this section we shall discuss some ideas that can be used to debug programs. Remember that you should not be discouraged by bugs in your programs. The experienced programmer knows that debugging is an integral part of the programming process. However, you should attempt to write programs in such a way as to minimize the number of errors and to make debugging them relatively easy.

In general, there are two types of errors, errors in syntax and errors in logic. An error in syntax occurs when the rules of Lisp have not been followed. In such cases either you will not be able to establish the procedure using DEFUN or the procedure, once established, will not run. In either of these cases the Lisp system will output an *error message* that should provide some help in debugging the system. When a logical error occurs, on the other hand, the program may be perfectly good Lisp and will run without any apparent difficulty, but it gives the wrong answers.

DEBUGGING OF SYNTAX ERRORS

Syntax errors often prevent the DEFUN expression from evaluating or, if it does evaluate, the procedure itself may not evaluate. In either case an error message will be output. If these error messages described the error exactly, debugging would be a very simple matter. Unfortunately, the error messages are not ideal. For instance, suppose that you have inadvertently omitted a right parenthesis from part of your Lisp program. The error message,

Unexpected end of file   (5-58)

might be output when you attempt to DEFUN your procedure. That is, the Lisp system realizes that it has come to the end of the text for the program, but the number of left parentheses is greater than the number of right parentheses. Thus, the Lisp system expects that there is additional text contained in the function. However, there is no additional text remaining. Unfortunately, the error message (5-58) gives you no information as to where the error has occurred. You must reread your program carefully to detect where a parenthesis was left out. Note that it is much easier to do this with a short procedure than with a long one. The editor programs provided with some Lisp systems indicate matched pairs of parentheses. For instance, when you type over a right parenthesis, the corresponding left parenthesis will blink. Such editors are a great help in keeping track of parentheses.

Unfortunately, if you omit a complete pair of parentheses, these procedures may not help you. In those cases you may receive an error message only after you attempt to evaluate the procedure. The error message may indicate that a valid statement is invalid. When this occurs, and you are sure that the expression is actually valid, check your parentheses carefully.

Pairs of double quotation marks are used to delimit strings of characters. If you forget the second quotation mark, the Lisp system may consider that the rest of the procedure is part of the string and strange error messages may result. In all of the previous cases, experience with the error messages produced by your system will help you identify the error. Reread your program carefully to find where the problem has occurred.

Some of these syntax errors will be detected when the DEFUN statement is evaluated; others will be detected when you attempt to run the procedure. For instance, if you omit one parenthesis, the error will be detected when you attempt to evaluate the DEFUN statement. On the other hand, if a pair of parentheses are omitted, then this may not be detected until you attempt to evaluate the procedure itself.

DEBUGGING OF LOGICAL ERRORS

Even if the program appears to run properly it, may contain logical errors. *You must check each program with several sets of data* to make sure that it computes the correct values. This is very important; every program must be tested with several sets of unrelated data. If you have a logical error, reread your program very carefully to make sure that you do not have a typographical error. For instance, there may be a + where a - should be. If this does not correct the error then compute each step of the program by hand and compare the results with the corresponding results of the program. This will enable you to see if the program is functioning as it should. In addition, this operation will enable you to check that the algorithm that you are using is correct. An *algorithm* is the general scheme of your program. In order to check your program step by step you nay have to include additional PRINT expressions at appropriate points in the program. Of course, after the program is debugged, these additional PRINT expressions should be removed.

DEBUGGING TOOLS

Many Lisp system provide you with tools that can be used to aid debugging. We have already discussed the TRACE procedure. Remember, *see* sec. 5-2, that TRACE indicates those procedures that have been called as well as the values returned by those procedures. If your program is modularized into small subprocedures then the TRACE operation will output many intermediate values without your having to add special debugging expressions to your program. Note that you can also determine if the correct subprocedures are called by using using TRACE.

There is another debugging tool called STEP. When STEP is invoked, your procedure will execute one expression at a time. Intermediate values will be output and you will be able to check each step of the operation without including any special debugging statements. The operation of STEP will vary from system to system, but the basic ideas are as we have discussed. Your system manual will describe how to use STEP and TRACE. You should practice using TRACE and STEP on your system to see how they function.

There are errors that occur with one set of data that do not occur when other data is used. Let us consider an example of this. Suppose that you are computing the following:

$$(/ (* A B) C) \tag{5-59}$$

That is, A and B are multiplied and the resulting product is divided by C. It is possible that the product may be so large that an overflow occurs, even though the final answer can be represented by the number system in use. The overflow could be avoided if (5-59) were rewritten as:

$$(* (/ A C) B) \tag{5-60}$$

In this case A would be divided by C and then the resulting quotient would be multiplied by B. Now the large product of A and B would never be computed and the overflow would be avoided.

Errors also can result because of the roundoff errors that occur when floating point calculations are performed. No warning is ever given when such errors occur. Each floating-point calculation usually produces a very small roundoff error. If there are very many calculations then these errors can accumulate, and a substantial error in the final answer can result. One way to check for the presence of roundoff errors is to repeat the calculations using greater precision. For instance, numbers of type LONG could be used. If the two answers are substantially different, then roundoff error is a problem. If the two answers are the same, then roundoff error is probably not significant. If there are differences in the two sets of calculations, you cannot be sure that the higher precision calculations are correct. In such cases you should perform a reasonable number of calculations by hand to verify your results.

Some calculations are especially prone to roundoff error. The subtraction of two large, almost equal, numbers is one such case. For instance, consider that you are subtracting 99 from 100. The answer should be 1. Now suppose that a one percent error was made in the 100, so that its value became 101. The result of the subtraction would be 2. Thus a one percent error in one of the numbers results in an 100 percent error in the answer.

Exercises

Check any procedures that you write by running them on your computer.

1. Write a procedure using &REST that has an arbitrary number of integers as its arguments. The procedure should return the largest integer argument.

2. Write a procedure whose first argument is a name that is to be removed from a sequence of names. The remaining arguments consist of a sequence of names that is arbitrarily long. Use &REST in the argument list. A list, containing all the names in the sequence except for the specified one is to be returned. Assume that no name is duplicated in the sequence.

3. Is it possible to repeat exercise 2 with the name removed from the sequence of names have a default value of JONES? If this is possible, write the procedure. If not, explain why.

4. Repeat exercise 2 but now have the sequence of names passed in a list. Also arrange for the name that is to be removed from the list names to have a default value of JONES.

5. Write a procedure that demonstrates the use of &AUX. Initial values should be given to the local variables.

6. A list contains a number of sublists. Each sublist contains a sequence of names. Assume that no name is duplicated in any sublist. Use the procedure of exercise 4 to remove a specified name from each of the lists in which that name occurs. A single list containing all the names, minus the specified one, should be returned.

7. Write a procedure that is passed an integer N and returns the sum of the first N integers. Use recursive calls.

8. Modify the procedure FINDER of figure 5.7 so that it can be used with nested lists. That is, there can be lists of names embedded in the input list. Assume that there is no more than one level of nesting.

9. Repeat exercise 8, but now assume that the level of nesting is arbitrary.

10. What is meant by a tail-recursive procedure? Why is it sometimes desirable for a recursive procedure to be written in a tail-recursive form?

11. Write a recursive procedure called COUNT-MEMBER that returns the number of times that an item is found in a list at any level.

12. Repeat exercise 5-9 but now modify the procedure so that it returns the number of times that either of two items are found.

13. Write a procedure that is passed a list as an argument. The procedure should return the total number of atoms in the entire list. The list can contain nested lists, etc.

14. Write a procedure as a LAMBOA definition that averages a list of numbers.

15. Use a lambda definition to determine if a list contains sublists.

16. What is meant by saying that a variable has lexical scope and indefinite extent?

17. What is meant by saying that a variable has indefinite scope and dynamic extent.

18. Discuss figure 5.11 by first assuming that there is lexical scope and indefinite extent and then assuming that there is indefinite scope and dynamic extent.

19. What is meant by shadowing?

20. Write a procedure that allows the person running the program to enter a procedure name and its arguments, then that procedure is to be run with the specified arguments. The person entering the data is assumed to enter both the name of an existing procedure and the correct number of arguments.

21. Write a procedure that generates an odd number each time that it is called. The same number should not be generated twice. Do not use ordinary free variables in your procedure.

22. Demonstrate that closures can be used with recursive function calls.

23. Why should programs be modularized?

24. If your Lisp system has a version of TRACE, then use it to trace the operation of a procedure that calls other procedures. One of the procedures should call itself recursively.

25. If your lisp system has a version of STEP, then use it to step the operation of the procedure used in exercise 24. Determine the information that is output by STEP.

6

Databases and Database Manipulation

In many applications we deal with the properties of objects. For instance, a table may be made of wood, brown in color and round in shape. In this simple example we have considered the following properties: made of, color, and shape. Lisp allows us to store this data in several convenient forms.

Let us consider an application for data of this type. Suppose that an expert system was needed to identify objects. An *expert system* is a program that functions as an expert would. Thus, the expert system program can be used to replace the "expert" in some functions. Suppose that our expert identifies things. For instance, if you show the expert a table, he tells you that it is a table, and if you show the expert a book, he tells you that it is a book. An expert system program would take the properties of the object and tell you what the object is. Note that we have only indicated one type of expert system here. Although the example that we have used is trivial, it does have features that are common to many expert systems. (The general problem of identifying objects is not a simple one.) For instance, an expert systems could return a medical diagnosis when a list of symptoms is supplied. Another expert system, used in conjunction with a visual scanner could "read" x-ray photographs and interpret them. Expert systems also are used to control robots in assembly lines.

Lisp provides three forms that can be used conveniently to store the properties of an object. These forms are the *property list*, or *p-list*, the *association list*, or *a-list*, and the *structure*. The ability to manipulate these forms is an important aspect of Lisp and is one of the reasons that it called the "language of artificial intelligence."

6-1. Association Lists

Three list forms generally are used to store property values in Lisp. These are the *property list,* which is often abbreviated *p-list,* the *association list,* which is often abbreviated *a-list,* and the *structure.* The p-list, the a-list, and the structure are different data forms and are manipulated using different procedures. However, they store the same kinds of information and often are used for similar applications. Actually a-lists can be contained within p-lists, and this versatility is useful in certain circumstances. We shall discuss association lists in this section. Property lists will be discussed in the next section. Structures will be discussed in sec. 6-6.

The association list consists of a list of lists. For instance, suppose that we list the properties of the object my-table as: type furniture, color brown, and shape round. In this simple example have listed the three properties type, color, and shape. These properties have the values furniture, brown, and round. Suppose that this information is to be stored in an association list, and that, furthermore that association list is to be bound to the atom MY-TABLE. The following will accomplish this:

```
(SETQ MY-TABLE '((TYPE FURNITURE) (COLOR BROWN)
                 (SHAPE ROUND)))                    (6-1)
```

Note that each sublist consists of a pair of elements. The first element is the property name or attribute; the second element is the "value" of the property. Lisp systems often use dotted pairs in association lists because this reduces storage requirements and can increase speed somewhat. For those systems (6-1) would be replaced by:

```
(SETQ MY-TABLE '((TYPE . FURNITURE) (COLOR . BROWN)
                 (SHAPE . ROUND)))                    (6-2)
```

There are similar procedures that manipulate the two different types of a-lists. Remember that your Lisp system may accommodate only one form of a-list.

There are various procedures that are used to manipulate a-lists; we shall consider some of them here. The primitive ASSOC is used to extract a property value from an a-list. For instance,

```
(ASSOC 'COLOR MY-TABLE)                               (6-3)
```

will return,

(COLOR BROWN)   (6-4a)

if dot notation is not used. On the other hand, (6-3) will return,

(COLOR . BROWN)   (6-4b)

if dot notation is used. The form of an ASSOC expression is the atom ASSOC followed by the property type, preceded by an apostrophe, and then the name of the variable that stores the list. If the property type is not found in the specified a-list, then ASSOC will return NIL. A property value could itself be NIL. In this case, ASSOC will return the pair consisting of the name of the property type and NIL. We shall assume that the dotted pair form of notation is used from this point on. The results are essentially the same when the alternative form is used.

Suppose that we want the word BROWN returned. This can be accomplished with the construction:

(CDR (ASSOC 'COLOR MY-TABLE))   (6-5)

Note that if dot notation was not used, the CDR of (6-5) would have to be replaced by CADR.

The property's name is referred to as the *key*. ASSOC uses the key to find the datum (item of data) associated with it. Conversely, the procedure RASSOC uses the datum to find the key. For instance if,

(RASSOC 'BROWN MY-TABLE)   (6-6)

is evaluated then,

(COLOR . BROWN)   (6-7)

will be returned. Note that if there are two different keys that have the same datum, the first one encountered will be returned by RASSOC.

The procedure ACONS is used to add a key-datum pair to the beginning of an a-list. For instance the evaluation of,

(SETQ MY-TABLE (ACONS 'MFGR 'SMITH-FURN-CO
                      MY-TABLE))   (6-8)

will result in MY-TABLE being rebound to the a-list:

```
((MFGR . SMITH-FURN-CO) (TYPE . FURNITURE)
    (COLOR . BROWN) (SHAPE . ROUND))                    (6-9)
```

Here we want each datum to be a single atom. Thus, the hyphens are used instead of blank spaces within the name of the manufacturer of the furniture.

The procedure ACONS is convenient to use when a single pair is to be added to the a-list. However, it is tedious to use if many pairs are to be added. The procedure PAIRLIS allows data is to be entered in list form. PAIRLIS is also used to initially set up lists. The use of PAIRLIS is very similar to the use of ACONS except that all the keys are put into one list and the associated data are put into a second list. For instance,

```
(SETQ MY-TABLE (PAIRLIS '(COLOR SHAPE)
                        '(BROWN ROUND)))              (6-10)
```

will result in the list,

```
((COLOR . BROWN) (SHAPE . ROUND))                      (6-11)
```

being bound to MY-TABLE. Of course,

```
(PAIRLIS '(COLOR SHAPE) '(BROWN ROUND)))               (6-12)
```

returns the list (6-11). PAIRLIS can be used to add new pairs to the beginning of a list. For instance, if we want MY-TABLE to be bound to (6-9), and its present form is (6-11), then the following should be evaluated:

```
(SETQ MY-TABLE (PAIRLIS '(MFGR TYPE)
              '(SMITH-FURN-CO FURNITURE) MY-TABLE))
                                                       (6-13)
```

The use of the list name is an optional third argument of PAIRLIS. When this third argument is included, the data is added to the a-list specified in that third argument. Note that ACONS and PAIRLIS return new lists, but they do not modify any existing lists. That is why SETQ was used in the previous examples.

The procedures discussed in sec. 3-4 to modify existing lists can be utilized here. For instance suppose that you want to change the SHAPE property of MY-TABLE from ROUND to OVAL, the following construction will accomplish this:

(RPLACD (ASSOC 'SHAPE MY-TABLE) 'OVAL)   (6-14)

when (6-14) is evaluated,

(ASSOC 'SHAPE MY-TABLE)

returns:

(SHAPE . ROUND)   (6-15)

   This becomes the first argument of RPLACD. The RPLACD procedure replaces all of the list that is its first argument, except that pointed at by the car of the first cons cell. The car of the list of (6-15) is SHAPE. Thus, the atom ROUND is replaced by OVAL. (Dot notation is used in (6-15) because that form has a single cons cell and its cdr does not point at NIL.) Remember that RPLACD is a destructive operation; that is, it actually changes the cons cell.
   Suppose that you want to remove an entry from an a-list. The procedure DELETE destructively removes an element from a list. For instance, the following removes the SHAPE property from the MY-TABLE list:

(DELETE (ASSOC 'SHAPE MY-TABLE) MY-TABLE)   (6-16)

Because

(ASSOC 'SHAPE MY-TABLE)   (6-17)

points to the actual (SHAPE . ROUND) in the list, that element will be removed form the list bound to MY-TABLE. The procedure DELETE uses EQL rather than EQUAL to locate the element in the list that is to be removed. Thus, we could not replace (6-16) by:

(DELETE '(SHAPE . ROUND) MY-TABLE)

That is, the result of the evaluation of (6-17) actually points at the element in the list MY-TABLE. Comments of this type could also be applied to RPLACA and RPLACD.
   We have assumed that each datum was an atom. In this case the a-list consisted of a list of dotted pairs. However, the data can consist of a list. Consider the cons cell for a dotted pair. Its car points at one atom and its cdr

points at another atom. It is a dotted pair because the cdr of the last cons cell, which is the same as first cons cell, does not point at NIL. Now consider that the data is replaced by a list. The car of the first cons cell still points at the key, but now the cdr of that cons cell points at a valid list, and the cdr of the last cons cell of that list points at NIL. The structure is now that of a valid list whose CAR is the key and whose CDR is the list of data. Let us illustrate this with an example. Suppose that we evaluate:

```
(SETQ BOOK (PAIRLIS '(COVER SUBJECT PUBLISHER)
                    '(HARD LISP (JONES BOOK CO))))
```

The list that BOOK is bound to is:

```
((COVER . HARD) (SUBJECT . LISP)
   (PUBLISHER JONES BOOK C0))
```

Thus, an a-list is a list whose elements are either lists or dotted pairs.

6-2. Property Lists

In Lisp a name of an entity is called a *symbol*. We have used symbols as both the names of variables and the names of functions. The same symbol can be used to represent different types of entities. For instance, we have seen that a variable and a procedure can have the same name. The Lisp system determines whether a symbol represents a variable or a procedure by the way that it is used. A symbol can also represent a property list. A property list associates the property types of an object with particular values. The programmer does not have to be concerned with the mechanism by which the Lisp system stores this information. Thus, the same symbol can represent at least three different objects. (Actually a symbol can represent other entities. We shall discuss this concept at more length subsequently.)

There are special procedures that are used to manipulate property lists. We shall consider some of them here. Property lists are set up using the procedure PUTPROP. In some systems this procedure is called PUT. For instance, suppose that a property list is to be set up with the name LISP-BOOK, the property type BK-TYPE, and with the value TEXTBOOK.

This could be established by evaluating:

(PUTPROP 'LISP-BOOK 'TEXT-BOOK 'BK-TYPE)   (6-18)

The form of the use is the atom PUTPROP followed by the symbol that is the p-list name, then the property value, and the property type. The property type is sometimes called an *attribute*. Some Lisp systems provide a procedure called DEFPROP, which functions in the same way as PUTPROP except that its arguments are not evaluated. As a practical matter this means that the apostrophes can be omitted from the list of arguments.

A p-list cannot be output to the screen simply by entering the symbol name or by using PRINT. For instance, if you type LISP-BOOK followed by RETURN, an error will result because LISP-BOOK is an unbound atom. (This assumes that you have not bound an atom called LISP-BOOK to a value.) The value of a property list can be output using the procedure SYMBOL-PLIST. In some Lisp systems this is simply called PLIST. For instance if, after (6-18) is evaluated, the following expression is evaluated,

(SYMBOL-PLIST 'LISP-BOOK)   (6-19)

then the following list will be returned:

(BK-TYPE TEXT-BOOK)   (6-20)

PUTPROP can be also used to add to an existing p-list. For instance, if,

(PUTPROP 'LISP-BOOK 'LISP 'SUBJECT)   (6-21)

is evaluated, the property SUBJECT with value LISP will be added to the p-list associated with the symbol LISP-BOOK. If (6-19) now is reevaluated, the output will be:

(SUBJECT LISP BK-TYPE TEXT-BOOK)   (6-22)

Note that SYMBOL-PLIST returns a list that consists of a sequence of pairs of property names and their values. The last entered property name-value pair will be returned first. This does not necessarily mean that the Lisp system stores the p-list as an ordinary list. However, SYMBOL-PLIST does return an ordinary list.

The value of a property can be retrieved by using the procedure called GET. Let us assume that the p-list named LISP-BOOK exists as in (6-22). The evaluation of,

(GET 'LISP-BOOK 'BK-TYPE)   (6-23)

will return TEXT-BOOK.

If you ask for a property that is nonexistent, GET will return NIL. There is a problem here. GET also will return NIL if you ask for a property that does exist, but happens to have the value NIL. (Note that this problem did not occur when ASSOC was used in conjunction with a-lists because ASSOC returns a pair of values as long as the key exists.) To resolve this difficulty, GET has an optional third parameter. Its value will be returned if the specified property does not exist in the p-list in question. For instance,

(GET 'LISP-BOOK 'COLOR 'NOT-VALID-PROPERTY)   (6-24)

will return NOT-VALID-PROPERTY. Note that if the second argument of GET is not a p-list, GET will also return NIL or its third argument, if it is present. Not all Lisp systems allow GET to have a third argument.

Now let us consider how a p-list can be modified. Suppose that the value of a particular property is to be changed. PUTPROP can accomplish this. We have used PUTPROP to add new properties and their values to lists. Property lists cannot have duplicate property types; Although different property types can have the same values. If the third argument of PUTPROP is the same as an existing property type in the named p-list, then the *value* of the existing property type will be changed. For instance, if the p-list named LISP-BOOK is as shown in (6-22) and the following is evaluated,

(PUTPROP 'LISP-BOOK 'LISP-AI 'SUBJECT)   (6-25)

then, reevaluation of (6-19) will return,

(SUBJECT LISP-AI BK-TYPE TEXTBOOK)   (6-26)

with LISP-AI replacing LISP as the value of the property SUBJECT.

The generalized procedure SETF also can be used to modify a p-list. Remember that SETF is a generalized form of SETQ where the first argument can be certain procedures. The entity returned by the procedure will be modified when the SETF expression is evaluated. For instance, the following will have the same effect as (6-25):

(SETF (GET 'LISP-BOOK 'SUBJECT) LISP-AI))   (6-27)

The procedure named REMPROP can be used to remove a property from a p-list. For example,

(REMPROP 'LISP-BOOK 'BK-TYPE)   (6-28)

will remove the property BK-TYPE and its associated value TEXTBOOK from the p-list named LISP-BOOK. If REMPROP cannot remove the specified property from the specified list, either because the property is not in the p-list, or because the named p-list does not exist, then it returns NIL. If REMPROP functions properly, it returns T. Some Lisp systems return specific values instead of T. Check your Lisp manual to see how REMPROP functions in your Lisp system.

The procedure GET-PROPERTIES can be used to determine if certain properties are in a p-list. Suppose that you want to determine if the properties COLOR and SUBJECT are contained in the p-list LISP-BOOK. Evaluation of the following would accomplish this:

(GET-PROPERTIES (SYMBOL-PLIST 'LISP-BOOK)
                '(COLOR SUBJECT))   (6-29)

Note the form. SYMBOL-PLIST is used to provide an actual list as a first argument for GET-PROPERTIES. The second argument is a *list* that contains the property types that are to be searched for. GET-PROPERTIES functions in the following way. The property types in the first list (the p-list) are searched for a match with the first element in the second list. If there is a match then three items are output: the property type, its corresponding property value, and the tail, which is the rest of the p-list starting with the property type in question. Once a match is found and the values are returned, the procedure terminates. If a match is not found using the first element of the second argument of GET-PROPERTIES, then the procedure is repeated with the second element of the second argument, etc. If no match is found, NIL is output three times. If the value returned by GET-PROPERTIES is simply passed to another procedure, it is the first returned value, i. e., the property type, that will be used by that procedure.

Note that the first argument of GET-PROPERTIES can be any list that is in the form returned by SYMBOL-PLIST. For instance the second argument of (6-29) could be:

'(SUBJECT LISP-AI BK-TYPE TEXTBOOK)

DIFFERENCES BETWEEN A-LISTS AND P-LISTS

An a-list is assigned to a symbol. That symbol can be used as is any other atom that is bound to a value. In particular, any a-list can be an argument of a procedure; it can be returned by a procedure, it can be assigned to another variable, and it can be tested using EQUAL, EQL, or EQ. Entities that possess these four properties are said to be *first class data objects*. (This notation has been promoted by The Lisp Company, developers of TLC Lisp.) A p-list, on the other hand, is not assigned to a symbol that can be evaluated in the usual sense. Thus, the p-list is not a first class data object and does not possess any of the four attributes that were enumerated above. However, the internal representation of p-lists requires less storage space than do a-lists. In addition, the p-list manipulations that we have discussed are, in general, faster than the corresponding a-list manipulations. Thus, each list form has its advantages and disadvantages.

6-3. An Example of a Database - Some Simple Database Manipulations

We are now in a position to use the power of Lisp to manipulate data in a significant way. We shall start by discussing the storage of data in a *database*. A database is an orderly collection of data. There are many forms for the storage of data. We shall set up a database as a collection of either a-lists or p-lists. A complete textbook can be written on databases and database manipulation. It is not our purpose to present an all inclusive study of databases here. However we shall consider a representative form of database and show how you can write pertinent Lisp procedures that manipulate databases. In this section we shall consider how a database can be set up and modified. In the following sections of this chapter we shall consider operations with the database that relate to artificial intelligence and expert systems.

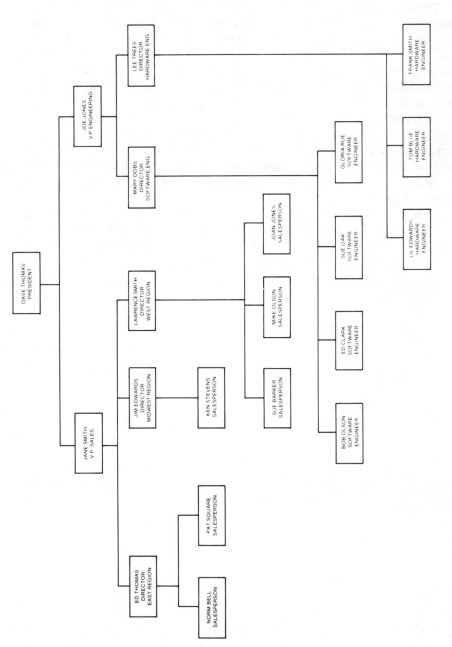

Figure 6.1. A company organization chart

The example that we shall use for a database is a personnel list for a small company. The structure of the company is not realistic in that not all personnel types are considered. This has been done so that the database can be kept small, but still be complex enough so that we can illustrate the features of Lisp that we want to consider. The company that we shall consider will have the structure illustrated in figure 6.1. There is a president, named ED WILSON and two vice presidents who report to the president. There is a vice president for sales and a vice president for research. Three directors report to the vice president for sales and two directors report to the vice president for research. Numerous salespeople and engineers report to the appropriate directors. Some levels of management and support personnel have been omitted from the database in order to keep it relatively simple so that the discussions are not obscured by too much detail.

Every employee will have a personnel file. We shall use a p-list for this file. (Subsequently we shall consider other forms that could be used to store this data.) The collection of p-lists for all the employees will constitute the database. The p-lists will contain the following properties:

```
NAME
SALARY
JOB-DESCRIPTION
AGE
YEARS-IN-COMPANY
YEARS-IN-PRESENT-JOB                                    (6-30)
EDUCATION
RATING-OF-SUPERVISOR
REPORTS-TO
SUPERVISES
```

Again, an actual personnel file probably would have additional data. However, this data is varied enough so that the database can be used to illustrate the features that we shall discuss.

```
(DEFUN ADD-ONE(NAME LST PROPS)
   (COND ((AND (> (LENGTH LST) 0) (> (LENGTH PROPS) 0))
                   (PUTPROP NAME (CAR LST) (CAR PROPS))
           )
   )
   (COND ((AND (> (LENGTH PROPS) 1) (> (LENGTH LST) 1))
                (ADD-ONE NAME (CDR LST) (CDR PROPS))
           )
     )
 )


(DEFUN ADD-PERSON(LST &AUX PROPS)
   (SETQ PROPS '(NAME SALARY JOB-DESCRIPTION AGE YEARS-IN-COMPANY
                 YEARS-IN-PRESENT-JOB EDUCATION
                 RATING-OF-SUPERVISOR REPORTS-TO SUPERVISES))
   (ADD-ONE (CAR LST) LST PROPS)
 )


(DEFUN GENERATE-NAME-LIST(LST)
   (COND ((> (LENGTH LST) 0) (SETQ NAME-LIST
                 (APPEND NAME-LIST (LIST (CAAR LST))))
           )
     )
   (COND ((> (LENGTH LST) 1) (GENERATE-NAME-LIST (CDR LST))))
 )
```

Figure 6.2. The procedures ADD-ONE and ADD-PERSON that are used to set up P-lists from lists of data and the preceding GENERATE-NAME-LIST that sets up an inside list.

We shall write various procedures to manipulate this database. The first one is called ADD-ONE and is illustrated in figure 6.2. It is used to set up a p-list from data supplied in list form. The properties are supplied in one list and the data is supplied in another list. The name of the p-list is an atom. Thus the arguments of ADD-ONE are an atom and two lists. ADD-ONE is analogous to the procedure PAIRLIS that is used in conjunction with a-lists. The property types that we shall use will be those in (6-30). The procedure ADD-PERSON calls ADD-ONE and supplies it with the proper arguments. The procedure ADD-PERSON has a single argument that is a list containing the data corresponding to the properties of (6-30). The name of the p-list will be the same as the name that corresponds to the NAME property in (6-30). The list of property types is called PROPS and is established when the SETQ expression of ADD-PERSON is executed. Note that (CAR LST) is the first atom in the list LST. This is assumed to be the name of the p-list. Next the procedure ADD-ONE is called using (CAR LST), LST, and PROPS as arguments and the property list is set up with the specific data for the employee associated with the corresponding attribute.

Procedure ADD-ONE takes the first element from each of the lists passed to it and makes them arguments of PUTPROP. Thus, a p-list containing a single pair is set up. If the lengths of each of the lists PROPS and LST is greater than one, then the lists are each replaced by their CDRs and ADD-ONE is called recursively. Each time this is done, an additional pair is added to the p-list. Thus, when ADD-ONE finally terminates, the desired p-list will be generated.

The procedures that are shown in figure 6.2 generate a property list with a specific set of property types. However, the procedure ADD-ONE is general in that its arguments are NAME, the name of the property list, LST, the list of data, and PROPS, the list of property types. Thus, ADD-ONE is a p-list analog of PAIRLIS.

Figure 6.2 also contains the procedure GENERATE-NAME-LIST. This procedure produces a list of the names of all the individual p-lists. This list can be considered to be an index for the database. The list LST, which corresponds to the argument of this procedure, must be a list of lists. Each sublist will contain the data for an individual p-list. The first element of the list will be the person's name which in turn, will be the name of the corresponding p-list and an element of the list set up by GENERATE-NAME-LIST. Assume that there is a variable called NAME-LIST that is bound to NIL. If the length of LST is greater than zero, then the CAAR of LST will be APPENDed to NAME-LIST. Thus, NAME-LIST will contain the first element in the first sublist of LST. We assume that this first element is an atom that is the person's name.

If the length of LST is greater than one, then LST is set equal to its CDR. That is, the first sublist is removed from LST and the procedure is called recursively. Thus, after GENERATE-NAME-LIST terminates, NAME-LIST will contain the desired list of names.

We have used a simple form of a database here. If there were very many employees, the name of the individual p-lists could be each person's ID number. For instance, a p-list name could be N101. In such a case the index list generated should be an a list of pairs of ID numbers and names. This list could be an a-list, a p-list, or simply a list containing alternating ID numbers and names.

```
(DEFUN GENERATE-DATABASE(&AUX BIG-LIST)
  (SETQ BIG-LIST
 '((ED-WILSON 150000.00 PRESIDENT 55 35 20 PHD 100 NIL (JANE-SMITH JOE-JONES))
   (JANE-SMITH 100000.00 VP-SALES 45 20 10 MASTERS 90 ED-WILSON
                (ED-THOMAS JIM-EDWARDS LAWRENCE-SMITH))
   (JOE-JONES 100000.00 VP-ENGINEERING 40 19 5 PHD 85 ED-WILSON
                (MARY-DOBS LEE-TREES))
   (ED-THOMAS 70000.00 DIR-EAST-SALES 35 28 20 BACHELORS 70 JANE-SMITH
                (NORMAN-BELL PAT-SQUARE))
   (JIM-EDWARDS 45000.00 DIR-MIDWEST-SALES 29 15 3 MASTERS 60 JANE-SMITH
                (KEN-STEVENS))
   (LAWRENCE-SMITH 60000.00 DIR-WEST-SALES 38 12 9 MASTERS 95 JANE-SMITH
                (SUE-BARKER MIKE-OLSON JOAN-JONES))
   (MARY-DOBS 65000.00 DIR-SOFTWARE-ENGINEERING 34 8 3 PHD 90 JOE-JONES
                (ROB-OLSON ED-CLARK SUE-OAK GLORIA-ROE))
   (LEE-TREES 75000.00 DIR-HARDWARE-ENGINEERING 41 20 12 MASTERS 75 JOE-JONES
                (LIL-EDWARDS TOM-BLUE FRANK-SMITH))
   (NORMAN-BELL 51000.00 SALESPERSON 42 14 14 BACHELORS 95 ED-THOMAS NIL)
   (PAT-SQUARE 49000.00 SALESPERSON 39 12 12 BACHELORS 90 ED-THOMAS NIL)
   (KEN-STEVENS 37000.00 SALESPERSON 32 8 8 BACHELORS 80 JIM-EDWARDS NIL)
   (SUE-BARKER 55000.00 SALESPERSON 36 9 7 MASTERS 98 LAWRENCE-SMITH NIL)
   (MIKE-OLSON 35000.00 SALESPERSON 26 4 2 BACHELORS 80 LAWRENCE-SMITH NIL)
   (JOAN-JONES 36000.00 SALESPERSON 27 5 3 BACHELORS 70 LAWRENCE-SMITH NIL)
   (ROB-OLSON 36000.00 SOFTWARE-ENGINEER 29 7 7 BACHELORS 75 MARY-DOBS NIL)
   (ED-CLARK 41000.00 SOFTWARE-ENGINEER 35 3 3 MASTERS 80 MARY-DOBS NIL)
   (SUE-OAK 29000.00 SOFTWARE-ENGINEER 26 1 1 PHD 99 MARY-DOBS NIL)
   (GLORIA-ROE 31000.00 SOFTWARE-ENGINEER 29 4 2 PHD 85 MARY-DOBS NIL)
   (LIL-EDWARDS 27000.00 HARDWARE-ENGINEER 22 1 1 BACHELORS 87 LEE-TREES NIL)
   (TOM-BLUE 42000.00 HARDWARE-ENGINEER 42 20 15 MASTERS 70 LEE-TREES NIL)
   (FRANK-SMITH 36000.00 HARDWARE-ENGINEER 31 5 5 PHD 98 LEE-TREES NIL)
   )
  )
  (MAPCAR #'ADD-PERSON BIG-LIST)
  (SETQ NAME-LIST NIL)
  (GENERATE-NAME-LIST BIG-LIST)
  )
```

Figure 6.3. The procedure that generates the database of figure 6.1 and its index list.

The procedure that actually generates the original database is shown in figure 6.3. The list BIG-LIST is set up. This consists of a list of lists. Each sublist consists of the data for one person. The ordering of the data in the sublists corresponds to the ordering of the properties in the procedure ADD-PERSON. After the SETQ expression that sets up BIG-LIST is evaluated, the database is established with the expression:

(MAPCAR #'ADD-PERSON BIG-LIST)   (6-31)

Each of BIG-List's sublists will be supplied to ADD-PERSON in turn. Thus, the desired set of lists will be generated. The index of names is generated using the last two expressions. The SETQ expression sets up a variable called NAME-LIST and binds it to NIL. The evaluation of the last expression causes GENERATE-NAME-LIST to be called and the index list to be generated.

The variable BIG-LIST contains all the data for the database and can itself be used as a database. However, when a p-list or an a-list is used, the property types as well as the corresponding property values are stored. BIG-LIST stores only the property values. As long as the order of the storage corresponds to a known list of property types, BIG-LIST conveys the same information as would a p-list or an a-list. In addition, BIG-LIST is a single list, while there are individual p-lists for each person. The use of multiple lists requires additional storage because the Lisp system must keep track of all these lists. However, it is much more convenient to use p-lists (or a-lists) when data is to be extracted from or added to the lists. For instance, suppose we want ED-CLARK's salary. If the data is as set up by GENERATE-DATABASE of figure 6.3, then all we need do is evaluate:

(GET 'ED-CLARK 'SALARY)   (6-32)

If the data was in the form of BIG-LIST, we would have to write specific procedures to extract the data. This is not difficult, but it is time consuming. If storage space is a limiting factor, then such procedures should be written.

If an a-lists is used to store an individual's data, all of the a-lists can be combined into a single structure. For instance, the individual a-lists could be stored in a p-list. In such a p-list, the property type would be the ID number and the corresponding property value would be the entire appropriate a-list. Thus, the pairs would be the ID number and the corresponding a-list. Actually, either an a-list or a p-list could be used to store the entire data structure.

We have used individual p-lists to avoid obscuring the discussion with unnecessary details. This form of database is practical as long as the number of individual p-lists does not become excessive. Note that the database can be queried for any specific information using GET. All the data for a particular individual could be obtained using SYMBOL-PLIST. For instance,

(SYMBOL-PLIST 'SUE-BARKER)   (6-33)

will result in all of SUE-BARKER's data being output. If an individual's data were to be changed, PUTPROP or SETF could be used. These operations are illustrated in (6-25) and (6-27). ADD-PERSON could be used to add data for an additional individual to the database. Once the database has been modified, the new database should be saved. This can be done by editing the database in figure 6.3 and then running the procedure GENERATE-DATABASE again. This procedure can also be used to add an individual to the database. However, this is a very tedious operation. The modified p-lists should be saved. The procedures for doing this vary with the Lisp system. Some Lisp systems allow you to save the entire environment on a disk file and then load it again at a later date. This would save all the p-lists. Other Lisp systems allow you to save data in other ways. Consult your Lisp manual to find out how to save your data.

In this section we have considered procedures for the generation of databases and procedures for extracting the data they contain. Modifications to the database also were discussed. In the next sections we shall discuss more complex operations with databases that are related to expert systems and artificial intelligence.

6-4. Database Searches - Elements of Expert Systems

We have discussed the setting up of a database and the extraction of elementary data from it. More generalized searches of databases are required by expert systems. Suppose that the database of sec. 6-3 represents the structure of the XYZ company. The XYZ company calls in an expert who studies the personnel data and decides who should be given raises and the amount that those raises should be. The expert provides the company with a list of the employees who deserve raises and the amounts of the raises. Now suppose that you write a computer program to do this. In as much as that program replaces the expert, the program becomes an *expert system.*

The expert system functions on the basis of rules. For instance, suppose that the management of the company has decided that they want to reward employees for continuing their education. Thus, a rule for raises could be that all technical people who have a PhD and a RATING-OF-SUPERVISOR (i.e., fitness rating) of at least 85 will receive a 20 percent raise. A second rule might be that all people in sales who have at least a masters degree, and a fitness rating of at least 80 percent will receive an 15 percent raise. Procedures can be written that search the database for the people that meet the qualifications. Thus obtaining the desired lists.

Similar procedures could be used with other databases. For instance, if a database of diseases and symptoms were available, an expert system could be written to perform medical diagnoses. Robots can be controlled by expert systems. In this case, the database could describe the robot's allowable moves. For instance, if the robot performs welds on an automobile, the database could contain data such as whether the robot's arm was extended or if the welding torch was turned on. There would be sensors that determine the position of the automobile on the assembly line. The automobile's position would also be included in the database. The database would be searched continuously to update the data and to apply the rules to determine the instructions for the robot. We shall discuss procedures for searching databases and extracting the desired information so that expert systems such as these can be set up. Of course, these programs need not be called expert systems: they could simply be called search programs.

We have illustrated the ideas of search programs using expert systems to demonstrate that there is nothing mysterious about expert systems. The real difficulty is in determining the data that should be in the database and in specifying the rules. People can perform remarkably complex operations. However, it is not clear if, or how, a computer could be programmed to perform those operations. Artificial intelligence research studies areas such as these.

We shall discuss several procedures that are used to search databases. Often, the database that is involved is very large and it could take an unduly long time to search the database exhaustively even with a fast computer. Thus, the strategy used to search the database often is important. We shall discuss several strategies here.

The database that we have set up is called a *tree structure*. The data is stored at the *nodes* of the tree. In the tree of figure 6.1, each node stores the data for a single individual. There are various levels in the tree. The top level is called the *root*. The tree then grows from the root. The lowest level nodes are called the leaves. Note that tree structures resemble upside-down botanical trees. The root of our tree structure is at the top of the page, while the leaves are at the bottom of the page. If a tree structure is to exist, then the data in each node must contain an item that points to the nodes in the next lower level. For instance, in the data base that we have set up the data type SUPERVISES contains the data that points at the next lower level in the tree.

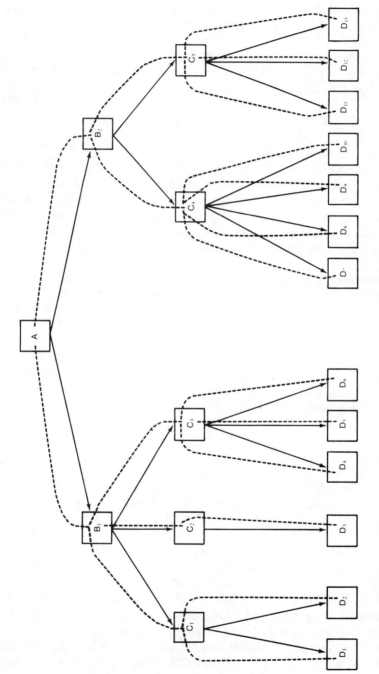

Figure 6.4. A diagrammatic representation of the database of figure 6.1. The tree structure is illustrated.

Tree structures generally are used because they shorten searches. Figure 6.4 is a representation of the tree structure of the database of figure 6.1. The root is labeled A. The next level has two nodes labeled B_1 and B_2. These represent the vice presidents in our database. Similarly the next level has five nodes labeled C_1, C_2, C_3, C_4, and C_5. This notation is repeated for each level as shown. For instance, suppose that you want to find the name of the vice president for engineering, represented by node B_2. Assume that only the root of the tree, ED-WILSON in the case of our database, is known. The root points at the two vice presidents. Thus, the data at nodes B_1 and B_2 should be retrieved first. After this data is read it can be determined that B_2 represents the vice president for engineering and the search is ended. If no tree structure had been set up, then *all* the records would have to be searched at random until the vice president for engineering was found. On the average, half of the nodes would have to be searched before the desired data was obtained. This simple example illustrates the advantage of the tree structure. Note that although the tree structure usually is advantageous, it is not always the best one to use.

Let us consider some terminology. The tree structure of figure 6.4 will be used in this discussion. If node A points at nodes B_1 and B_2, then nodes B_1 and B_2 are said to be the *children* of A. Similarly A is said to be the *parent* of B_1 and B_2. In a similar way C_1 to C_5 can be said to be the grandchildren of A; equivalently, A is said to be the grandparent of C_1, etc.

Now let us consider some actual search procedures. We shall begin by considering what is called a *depth-first search*. We shall assume that we do not know any data that could be used to narrow the search. For instance, if we are searching for the names of all the software engineers, we shall assume that we do not know that they are descendents of the vice president for research, etc. There are circumstances in database searches when such data is not known.

Suppose that we are searching for one person whose JOB-DESCRIPTION is SOFTWARE-ENGINEER. Thus, the rule of our search is that the person to be found is the first one for whom the value of JOB-DESCRIPTION is SOFTWARE-ENGINEER. In a depth-first search, we would start by searching from A to B_1 to C_1 to D_1. At each node, the data would be checked to determine if the rules were satisfied. Once a person who meets the conditions of the rules is found, the data corresponding to NAME is output and the search terminates. Since the only nodes that have the value of SOFTWARE-ENGINEER for JOB-DESCRIPTION are on the fourth level, the first possible output would be for a person at the D level of figure 6.4. Because the children of a node are searched from left to right, node D is examined. However the search test returns false for that individual because his JOB-DESCRIPTION is SALESPERSON. Now, the search would back up the tree to C_1 and then the data for D_2 would be checked. Note that this backing up is symbolic in nature in that the data for C_1 is not checked again. If the search test at node D_2 also fails then the search would back up to C_1 again. Because C_1 has no other children, the search would back up to B_1 and then down to C_2 and then to D_3. The procedure would continue in this way until either the search test returned true, or the entire tree was searched. The various paths for a depth-first search are shown by the dashed lines in figure 6.4.

We have searched for a single person who meets the search-test criteria set forth by the rules. Searches like this are common. For instance, we might want to find a route from one city to another. On the other hand, we might also want to find all the SOFTWARE-ENGINEERS rather than just one instance of that category. The basic search procedure is the same in both cases. In one case, the search terminates after a single person is found; in the other case, the search proceeds through the entire list and finds all the people that meet the specifications.

```
(DEFUN DEPTH-SEARCH(START &AUX SEARCH-LIST)
    (SETQ ANSWER NIL)
    (SETQ SEARCH-LIST (GET START 'SUPERVISES))
    (DEPTH-SEARCH-INT START)
)

(DEFUN DEPTH-SEARCH-INT(START)
    (COND ((EQUAL (GET START 'JOB-DESCRIPTION) 'SOFTWARE-ENGINEER)
               (SETQ ANSWER (APPEND ANSWER (LIST (GET START 'NAME))))
          )
    )
    (COND ((NULL SEARCH-LIST) NIL)
          (T (SETQ START (CAR SEARCH-LIST))
             (SETQ SEARCH-LIST (CDR SEARCH-LIST))
             (SETQ SEARCH-LIST (APPEND (GET START 'SUPERVISES) SEARCH-LIST))
             (DEPTH-SEARCH-INT START)
          )
    )
    ANSWER
)
```

Figure 6.5. A set of procedures that perform a depth-first search

SEARCH binds the global variable ANSWER to NIL, next the variable SEARCH-LIST is bound to (GET START 'SUPERVISES). For instance, if START is bound to bound to ED-WILSON, SEARCH-LIST will be bound to (JANE-SMITH JOE-JONES). Note that SEARCH-LIST is local to DEPTH-SEARCH and any procedures that it calls. Finally, the procedure DEPTH-SEARCH-INT is called. The first procedure is used only to set up the variables ANSWER and SEARCH-LIST and to establish their initial values. The argument START is passed from DEPTH-SEARCH to DEPTH-SEARCH-INT. START represents the starting point in the search. For instance, if the entire database of figure 6.1 is to be searched, then START will be the root, ED-WILSON. We assume that the search is to find all people whose JOB-DESCRIPTION is SOFTWARE-ENGINEER. (The condition of the first COND expression should be changed if the procedure is to search on the basis of another condition.)

If the condition of the first COND expression is true, then the search condition has been satisfied and the value of the NAME property will be appended to ANSWER. Now the second COND expression will be evaluated. If SEARCH-LIST is empty operation ceases. If the list is not empty then START is bound to the first name in the list. At the start this is JANE-SMITH. This name is then removed from SEARCH-LIST. Next the "children" of the (new) START are added to the *beginning* of SEARCH-LIST. Thus, after the first iteration SEARCH-LIST will consist of (ED-THOMAS JIM-EDWARDS LAWRENCE-SMITH JOE-JONES). Then DEPTH-SEARCH-INT will be called recursively using the (new) value of START. (JANE-SMITH if this is the first iteration.) Because DEPTH-SEARCH-INT is called recursively, and because the children of START are added to the beginning of SEARCH-LIST, the search will proceed down a path to its end. Thus, a depth first search has been achieved. If a match with the test condition is found, the appropriate NAME value will be appended to ANSWER. Remember that the database we are using is only an example. This procedure could be used with databases with different kinds of data. The only requirement is that each p-list have a property that points to the level below it.

After the procedure has completed, ANSWER will contain a list of all the found names. This list will be returned to DEPTH-SEARCH which, in turn, returns it and the procedure terminates.

```
(DEFUN DEPTH-SEARCH(START &AUX SEARCH-LIST)
    (SETQ ANSWER NIL)
    (SETQ SEARCH-LIST (GET START 'SUPERVISES))
    (DEPTH-SEARCH-INT START)
)

(DEFUN DEPTH-SEARCH-INT(START)
    (COND ((EQUAL (GET START 'JOB-DESCRIPTION) 'SOFTWARE-ENGINEER)
              (SETQ ANSWER (APPEND ANSWER (LIST (GET START 'NAME))))
              )
    )
    (COND ((NULL SEARCH-LIST) NIL)
           (ANSWER NIL)
           (T (SETQ START (CAR SEARCH-LIST))
              (SETQ SEARCH-LIST (CDR SEARCH-LIST))
              (SETQ SEARCH-LIST (APPEND (GET START 'SUPERVISES) SEARCH-LIST))
              (DEPTH-SEARCH-INT START)
           )
    )
    ANSWER
)
```

Figure 6.6. A modification of the procedures of figure 6.5 that return only the first round name.

The procedure of figure 6.5 will find all persons who meet the search condition. There are applications where only the the first match found is to be returned. Note that in our application we are searching for people in the database. However, with only minor modification this procedure could be used with other databases. For instance, the search might find a list that contains a route from one city to another. In figure 6.6 we have modified the procedures of figure 6.5 so that the search will terminate once the search conditions have been met. A second condition has been added to the second COND expression. It is:

(ANSWER NIL)   (6-34)

Thus, the operations will terminate as soon as ANSWER becomes nonNIL. The procedure will terminate after the first time that the search condition is met.

```
(DEFUN DEPTH-SEARCH(START END &AUX SEARCH-LIST)
    (SETQ ANSWER NIL)
    (SETQ SEARCH-LIST (GET START 'SUPERVISES))
    (DEPTH-SEARCH-INT START END)
)

(DEFUN DEPTH-SEARCH-INT(START END)
    (COND ((EVAL END)
            (SETQ ANSWER (APPEND ANSWER (LIST (GET START 'NAME))))
          )
    )
    (COND ((NULL SEARCH-LIST) NIL)
          (T (SETQ START (CAR SEARCH-LIST))
             (SETQ SEARCH-LIST (CDR SEARCH-LIST))
             (SETQ SEARCH-LIST (APPEND (GET START 'SUPERVISES) SEARCH-LIST))
             (DEPTH-SEARCH-INT START END)
          )
    )
    ANSWER
)
```

Figure 6.7. A modification of the procedure of figure 6.5 that allows the search parameters to be passed as an argument.

The procedures of figure 6.5 and 6.6 are written with a specific search condition. That is, they search only for people whose JOB-DESCRIPTION is SOFTWARE-ENGINEER. If a different search condition is needed, the procedures must be rewritten. It would be convenient if the search condition could be passed to the procedure as a parameter. This is done in the procedure of figure 6.7. Now there are two parameters. START is the starting point of the search, as before. END contains the search parameters. Let us see how search conditions can be passed to a procedure as a parameter. Assume that a variable contains the search condition. For instance, suppose that we evaluate:

$$(SETQ\ XX\ '(AND\ (EQUAL\ (GET\ START\ 'JOB\text{-}DESCRIPTION)$$
$$'SOFTWARE\text{-}ENGINEER)$$
$$(>\ (GET\ START\ 'AGE)\ 30)))$$

(6-35)

That is, the search is to be for software engineers over the age of 30. The variable XX is bound to the list containing the conditions. If we want to evaluate the condition to obtain either true or false, then the following expression should be evaluated:

$$(\text{EVAL XX}) \hspace{6cm} (6\text{-}36)$$

The EVAL primitive forces the evaluation of its argument so that the desired result is obtained. Now consider figure 6.7. The test condition is replaced by

$$(\text{EVAL END})$$

Thus, the search condition, or *rule*, has been passed as the argument END. Note that the form of the passed parameter should be as shown in (6-35). That is, it could be a variable that has been set equal to a list or it could be the list itself. The list must be preceded by an apostrophe.

Now let us consider a *breadth-first search*. In this case, each level in the tree is searched before the next one is searched. For instance, for the tree structure of figure 6.4 the search order would be:

$$
\begin{aligned}
&A\\
&B_1\ B_2\\
&C_1\ C_2\ C_3\ C_4\ C_5\\
&D_1\ D_2\ D_3\ D_4\ D_5\ D_6\ D_7\ D_8\ D_9\ D_{10}\ D_{11}\ D_{12}\ D_{13}
\end{aligned}
$$

$$(6\text{-}37)$$

The search order can affect the speed of search substantially. For instance, suppose that the object of the search is the node B_2. If a breadth-first search is made, then the desired node would be found after three tries. On the other hand if the depth-first search shown in figure 6.4 is made, then 12 tries will be required to reach the desired node. If the database was larger, then the difference between these two searches would be even more impressive. The breadth-first search will not always be faster. For instance, if the object of the search is the node D_1, then the breadth-first search would require nine tries, while the depth-first search would require only four tries. Thus, it is desirable to have both types of searches available. Note that if the search is to find all possible candidates from the entire list who meet the search conditions, then it does not matter if a breadth-first or a depth-first search is performed, because all the nodes have to be searched.

```
(DEFUN BREADTH-SEARCH(START &AUX SEARCH-LIST)
   (SETQ ANSWER NIL)
   (SETQ SEARCH-LIST (GET START 'SUPERVISES))
   (BREADTH-SEARCH-INT START)
)

(DEFUN BREADTH-SEARCH-INT(START)
   (COND ((EQUAL (GET START 'JOB-DESCRIPTION) 'SOFTWARE-ENGINEER)
          (SETQ ANSWER (APPEND ANSWER (LIST (GET START 'NAME))))
          )
   )
   (COND ((NULL SEARCH-LIST) NIL)
         (T (SETQ START (CAR SEARCH-LIST))
            (SETQ SEARCH-LIST (CDR SEARCH-LIST))
            (SETQ SEARCH-LIST (APPEND SEARCH-LIST (GET START 'SUPERVISES)))
            (BREADTH-SEARCH-INT START)
         )
   )
   ANSWER
)
```

Figure 6.8. A set of procedures that perform a breadth first search

The procedures of figure 6.8 implement a breadth-first search. The procedure is almost the same as that for the depth-first-search that was implemented in figure 6.5. The only difference is that names are appended to the *end* of SEARCH-LIST, rather than to its beginning. That is the APPEND statement is of the form,

> (APPEND SEARCH-LIST (GET START 'SUPERVISES))
>
> (6-38a)

rather than,

> (APPEND (GET START 'SUPERVISES) SEARCH-LIST)
>
> (6-38b)

For instance after the first iteration, SEARCH-LIST will be (JOE-JONES ED-THOMAS JIM-EDWARDS LAWRENCE-SMITH), and the value of START will be JANE-SMITH. Note that the difference between the depth-first search and the breadth-first search is simply the order in which elements are added to SEARCH-LIST.

```
(DEFUN BREADTH-SEARCH(START END &AUX SEARCH-LIST)
    (SETQ ANSWER NIL)
    (SETQ SEARCH-LIST (GET START 'SUPERVISES))
    (BREADTH-SEARCH-INT START END)
)

(DEFUN BREADTH-SEARCH-INT(START END)
    (COND ((EVAL END)
            (SETQ ANSWER (APPEND ANSWER (LIST (GET START 'NAME))))
          )
    )
    (COND ((NULL SEARCH-LIST) NIL)
          (T (SETQ START (CAR SEARCH-LIST))
             (SETQ SEARCH-LIST (CDR SEARCH-LIST))
             (SETQ SEARCH-LIST (APPEND SEARCH-LIST (GET START 'SUPERVISES)))
             (BREADTH-SEARCH-INT START END)
          )
    )
    ANSWER
)
```

Figure 6.9. A modification of the procedures of figure 6.8 allows the search parameters to be passed as arguments.

The procedure of figure 6.8 will search only for one fixed condition. In figure 6.9 we have modified the procedure so that the search condition can be passed as a parameter. The principles here follow those presented in relation to figure 6.7.

Combinations of searches can be used if you have some information about the tree structure. For instance, suppose that you want to find the names of all the software engineers. A breadth-first search could be used to find the name of the person whose JOB-DESCRIPTION is DIR-SOFTWARE-ENGINEERING, and then a depth-first search would be performed starting with that name (MARY-DOBS). The depth-first search would be initiated by evaluating:

(DEPTH-SEARCH 'MARY-DOBS)   (6-39)

This assumes that the procedure of figure 6.5 is used for the depth-first search.

The search order that has been used has been that specified by the data of the tree structure. For instance, the order of the breadth-first search is as indicated in (6-37). There are times when the search procedure could be shortened if this search order could be modified. For instance, consider the fourth level of the tree structure of figure 6.4. If a breath-first search was performed, the search would be at the fourth level from D_1 to D_{13}. This data can be divided into four groups, D_1 to D_2, D_3 to D_6, D_7 to D_{10}, and D_{11} to D_{13}. Suppose that the node being searched for is in the group D_7 to D_{10}. The search would be speeded if this third group were searched first. Such a search would be called a type of *best-first search*.

You might ask why not simply start the search at node C_4. Often, however, not all the information about the tree structure is known. For instance, the name corresponding to node C_4 (MARY-DOBS) might not be known. In addition, the information about the best way to search might only be a guess based on some information seen previously. Such a guess is termed an *heuristic*. For instance, you might guess that the data would be in the part of the tree structure under the node whose JOB-DESCRIPTION was DIR-SOFTWARE-ENGINEERING. However, because this is only a guess, you cannot exclude any part of the tree from the search. The guess should be used only to influence the search *order* and not to exclude any part of the tree from the search.

The procedure of figure 6.9 could be modified to accomplish this best-first search. Instead of SEARCH-LIST being ordered as in figure 6.9, the ordering of the list would be determined by an additional parameter(s) that was passed to the procedure. For instance, if any of the names were obtained from a node whose JOB-DESCRIPTION was DIR-SOFTWARE-ENGINEERING, then those names would be placed at the start of the SEARCH-LIST. The actual construction of this procedure will be left as an exercise. Best-first searches can have other forms. For instance, the previously discussed example of a breadth-first search followed by a depth-first search could be called a best-first search.

When a tree is set up, each node has pointers to the nodes below it in the tree. For instance, in the tree structure that we have been using, the data for SUPERVISES contains the pointers. Suppose that one of these pointers is in error and points, instead, back up the tree. The tree structure now contains a *loop*. It is possible for a search procedure to become "stuck" in such a loop. In this case the procedure will never terminate. Safety features can be incorporated into the search programs so that they do not allow any node to be searched more than once. If a loop occurs, the search path could be output so that the database could be repaired. The use of such safety features will slow the operation of the program because there will be additional checking at each step in the program. For this reason, this type of safety feature is often omitted from search programs. There are some database structures that deliberately incorporate loops. Search procedures for such databases must contain routines that prevent a node from being searched more than once.

RULES AND DATA

We have written a database wherein data about each individual is stored in a p-list. Expert systems are often *rule based*. This means that each node of the the tree contains the data for a rule. For instance, suppose that you are working with an expert system that tells you what computer to buy. A rule might be as follows: if you need a hard disk, at least 512K of memory and a color monitor, then buy Brand XYZ. This could be stored in a property list that had the property types: DISK, MEMORY, MONITOR, and BRAND. The data corresponding to these property types would be: HARD, 512, COLOR, and XYZ. On the other hand, suppose that we were simply storing data about the Brand XYZ computer, we could use the *identical* property list. That is, the rules and the data are equivalent. The expert system could be written so that the rules were searched, or it could be written so that the data was searched. These procedures are essentially equivalent. The primary difference between the two procedures is how programmers think about them.

6-5. Pattern Matching

The search procedures discussed in the last section required that the person running the program enter the data in a specific way. For instance, consider the procedures of figure 6.7 and 6.9. The test conditions were passed to the procedures as parameters. These parameters had to be in the form of precise Lisp expressions. Thus, the person running the program would need some knowledge of Lisp. However, the person running the program often knows nothing about computer programming. One way of overcoming this problem is to have the program output a menu so that the person running the program only has to input a letter or number to indicate what the program is to do. There is another alternative. The person running the program could enter his requirements in some imprecise way and the program could then "figure out" what is required. This seems to violate what we know about programming wherein everything must be stated very precisely. What actually occurs is a search by the program of the input statement for certain *patterns*. If these patterns are present, then certain assumptions are made about the entry precise meaning of the entry.

As an example of this, let us consider a program that helps you either buy an automobile or pick out a restaurant. (We choose these diverse topics here simply for purposes of example; a single program would probably not be concerned with such totally unrelated topics.) Let us see what might happen when such a program was run. Suppose that the program causes the following output to appear on the screen:

What do you want to do?   6-40)

The response by the person running the program could be one of the following:

BUY A CAR   (6-41a)
I WANT TO BUY A CAR NOW   (6-41b)
EAT MY LUNCH   (6-41c)

The program must recognize that either of the first two inputs should trigger the "car buying mode" while the third input should trigger the "restaurant choosing mode."

We want to write a procedure that will search through text for certain patterns and be able to ignore extraneous data. This is called *pattern matching*. For instance, in the case of (6-41a) and (6-41b) the words BUY followed by CAR represent a pattern, regardless of the words before, between, or after them.

```
(DEFUN MATCH(PATTERN INPUT)
    (COND ((AND (NULL PATTERN) (NULL INPUT)) T)
          ((OR (NULL PATTERN) (NULL INPUT)) NIL)
          ((EQUAL (CAR PATTERN) (CAR INPUT)) (MATCH (CDR PATTERN) (CDR INPUT)))
    )
)
```

Figure 6.10. A simple pattern matching procedure

Let us start by writing a procedure called MATCH that determines if two lists of atoms are exactly the same. If so, the procedure returns T; otherwise it returns NIL. This procedure will not do all that we want because it will not ignore the extraneous data. However, we shall subsequently modify this initial MATCH procedure.

The basic procedure is shown in figure 6.10. This is a recursive procedure. The procedure is passed to two lists. The parameter PATTERN is the pattern that is to be matched and INPUT is the data that is scanned to see if it is EQUAL to PATTERN. Now consider the COND expression. If PATTERN and INPUT are both empty lists, then they are EQUAL and T will result. On the other hand if one of PATTERN or INPUT is empty, but the other is not, then they cannot be EQUAL and NIL will result. If both first elements of PATTERN and INPUT are EQUAL, then further testing is required. The first elements are stripped from both PATTERN and INPUT and the remaining lists are used as arguments in a recursive call of MATCH. Note that this is accomplished by passing the CDRs of PATTERN and INPUT as parameters of MATCH in the recursive call. Thus, after the procedure cycles completely, T will be returned if PATTERN and INPUT are the same and NIL will be returned otherwise. Note that the T and NIL in figure 6.10 could be omitted because the AND and OR operations will, themselves, return T or NIL. In a similar way, we did not include an expression,

(T NIL)   (6-42)

in the COND expression because COND will return NIL if none of its conditions are true.

WILD CARDS

There are times when we do not require an exact match for a particular pattern. In these cases *wild cards* are inserted into the pattern. A wild card is a symbol that matches *any* atom or sequence of atoms. We shall start by considering the wildcard ?, that matches a single atom only. For instance, if the pattern is,

(THE BOOK IS ? THE TABLE)   (6-43)

it can be matched by any of the following:

(THE BOOK IS ON THE TABLE)   (6-44a)
(THE BOOK IS NEAR THE TABLE)   (6-44b)
(THE BOOK IS HOUSE THE TABLE)   (6-44c)

On the other hand the pattern of (6-43) *does not* match,

(THE BOOK IS CLOSE TO THE TABLE)   (6-45)

because the wild card ? matches a single atom only.

```
(DEFUN MATCH(PATTERN INPUT)
  (COND ((AND (NULL PATTERN) (NULL INPUT)) T)
        ((OR (NULL PATTERN) (NULL INPUT)) NIL)
        ((EQUAL (CAR PATTERN) (CAR INPUT)) (MATCH (CDR PATTERN) (CDR INPUT)))
        ((EQUAL (CAR PATTERN) '?) (MATCH (CDR PATTERN) (CDR INPUT)))
  )
)
```

Figure 6.11. A pattern matching procedure that allows the use of wild cards to match a single atom.

The procedure that implements the ? wildcard is shown in figure 6.11. It is essentially the same as that of figure 6.10 except that the clause,

$$((EQUAL (CAR PATTERN) '?) (MATCH (CDR PATTERN) (CDR INPUT))) \qquad (6\text{-}46)$$

is added to the COND expression. Thus, the atom ? is *not* compared with an atom of INPUT. If the atom ? occurs, then MATCH is called recursively using the CDRs of PATTERN and INPUT just as if an exact match did occur. Thus, any atom matches the ? wild card.

The * wildcard is used to replace an arbitrary sequence of atoms. For instance, the following pattern will be matched by (6-45):

$$(THE BOOK IS * THE TABLE) \qquad (6\text{-}47)$$

For the case of (6-45) the * wild card matches the two atoms CLOSE TO. The asterisk can match a sequence of any length including zero. Note that this is not the case for the ? wild card; it matches exactly one atom only.

```
(DEFUN MATCH(PATTERN INPUT)
  (COND ((AND (NULL PATTERN) (NULL INPUT)) T)
        ((AND (EQUAL PATTERN '(*)) (NULL INPUT)) T)
        ((OR (NULL PATTERN) (NULL INPUT)) NIL)
        ((EQUAL (CAR PATTERN) (CAR INPUT)) (MATCH (CDR PATTERN) (CDR INPUT)))
        ((EQUAL (CAR PATTERN) '?) (MATCH (CDR PATTERN) (CDR INPUT)))
        ((EQUAL (CAR PATTERN) '*)
                  (COND ((MATCH (CDR PATTERN) (CDR INPUT)) T)
                        ((MATCH PATTERN (CDR INPUT)) T)
                        ((MATCH (CDR PATTERN) INPUT) T)
                  )
        )
  )
)
```

Figure 6.12. A pattern matching procedure that allows the use of the ? wild card to match a single atom and the use of the * wild card to match a sequence of atoms of arbitrary length

The procedure that implements the * wildcard is shown in figure 6.12. It is the same as that of figure 6.11 except for the addition of two expressions to the COND construction. The first expression is:

((AND (EQUAL PATTERN '(*)) (NULL INPUT)) T)   (6-48)

This will return true if PATTERN consists of a list containing only a single atom; that single atom is the *; and if INPUT is an empty list. This test will return true when the last atom in PATTERN is the * wild card and the last atom in INPUT has been matched by the atom in PATTERN that precedes the wild card.

The second added expression is:

```
((EQUAL (CAR PATTERN) '*)
    (COND ((MATCH (CDR PATTERN) (CDR INPUT)) T)
          ((MATCH PATTERN (CDR INPUT)) T)
          ((MATCH (CDR PATTERN) INPUT) T)
    )
)
```
                                                    (6-49)

Consider this COND construction. MATCH will be called recursively using the CDRs of PATTERN and INPUT as arguments. If there is a match, then T will be returned. There are three clauses in the COND construction. If the part of PATTERN that follows the * matches INPUT after one character has been stripped off, then a match has been found. If this first clause of the COND construction does not return T, the second expression will be evaluated. In this case MATCH will be called recursively using PATTERN, which includes the * wild card, and the CDR of INPUT as arguments. The test continues, but now one atom has been stripped from INPUT. The recursive nature of the procedure permits several atoms to be striped from INPUT in search of a matching atom.

Note that there many be some confusion when recursive procedures are described, because the same name is used for different variables in different recursive calls. For instance, INPUT will be different with each recursive call to MATCH. The Lisp system has no trouble keeping track of this, but it can become confusing to people. The third part of the COND expression (6-48) recursively calls MATCH. Now its arguments are the CDR of PATTERN, and INPUT. In this case, the wild card has been stripped from pattern while INPUT remains unchanged. This is used to check for the match of * against a sequence of zero length.

There can be several wild cards embedded within PATTERN; the recursive nature or the procedure automatically processes them. Suppose, for instance, that there are several * wild cards throughout the pattern. After the first * is processed, the particular PATTERN that is passed as an argument will contain the second wild card and the recursive calls to MATCH will process this PATTERN.

```
(DEFUN TEST(LST)
   (TERPRI)
   (COND ((MATCH '(* BUY * CAR *) LST)
                (PRINC "TELL ME ABOUT THE CAR YOU WANT TO BUY")
          )
          ((OR (MATCH '(* EAT * LUNCH *) LST) (MATCH '(* BUY * LUNCH *) LST))
                (PRINC "WHAT TYPE OF LUNCH DO YOU WANT TO EAT")
          )
    )
)
```

Figure 6.13. The procedure TEST that utilizes the procedure MATCH

A simple procedure that uses MATCH is shown in figure 6.13. This is a simulation of the kind of querying that was discussed at the beginning of this section. A list is passed to TEST as an argument. The first test of the COND statement is:

$$(MATCH \ '(* \ BUY * CAR *) \ LST) \tag{6-50}$$

Thus any input such as,

(I WANT TO BUY A GOOD CAR TODAY)   (6-51a)
(BUY CAR)   (6-51b)
(BUY ME A CAR)   (6-51c)

will result in,

TELL ME ABOUT THE CAR YOU WANT TO BUY

being output. The PRINC expression simulates the rest of the program.
The second test of the COND expression is:

(OR (MATCH '(* EAT * LUNCH) LST)
    (MATCH '(* BUY * LUNCH) LST))   (6-52)

Note that this considers the possibility of several different answers. That is, one person might express his request as wanting to buy lunch while another person might want simply to eat lunch. In general, when the computer is to be instructed in a *natural language*, there are many possible forms for a proper answer. If the computer is to appear to have a large vocabulary and to understand a wide variety of speech patterns, then the number of potential patterns against which the input must be checked will be large. In such cases the patterns, with the appropriate wild cards, could be stored in a database that is searched for the appropriate matches.

The pattern matching procedures that we have discussed are recursive in nature. However, nonrecursive procedures can be used also. For instance, the LENGTH of PATTERN and INPUT could be established and then looping used to search for a match. Such procedures will be much longer than the recursive ones. Therefore, the recursive procedures will be easier to write and be less error prone. However, the nonrecursive procedures may run faster. The discussion of tail recursion, see sec. 5-3, considers this in greater detail.

6-6. Structures and Frames

We have seen how databases can be built up by using a-lists and/or p-lists. Each list can represent the node of a tree. The format of each node can be relatively complex. For instance, one item of data stored in one list may itself be a list. If we want to access, add to, or change this data then Lisp primitives must be used to write the necessary procedures. It can be tedious to write such procedures every time a database with a new format is developed. Fortunately, many versions of Lisp provide mechanisms that write these procedures for you when the proper data form is used. These forms are called *structures*. The procedures needed to access, add to, or change structures are automatically provided when you initially set up the format of the structure. Because structures are represented by variables, they are easy to manipulate.

If the database is large, then it will contain many different structures just as many different p-lists were contained in the database of Sec. 6-4. For instance, a structure rather than a p-list could be used to represent the data for each individual in the tree database of figure 6.1.

When programmers set up complex data structures, they must remember how each piece of data is to be accessed. For instance, if an ordinary list is set up, then the position of the data in the list must be remembered. If some data is stored in an a-list and other data is stored in a p-list, then this too must be remembered because different functions are used to access data from a-lists and from p-lists. If the programmer does not have to remember these details but, instead, can use standard functions to access the data, then his job becomes much less tedious. If such standard functions can be used, then *data abstraction* is said to have been achieved. The use of structures, or a generalization of these called *frames*, is one means of achieving data abstraction. Note that data abstraction is not some obscure concept, but merely a general way of storing data and writing the procedures to access the data thus making the programmer's life easier.

The procedure DEFSTRUCT is used to establish structures. Actually, a structure is not set up when DEFSTRUCT is invoked. Rather, a number of other procedures are created; these procedures are used to set up structures, to extract the data from them, and to change the structures. The general names for procedures that perform these types of operations are called *constructors*, *selectors*, and *mutators*, respectively. Selector functions are also called *access* functions. A structure consists of a set of *fields* or *slots* that store data. The data is called a *field value* or a *slot value*. A field is simply a place where data is stored. For instance, suppose that you were setting up a structure in the form of table on a piece of paper, and that the data to be stored is the copyright date of a book, the type of cover (hard or soft), and the name of the publisher. You could state that the copyright date would be placed in the first six columns, the type of the cover in the next eight columns, and the publishers name in the next 20 columns. The fields would be represented by the number and position of the columns, the field values would be the actual data such as 1985, hard cover, and XYZ publishing company. The actual mechanism used to store the data is taken care of by the Lisp system and the programmer need not be concerned with it.

```
(DEFSTRUCT BOOK
    (COPYRIGHT 1984)
    (COVER 'HARD)
    (PUBLISHER 'XYZ-CO)
)
```

Figure 6.14. An illustration of the use of DEFSTRUCT. Evaluation of this construction will result in the establishment of the constructor, selectors, and mutators for type BOOK.

Now let us consider an example of the use of DEFSTRUCT. As previously stated DEFSTRUCT establishes procedures that work with structures. Figure 6.14 illustrates a DEFSTRUCT expression. The name that is to be associated with the procedures that are set up when the DEFSTRUCT of figure 6.14 is evaluated is BOOK. We can say that the structures that are set up will be of type BOOK. That is, BOOK is now a data type. These structures will have three fields called COPYRIGHT, COVER, and PUBLISHER. Note that the fields are set up by simply listing them after the word BOOK. Each field is enclosed in parentheses and followed by a default value. Unless otherwise specified, the default value will become the field value when a specific structure is set up. Note that it is not necessary to include a default value in a DEFSTRUCT expression. If none is used, then the default will be assumed to be NIL, or 0, depending on the Lisp system. If no default value is specified, then it is not necessary to enclose the field name in parentheses. The DEFSTRUCT construction is ended with a right parenthesis, as shown in figure 6.14.

When the expression of figure 6.14 is evaluated, four procedures are set up; MAKE-BOOK which is used to set up structures of type BOOK and BOOK-COPYRIGHT, BOOK-COVER, and BOOK-PUBLISHER which are used to read the COPYRIGHT, COVER, and PUBLISHER fields. Note that the constructor procedure consists of the word MAKE followed by a hyphen and the type name, BOOK in this case. There is one selector set up for each field. The name of the selector is the type name, BOOK in this case, followed by a hyphen, and the name of the field. No specific data mutator is set up. SETF is used to change data in the fields.

We have not as yet set up any structures. Now suppose that we want to set up a structure called STANDARD_BOOK that will be of type BOOK. Note that we have used an underscore, rather than a hyphen to connect the two words in the name STANDARD_BOOK. This was done because the hyphen is needed for use in the constructors and selectors. These hyphens *must* be used. Although the underscores could be replaced by hyphens we will use underscores to avoid confusion. Note that most modern programming languages use underscores to join words in this way. The structure STANDARD_BOOK is to have all the default field values. The following expression can be used to establish STANDARD_BOOK:

(SETF STANDARD_BOOK (MAKE-BOOK))   (6-53)

Note that SETQ could be used as well as SETF in expression (6-53). After (6-53) is evaluated, there will be a variable called STANDARD_BOOK that will have the (default) values 1984, HARD, and XYZ-CO in its fields.

When a structure is set up as in (6-53), the defaults can be overridden by including the field name, preceded by a colon, and followed by the desired field value. For example,

(SETF OTHER_BOOK (MAKE-BOOK :COPYRIGHT 1985
                    :PUBLISHER 'AAA_BOOK_CO))
                                                    (6-54)

will set up a structure called OTHER_BOOK that stores 1985, HARD, and AAA_BOOK_CO in its COPYRIGHT, COVER, and PUBLISHER fields, respectively.

Now let us consider the reading of the data stored in a structure. The selector (access) procedures are used here. For instance,

    (BOOK-COPYRIGHT STANDARD_BOOK)   (6-55)

will return 1984. Similarly,

    (SETQ XX (BOOK-PUBLISHER OTHER_BOOK))   (6-56)

will result in XX being bound to AAA_BOOK_CO.

Now let us consider how SETF is used to modify the data in a field (slot). For instance, suppose that we want to change the value of the COPYRIGHT field of STANDARD_BOOK. The following will accomplish this:

    (SETF (BOOK-COPYRIGHT STANDARD_BOOK) 1980)   (6-57)

Note that SETQ cannot be used in place of SETF for this purpose.

Structures can be used in place of either a-lists or p-lists. Structures use less storage space than do either a-lists or p-lists because the field names are not stored with the data. The field names, as well as their positions in the structure, are stored in the constructors and selectors. In most cases, there are many fewer constructors and selectors than there are structures themselves. Remember that although there will be at least one structure for each node in a database it is probable that the same constructor was used to establish each of them. Therefore, the same selectors will apply to each node, as well.

```
(DEFSTRUCT TEXTBOOK
    (OLDDATA STANDARD_BOOK)
    (NEWDATA)
    (SUBJECT)
    (PAGES 450)
    (LEVEL 'COLLEGE)
    (DIFFICULTY 'MODERATE)
)
```

Figure 6.15. The use of DEFSTRUCT with a structure that contains another structure.

One of the fields in a structure can itself represent another structure. In figure 6.15 we define a structure whose type is TEXTBOOK. It has the fields OLDDATA, NEWDATA, SUBJECT, PAGES, LEVEL, and DIFFICULTY. The names OLDDATA and NEWDATA have no significance to the Lisp system. The default value for OLDDATA is STANDARD_BOOK. In this case the variable name STANDARD_BOOK represents the variable that stores a structure of type BOOK. The actual structure STANDARD_BOOK will not stored in any structure of type TEXTBOOK, but we can reference the data in STANDARD_BOOK by a reference to the appropriate slot in a structure of type TEXTBOOK. Suppose that the following is evaluated:

(SETF LISP-BOOK (MAKE-TEXTBOOK :SUBJECT 'LISP))   (6-58)

Then LISP-BOOK will be a structure of type TEXTBOOK. Its SUBJECT slot will contain the data LISP. Thus,

(TEXTBOOK-SUBJECT LISP_BOOK)   (6-59)

will return LISP. In addition,

(TEXTBOOK-OLDDATA LISP-BOOK)   (6-60)

will return STANDARD_BOOK. Suppose that we wanted to extract some STANDARD_BOOK data from LISP_BOOK. This can be done by applying one of BOOK's extractors to the result of (6-60). For instance, the following will obtain the value of the PUBLISHER field of STANDARD-BOOK:

(BOOK-PUBLISHER (TEXTBOOK-OLDDATA LISP-BOOK))
                                               (6-61)

The evaluation of (6-61) actually causes the reading of the STANDARD_BOOK structure. Thus, if the value of a field in STANDARD_BOOK is changed, the result of the evaluation of (6-61) will be changed also.

The programmer must remember to use two different forms of access operations with structures of type TEXTBOOK. The form illustrated in (6-59) would be used for data that was private while the form illustrated in (6-61) would be required for data "inherited" from STANDARD_BOOK. Functions can be written to remove this restriction. Such functions are illustrated in figure 6.17. After these functions are evaluated, all the access functions for type TEXTBOOK will have the same format.

For instance, (6-61) could now be replaced by:

    (TEXTBOOK-PUBLISHER LISP-BOOK)   (6-62)

```
(DEFUN TEXTBOOK-COPYRIGHT(X)
       (BOOK-COPYRIGHT (TEXTBOOK-OLDDATA X))
)


(DEFUN TEXTBOOK-COVER(X)
       (BOOK-COVER (TEXTBOOK-OLDDATA X))
)


(DEFUN TEXTBOOK-PUBLISHER(X)
       (BOOK-PUBLISHER (TEXTBOOK-OLDDATA X))
)
```

Figure 6.16. Functions that allow data abstraction to be used with the access functions for structures of type TEXTBOOK.

Note that the functions of figure 6.16 cannot be used in conjunction with SETF to change any of the data stored in STANDARD_BOOK. The access functions for type BOOK would have to be used for this purpose. This is reasonable; the "inheriting" structure should not be able to control the date in the structure from which it "inherits" the data.

Suppose that we want to use values from one structure in a second structure, however the data in the new structure is to be unaffected by subsequent changes of that data in the first structure. This can be done by including the appropriate Lisp expression into the constructor expression. For instance, evaluation of the following expression will enter the current value of the PUBLISHER field in STANDARD_BOOK into the NEWDATA field of a structure of type TEXTBOOK:

    (SETF A_BOOK (MAKE-TEXTBOOK :NEWDATA
                     (BOOK-PUBLISHER STANDARD_BOOK)))
                                                      (6-63)

Note that STANDARD-BOOK is read at the time that the structure A_BOOK is set up and the data associated with PUBLISHER in STANDARD_BOOK is put into the NEWDATA field of A_BOOK. The value of the NEWDATA field of A-BOOK then contains a specific value, XYZ_CO in this case. If the

PUBLISHER field of STANDARD_BOOK is changed subsequently, the NEWDATA field of A_BOOK will *not* be changed.

When the construction of the form of figure 6.15 is used, one structure is said to have *inherited* the characteristics of another structure. For instance, in the case of figure 6.15, any structures of type TEXTBOOK are said to have inherited the characteristics of STANDARD_BOOK. When access functions of the type illustrated in figure 6.16 are used, the inherited characteristics appear to be part of the structure although they are actually not. Inheritance is a convenient way of passing large amounts of data. Note that copies of this data are not stored in each inheriting structure. For instance, LISP_BOOK does not actually store the data for STANDARD_BOOK; it stores only its name. Thus, inheritance is economical of data space as well as being convenient in that it reduces the amount of typing that must be performed.

SLOT OPTIONS - FIELD OPTIONS

Each slot specifier in the DEFSTRUCT expression can include several options that are used to restrict the data that is stored in that slot. The type of data that is stored in a slot (field) can be specified. For instance, suppose that the slot specifier is of the form:

(AVERAGE 100.00 :TYPE SHORT-FLOAT)　　　　　　　　(6-64)

Here we have specified a slot with a name of AVERAGE and a default value of 100.00. The type of data in this field is restricted to a short floating-point number. Note the form of the TYPE specification; it follows the default value and consists of a colon, followed by the word TYPE, which is followed by the type name. An error will result if there is an attempt to enter data of the wrong type into this slot.

A second option is READ-ONLY. Data in a slot so specified cannot be changed subsequently. In such cases, the default data specified in the DEFSTRUCT expression cannot be changed by subsequent use of SETF. The form of the use of this optional statement is:

(PUBLISHER 'XYZ_CO :READ-ONLY T)　　　　　　　　(6-65)

Note the T, if this is replaced by NIL, the READ_ONLY slot option will be ignored. Note that the T or NIL is not evaluated. If both TYPE and READ-ONLY are used, then the TYPE specification should precede the READ-ONLY specification. Optional data must be specified when slot options are used.

In addition to the options associated with the slots, there are options associated with the complete DEFSTRUCT expression. Some of these allow the names of the constructor and selector functions to be changed. For instance we have indicated that the constructor function will be named MAKE followed by a hyphen and the name of the particular structure type. This name can be changed. Consult your Lisp manual to see what options are available for your system.

In the interest of simplicity, we have not demonstrated the setting up of trees using structures. Of course, trees could be implemented using structures in conjunction with the procedures discussed in sec. 6-4. That is, the p-lists of sec. 6-4 could be replaced by structures.

FRAMES

We have discussed the ideas of structures *including* other structures. (Note that the including structure simply contained a pointer to the included structure. It did not actually contain the data.) We saw that access functions could be written so that data abstraction was achieved. A *frame* is a generalized type of structure that extends these ideas. The frame often has three levels of inclusion of structures. Another feature of frames is that they are usually arranged in a tree format. In a three-level frame, there would be a structure at each node of the tree and each of these structures would have slots whose data points at other structures. Note that an entire database could be placed in a single frame. These structures would in turn, have slots, called *facets*, that point at other structures. An important feature of frames, as well as of many other database constructions, is that the general layout of each node of the tree is the same as that of any other node. Thus, generalized access procedure could be used to obtain particular data at any node. When frames are implemented, on some Lisp systems, these generalized types of constructor, selectors and mutators are automatically written for the data structure that is being used. Thus, the programmer would have to remember only one form of access function.

We have illustrated frames using structures. However, the same ideas could be applied to a-lists or to combinations of a-lists and p-lists. These ideas were alluded to in sec. 6-4, although we did not actually mention frames there. Remember that structures use less memory than do a-lists or p-lists. Thus, structures should probably be used for most databases if your system implements them.

Exercises

Check any procedures that you write by running them on your computer.

1. Use a-lists to set up a family tree database. Each a-list should contain the following data for an individual: LAST-NAME, FIRST-NAME, DATE-OF BIRTH, MOTHER, FATHER, CHILDREN. Enter data for 24 related persons. There should be at least four generations. Note that each item of data should be a single atom. For instance, the date could be written as 11-17-35. The data for each person should be stored in a separate a-list. Write a procedure that reduces the work involved in setting up the database. Assume that there is only one known oldest ancestor in the family tree. There may be unknown ancestors. The data for MOTHER and FATHER should be single atoms such as JOHN-SMITH. That atom should also be the name of JOHN SMITH's file.

2. Write a procedure that will determine if a person, JOHN-SMITH for example, is the FATHER of a member of the database of exercise 1.

3. What is the difference between the procedures ACONS and PAIRLIS?

4. Write a procedure called CORRECT, that is used to change a datum in one of the a-lists set up in exercise 1. The procedure is passed no data but it queries the user as to the name of the a-list of the datum to be changed and for the changed data.

5. Write a procedure called ADD-MORE-DATA that functions in a manner similar to the procedure of exercise 4. It is used to add additional data pairs to an a-list.

6. What is the difference between an a-list and a p-list?

7. Repeat exercise 1 but now put the data into p-lists. Write a procedure that performs this transformation automatically. That is the user supplies the name of the a-list and the p-list is generated automatically. Then write a procedure that transforms all the a-lists into p-lists.

8. Check the p-lists that you have generated using SYMBOL-PLIST.

9. Write a procedure that will determine if a person, JOHN-SMITH for example, is the FATHER of any member of the database set up in exercise 7.

10. Repeat exercise 4, but now work with the p-lists of exercise 7. Do not use SETF in this procedure.

11. Repeat exercise 10 using SETF.

12. Repeat exercise 5, but now work with p-lists.

13. Write a single procedure that will read either the a-lists of exercise 1 or the p-lists of exercise 7. The procedure is to be passed the name of the list and either the letter A or P, for a-list or p-list. The entire list is to be output.

14. Repeat exercise 13, but now assume that the names of the a-list and the p-list are different. Therefore, the second argument (A or P) does not have to be passed to the procedure. When procedures such as this are used, the programmer does not have to remember to use different procedures for a-lists and p-lists. This is a form of fidata abstraction.

15. What is meant by a tree-structured database?

16. The databases constructed in either exercise 1 or 7 should be in the form of a tree. Draw a diagram that illustrates this structure.

17. Write a procedure using the database set up in exercise 1 that will list the children of a name that is passed to it.

18. Repeat exercise 17, but now find all the grandchildren of the name that is passed to the procedure.

19. Repeat exercise 17, but now use a depth first search to find all the descendents of the name passed to the procedure.

20. Repeat exercise 19 using a breadth-first search.

21. Repeat exercise 17 using the database of exercise 7.

22. Repeat exercise 18 using the database of exercise 7.

23. Repeat exercise 19 using the database of exercise 7.

24. Repeat exercise 20 using the database of exercise 7.

25. Use the data given in figure 6.3 to construct a database that stores its data in the form of a-lists.

26. Use the database of exercise 25 to output a list of all the engineers who have a RATING-OF-SUPERVISOR of 80 or over. Those people are to receive raises. The amount of the raise, in per cent, is to be equal to the RATING-OF-SUPERVISOR minus 70. A second list is to be generated containing the dollar amount of each of the raises. Perform a depth-first search.

27. Use the lists of exercise 26 to update the database automatically.

28. Repeat exercise 26 using a breadth-first search.

29. Repeat exercise 26, but now assume that you know the structure of the database, but not specific names. That is you know that there is a president, a vice president for sales, a vice president for engineering, but you do not know any of the names, except ED-WILSON. Use a combination of breadth-first and depth-first searches so that the shortest possible search is performed. A single call procedure should be required of the user.

30. Repeat exercise 26 using the p-list form of the database.

31. Repeat exercise 27 using the p-list form of the database.

32. Repeat exercise 28 using the p-list form of the database.

33. Repeat exercise 29 using the p-list form of the database.

34. Write a procedure that prompts the user to enter a sentence and then makes a suitable response. If one of the words MOTHER, FATHER, SISTER, or BROTHER is entered, the response should be:

TELL ME MORE ABOUT YOUR FAMILY

35. Modify the procedure of exercise 34 in the following way: If the words specified in exercise 34 are preceded by LOVE, then the response should be:

YOU HAVE A HAPPY FAMILY LIFE

If the specified words are preceded by HATE, then the response should be:

WHY ARE ARE YOU TROUBLED?

36. Modify the procedure of exercise 35 so that words that negate the input are searched for. For instance DON'T or DO NOT HATE. The response should be suitably modified in these cases.

37. Modify the database of exercise 1, now use structures to store the data for each individual. Have the database generated automatically from that of exercise 1.

38. Repeat exercise 2 using the database of exercise 37.

39. Repeat exercise 4 using the database of exercise 37.

40. Write procedures that can be used to access the data of the CHILDREN in the database of exercise 37. It should "appear" as though the structures of the parents are being accessed.

41. Use the data given in figure 6.3 to set up a database that consists of a set of structures.

42. Repeat exercise 26 using the database of exercise 41.

43. Repeat exercise 27 using the database of exercise 41.

44. Repeat exercise 28 using the database of exercise 41.

45. Repeat exercise 29 using the database of exercise 41.

46. Place the entire database of exercise 41 into a single structure.

47. What is meant by a frame?

48. Discuss the use of the READ-ONLY slot option.

7

Macros

A macro is a procedure that allows the programmer to define a sequence of operations to which parameters can be passed and from which results are obtained. These "results" can be in the form of returned values and/or side effects. As we have seen, the writing of procedures is a powerful programming technique that is used when an operation is to be performed repeatedly. Procedures also make the programmer's life easier because they can substitute an easily remembered single name for a sequence of operations that are not so easily remembered. All the procedures that we have discussed evaluated all of their arguments. (The logical AND and OR operations are an exception to this in that all their arguments were not always evaluated.) This provided for very versatile operation because after a variable name is passed to a procedure, the *value* of that variable could be used in operations within the procedure.

Lisp provides another feature called a *macro*. Although the construction of a macro is similar to that of a procedure, its operation differs from that of a procedure. A macro can represent a complex set of operations, just as a procedure does. However, a procedure always produces a result. A macro combines all its operation into one, possibly long, Lisp expression. This Lisp expression can contain a number of subexpressions. That is, it can be a list that contains lists. The Lisp expression is substituted for the call to the macro wherever that call appears in the program. The arguments passed to the macro are entered into the Lisp expression that is substituted for the call to the macro. However, these arguments are *not evaluated*. They are simply substituted into the Lisp expression that replaces the call to the macro.

229

Macros are used in those cases when not all of the arguments should be evaluated. In addition, in some circumstances macros execute faster than procedures. Macros should be used in place of procedures in such cases. However, as we shall discuss in the next section, there are many occasions when procedures are more appropriate than macros.

7-1. Macros - The DEFMACRO Construction

Let us start the discussion of macros by considering some aspects of procedures and then comparing them to macros. We will begin by assuming that we are dealing with an interpreted Lisp system. When a DEFUN construction is evaluated, the Lisp expressions of that procedure are stored in a sequence of memory locations. The first one of these is called the address of the procedure. When there is a call to the procedure, control of the program jumps to the procedure. That is, the expressions at the address of the procedure now control the operation. Without a procedure call, the expressions of a program are evaluated sequentially, one after the other. In this discussion we use the word program to represent the main, or outer, procedure. When a procedure is called, the system must keep track of where in the program that call occurred so that evaluation of the expressions of the program can resume after the operation of the procedure terminates. This keeping track involves saving of data such as the address of the next expression in the program. In addition, there are variables that must be saved. The time required to accomplish all of this is the overhead involved in calling a procedure.

Evaluation of the DEFUN construction also consumes time. The procedure must be placed into memory and the Lisp system must be informed of this location. Additional expressions may be added to the procedure. For instance, if you call a procedure using the improper number of arguments, an error message is output and the procedure does not function. This is the result of a COND construction that is automatically added to the beginning of the procedure by the Lisp system. This evaluation of a DEFUN construction takes place only once. That is, the DEFUN construction is not evaluated each time that the procedure is called, therefore the time involved in its evaluation does not add to the overhead.

Macros are set up using the DEFMACRO construction. The form of its use is the same as that of the DEFUN construction. When a macro is evaluated, it too is placed in memory and the Lisp system is given its address. However, when the macro is called, the macro is said to be *expanded*. This expansion consists of generating the sequence of expressions which, as in the case of DEFUN, may contain expressions other than the ones that you have written explicitly. When the macro is called the expanded list comprising the entire sequence of instructions is placed into the program in place of the macro call. This sequence will, in general, consist of a list of lists. The arguments are substituted into the expanded list in the appropriate places. The arguments are *not evaluated*. This process is a two-stage operation; the macro is expanded and then the unevaluated arguments are substituted in the resulting list of instructions. If the macro had to be expanded each time that it was called, the operation would be slowed appreciably. However, many Lisp systems remember the expanded form of the macro so that the expansion stage does not have to be performed more than once. If the expansion stage of the macro does not have to be performed at each call, then the operation of a macro call can be faster than that of a procedure call.

Now let us consider the compiled case. The program, procedures, and macros are all converted into a sequence of machine-language instructions. The procedures and the "main" program will be stored in different locations. When a procedure is called, the previously discussed overhead will result. The resulting slowing of the operation may or may not be significant. If the procedure is not called often, the loss in time may not be apparent to the user of the program.

When the program is compiled, the macro calls are replaced by the actual compiled form of the macro expansion. If that macro is called at ten different points in the program, then the compiled macro expansion will appear in the compiled program ten times. There will be no overhead spent in saving and recovering values because the macro will have become part of the program. This will speed the operation. However, the resultant program will be longer because of the insertion of all the macro code. Thus, macros and procedures each add different types of overhead.

We have compared macros and procedures on the basis of speed of operation and size of program. However, there may be other overriding considerations. Macros do not evaluate their arguments, while procedures do. In many instances it is desirable for the arguments to be evaluated and, in those cases, procedures should be used. On the other hand, there are occasions when the converse is true; in those cases, macros should be used.

There are operations that cannot be performed with macros. Consider a recursive call in a compiled program. When a macro is compiled, all of its machine language must be inserted into the program. Note that a macro cannot call itself. The code is simply inserted into the program when the program is compiled. There is no record of the macro name or of its address. When the program is executed, there is no distinction between the instructions resulting from the expansion of the macro and the instructions that were written into the program. There is no address to "jump" to as there is in the case of a procedure. If recursive calls were to be inserted into the program, then the compiler would have to know exactly how many calls to make. Because this would not be known until the program was run and data was entered, recursive macro calls cannot be made with true compiled Lisp. There are some Lisp interpreters that allow recursive macro calls. However, these calls should be avoided even if you have such a Lisp system. Most substantial Lisp programs will eventually be compiled to increase their speed. Thus, any operation that cannot be compiled should be avoided.

```
(DEFUN TEST(A B C)
   (+ A B C)
)


(DEFMACRO MTEST(A B C)
   (+ A B C)
)
```

Figure 7.1. The implementation of a function and a macro

Now let us consider the details of writing a macro. In figure 7.1 we illustrate the setting up of a function TEST and of the macro MTEST. Each of these causes three numbers to be added. Note that the forms of these constructions is the same except for the words DEFUN and DEFMACRO. For instance, the first line of the macro definition of figure 7.1 is:

$$(DEFMACRO\ MTEST(A\ B\ C) \tag{7-1}$$

Note that some Lisp systems do not establish a macro in exactly this way. Consult your Lisp manual to determine the syntax for implementing macros on your system.

The function TEST and the macro MTEST operate differently. As we have discussed, macros do not evaluate their arguments, while procedures do. If we evaluate,

$$(TEST\ 3\ 4\ 5) \tag{7-2a}$$

12 will be returned. Similarly, if we evaluate,

$$(MTEST\ 3\ 4\ 5) \tag{7-2b}$$

12 will be returned. In each case numbers were passed. Numbers do not have to be evaluated. Now suppose that we evaluate,

(SETQ X 3)   (7-3)

and then evaluate:

(TEST X 4 5)   (7-4a)

12 will again be returned. On the other hand, if we attempt to evaluate,

(MTEST X 4 5)   (7-4b)

an error will result because,

(+ X 4 5)

cannot be evaluated. This is because the + operation requires numbers as it arguments, and the unevaluated X is a symbol. The evaluation of the arguments can be forced using the EVAL operation. In this case, an error would not result, and the sum of the three numbers would be returned if the second line of the DEFMACRO construction was replaced by:

(+ (EVAL A) (EVAL B) (EVAL C))   (7-5)

The construction of (7-5) is awkward; a function rather than a macro would be used in this instance. Of course, this example is so simple that probably neither a function nor a macro would be used.

```
(DEFMACRO PAIRPLIS(NAME LST PROPS)
   (DO ((I 1 (+ I 1)))
         ((NULL LST) NIL)
          (PUTPROP NAME (CAR LST) (CAR PROPS))
          (SETQ LST (CDR LST))
          (SETQ PROPS (CDR PROPS))
      )
)
```

Figure 7.2. The macro PAIRPLIS.

To illustrate the writing and use of a more complex macro in figure 7.2, we have modified the procedure ADD-ONE of figure 6.2. The macro, called PAIRPLIS, does for p-lists what PAIRLIS did for a-lists. That is, the arguments of PAIRPLIS are the name of the p-list to be set up and two lists. The first is a list of property values and the second is a list of corresponding property types. There are some major differences between the macro PAIRPLIS of figure 7.2 and the procedure ADD-ONE of figure 6.2. ADD-ONE used recursive procedure calls. As we have discussed, recursion should not be used with macros. For this reason, PAIRPLIS uses looping rather than recursive calls.

Let us continue the discussion of PAIRPLIS. It is assumed that both LST and PROPS have the same length. Although it has not been done here, local variables can be established using &AUX. This follows the usage in procedures. Optional arguments can be specified using &OPTIONAL. Of course, the default values of these arguments will not be evaluated. There are other operations that can be performed in conjunction with the formal parameter list. Consult your Lisp manual to determine those operations that are available with your Lisp system.

Note that LST and PROPS are set equal to their respective CDRs after PUTPROP is called. This replaces the CDR operations in the recursive calls in ADD-ONE. The macro terminates when LST becomes empty.

An example of the use of the macro PAIRPLIS follows:

```
(PAIRPLIS JOHN-SMITH (JOHN SMITH 23)
          (FIRST-NAME LAST-NAME AGE))                 (7-6)
```

After evaluation of (7-6) the p-list JOHN-SMITH will have the property types FIRST-NAME, LAST-NAME and AGE with the corresponding property values JOHN, SMITH, and 23. Note that apostrophes are not used in conjunction with the lists that are arguments in (7-6). Because the arguments of macros are not evaluated, there is no reason to inhibit evaluation. Note if PAIRPLIS was a procedure, it would function in the same way as the macro of figure 7.2 except that the input lists and the name would have to be preceeded by an apostrophe.

PAIRPLIS cannot be used in place of ADD-ONE when the database representing figure 6.1 is generated using the procedures of figures 6.2 and 6.3. The procedure ADD-ONE is passed a variable by ADD-PERSON and the procedure evaluates that variables to obtain its value. The macro does not do this. Of course, we could modify the macro as discussed previously to cause it to evaluate the variables within its own body.

Most Lisp systems provide primitives that are procedures and primitives that are macros. For instance, SETF is a macro.

Usually the Lisp system provides a function that allows the programmer to see the expanded form of macros. One such function, that is used in Common Lisp, is MACRO-FUNCTION. Actually it is a predicate that returns the expanded macro if its argument is a macro and it returns NIL if its argument is not a macro. For example,

(MACRO-FUNCTION 'PAIRPLIS) (7-7)

will return the expanded macro for PAIRPLIS. Note that the expansion may differ from the expressions in your DEFMACRO form. There will be additional expressions that manipulate the arguments. Also, if you used additional macros in the definition, these will be expanded. If the Lisp system is sophisticated, then the expressions will be modified to speed the operation, if possible. In the next section we shall consider an example of a case where a macro must be used to avoid the evaluation of the arguments.

7-2. The Backquote Macro

We have used the apostrophe to inhibit evaluation. For instance, in the expression,

(PRINC '(THE ANSWER IS X)) (7-8)

the apostrophe, or single quote, prevents the list from being evaluated, and thus the list,

(THE ANSWER IS X) (7-9)

is output. However, there are occasions when it would be desirable to evaluate *some* of the items in the list. For instance, suppose that X is a variable that is bound to 2. We then might want the list,

(THE ANSWER IS 2) (7-10)

to be output. Until now the only way that this could be accomplished is by using two PRINC statements or by using a FORMAT statement. However Lisp systems provide a useful macro, called the *backquote macro*, that allows us to accomplish such tasks easily. The backquote (`) is the symbol that is used for these operations. We shall see that the backquote macro simplifies many programming tasks. Note that the backquote is also called the accent mark and is a single quotation mark that "leans" in a direction opposite to that of the apostrophe.

The backquote inhibits evaluation of the list following it, as does the apostrophe. However, any atom, in the list following the backquote, that is preceded by a comma will be evaluated. For instance, if X has been bound to 2, then evaluation of,

(PRINC `(THE ANSWER IS ,X))   (7-11)

will result in the output given in (7-10). Note that there can be more than one comma in the list. In fact, every atom in the list could be preceded by a comma. The backquoted list could contain sublists as well as atoms. If any of these sublists are preceded by a comma, then they will be evaluated.

Now suppose that,

(SETQ Y '(BOOK))   (7-12)

is evaluated and subsequently,

(PRINC `(THE ,Y IS ON THE TABLE))   (7-13)

is evaluated. The output will be:

(THE (BOOK) IS ON THE TABLE)   (7-14)

This is probably not what is desired. A single list with BOOK inserted into it would be the normal output, such as:

(THE BOOK IS ON THE TABLE)   (7-15)

If the comma is followed by an @ then the next symbol will be evaluated as it would if it was preceded by a comma. Now, however, the elements of the list resulting from the evaluation, rather than the list itself, will be inserted into the associated list. Do not use ,@ before an atom that is bound to something other than a list. Unpredictable results will occur in this case. As an example of the use of ,@ the evaluation of,

(PRINC `(THE ,@Y IS ON THE TABLE))   (7-16)

will produce the output shown in (7-15). Note that BOOK is not a sublist of the list of (7-15). The backquote allows us to set up forms containing blank spaces and then fill in the blank spaces with variables. Expression (7-16) is a simple example of this. The form consists of THE blank IS ON THE TABLE. The value of the variable Y replaces blank in the form. This type of operation is called *template filling*.

```
(DEFMACRO AND-IF(TEST1 TEST2 TRUE-ACTION FALSE-ACTION)
  `(COND ((AND ,TEST1 ,TEST2),TRUE-ACTION)
         (T ,FALSE-ACTION)
     )
  )
```

Figure 7.3. The macro AND-IF

In cases where it is is necessary that arguments not be evaluated, macros rather than procedures *must* be used because the arguments of a macro are never evaluated. An illustration of this is shown in figure 7.3 where we have written a macro called AND-IF. This is an extension of the primitive IF, which is also a macro. AND-IF is supplied four arguments, two tests and two actions. If the results of both tests are true then the first action is performed. If the results of either, or both of the tests is false, then the second action is performed. Let us consider the operation of AND-IF. The first line of figure 7.3 is:

$$(DEFMACRO\ AND\text{-}IF(TEST1\ TEST2\ TRUE\text{-}ACTION\ FALSE\text{-}ACTION) \tag{7-17}$$

Note that AND-IF has the parameters TEST1, TEST2, TRUE-ACTION, and FALSE-ACTION. If TEST1 and TEST2 are both true, then TRUE-ACTION will be evaluated. If TEST1 and TEST2 are not both true, then FALSE-ACTION will be evaluated. For instance if we evaluate,

$$(AND\text{-}IF\ (>\ 5\ 3)\ (=\ 2\ 2)\ (PRINC\ 'YES)\ (PRINC\ 'NO)) \tag{7-18}$$

YES will be output because both conditions are true. If AND-IF were a procedure, the operation would not be as desired because all the arguments would be evaluated. Thus, when (7-18) was evaluated both YES and NO would be output at the start because of the side effects of the evaluation of the arguments.

Now consider the COND statement. It is backquoted. Thus, all the atoms that are not preceded by a comma will be treated simply as text. When the macro is expanded, the evaluated backquoted list will be used to form a nonbackquoted list that will replace the macro call. In this list, COND, AND, and T will appear simply as written. The items that are preceded by commas will be replaced by the appropriate arguments of the macro. For instance, evaluation of TEST1 results in its replacement by the actual test that is the first argument of the macro; it does not result in its replacement by the *evaluation* of this argument (test). After the list replaces the macro call, the list will be evaluated. Thus, when the macro is called, TEST1, and TEST2 will always be evaluated. However, because of the COND operation, TRUE-ACTION will be evaluated only if TEST1 and TEST2 are both true. FALSE-ACTION will be evaluated only if TEST1 and TEST2 are not both true. In figure 7.3 we have again used the backquote to provide a template into which data is inserted. In this case the data are the arguments of a macro.

When we discussed the IF macro (in an earlier chapter, although it was not referred to as a macro there) we stated that the operations that correspond to TRUE-ACTION and FALSE-ACTION could be only a single Lisp expression. The same comments could apply to the AND-IF macro. However, the backquote macro allows us to replace a single expression with a *compound expression*. This is a sequence of expressions that acts as a single expression. Let us consider an example of this:

```
(AND-IF (> 5 4) (> 7 2)
           `(,(PRINC 'YES) ,(SETQ X 3))
        (PRINC 'NO)
)                                                            (7-19)
```

Both tests are true. Now YES will be output and X will be bound to 3. The compound expression is:

```
`(,(PRINC 'YES) ,(SETQ X 3))                                (7-20)
```

This is a single list containing sublists. The backquote prevents evaluation of all terms except those preceded by commas. In this case all the sublists are preceded by commas. Thus, they are all evaluated. Note how the backquote macro often can simplify tasks that would otherwise be very tedious. Note that compound expressions can also be set up using PROG1 and PROGN. See sec. 4-6.

Macros are often used to modify existing Lisp primitives or to change their names. For instance, suppose that we want to have an operation called FOR that performs the same function as DO. The following macro definition will accomplish this:

```
(DEFMACRO FOR(INIT TEST &REST BODY)
   `(DO ,INIT ,TEST ,@BODY)                                 (7-21)
)
```

When the macro is expanded the first and second arguments will replace INIT and TEST, respectively in the DO construction. The body of the DO construction will be replaced by BODY. Note that BODY is preceded by an @ in (7-21). This is done to avoid having an extra set or parentheses in the DO construction when the macro is expanded. Note that FOR is used in exactly the same way as is DO.

Exercises

Check any procedures or macros that you write by running them on your computer.

1. What is the difference between a macro and a procedure?

2. Write a macro that prints lists literally without requiring that they be preceded by an apostrophe. Hint; end the macro with a (TERPRI) so that the argument of the PRINT is not evaluated.

3. Write a macro that obtains the average of a list of numbers.

4. Write a macro called DEFPROC that is used to replace DEFUN. The defining statement should have the same form as the procedure call. For instance if a procedure called FOO that is to be passed three arguments is to be set up, then the first line of the DEFPROC should be:

    (DEFPROC (FOO A B C)

The body of the procedure definition should be the same as if DEFUN was used.

5. Write a macro that puts a test condition and a list of s-expressions into a DO loop. Use I as the index of the loop. I should be incremented with each pass through the loop.

6. Write a macro that will fill in a table of the form:

(NAME blank)
(ADDRESS blank)
(PHONE NUMBER blank)

The blanks are to be supplied as variables that are the arguments of the macro.

7. Modify the macro AND-IF of figure 7.3 so that the FALSE-ACTION becomes an optional parameter. The default value should be NIL.

8. Write a macro that has the following arguments: TEST1, ACTION1, TEST2, and ACTION2. There is to be a fifth optional argument ACTION3 that has the default value NIL. If TEST1 is true, then ACTION1 is to be evaluated. If TEST1 is false and TEST2 is true, then ACTION2 is to be evaluated. If both TEST1 and TEST2 are false, then ACTION3 is to be evaluated.

8

Some Additional Data Types

Thus far we have encountered several data types. For instance, we have discussed the list, several integer and floating-point numerical types, and boolean types. In addition, we have seen that structures represent a data type. Every time that a DEFSTRUCT construction is evaluated a new data type is established. The a-list and the p-list are each data types. We shall introduce additional data types in this chapter.

8-1. Arrays - Vectors

We have seen that lists are very versatile and can be used to store all types of data. However, there are times when a somewhat different type of structure is desired. If list is long, accessing a particular element of that list can be tedious. For instance, suppose that the list has 100 elements and you want to read element number 75. We could write a procedure that would apply CDR 74 times and then apply CAR. Indeed, this procedure could be easily generalized to read any element of the list. However, it would be convenient, at times, if we could simply refer to an element of the list by number.

Now consider a more complex structure. Suppose that data is stored in a table. For instance, the rows could each represent different students and the columns could represent their grades in each of ten tests. The table might have 100 rows, representing 100 students, and 10 columns, representing the 10 tests. Such data could be stored in a list of 100 elements wherein each element was a list of 10 elements. We could write a procedure to access a particular element of the table. The arguments of that procedure would be the row and column of the table. Again, it would be convenient if we did not have to write procedures of this type but could access the elements of the table simply by specifying the row and column.

Lisp, like every other programming language, provides a data type called an *array* that allows the programmer to store lists of data and then to reference a particular item of data by a number or a sequence of numbers. The length of an array is called its *dimension*. Arrays can be *multidimensional*. For instance, a table is an array of two dimensions. In this case, each element of the array is referred to by two numbers, one for the row and one for the column. Arrays can have more than two dimensions. For instance, the Common Lisp standards call for arrays with at least seven dimensions. Another name for a one-dimension array is a *vector*.

Lists are dynamic objects. That is, the size of a list can be changed during the running of a program. Data can be added, and the list becomes longer. Similarly, the list can be shortened by removing data. Arrays are static objects. We shall see that when an array is set up, the number of elements that it contains is specified. Actually, in some cases, we can change the size of an array. However, a special procedure must be invoked to do so.

Each array must be set up before it can be used. The procedure MAKE-ARRAY is used to set up a general array. For instance, suppose that we want to set up an array with three rows and ten columns and call that array X. Evaluation of the following construction will accomplish this:

```
(SETQ X (MAKE-ARRAY '(3 10)))                    (8-1)
```

Note the apostrophe. The array X is said to be a two-dimensional array whose dimensions are 3 and 10. Suppose that we want to set up a vector with 15 elements and call it Y. Evaluation of the following will accomplish this:

```
(SETQ Y (MAKE-ARRAY 15))                         (8-2)
```

Note that for a one-dimensional array the dimension need not be a list, although a single element list could be specified. (Note that some Lisp systems require that list *not* be used for one-dimensional arrays.) The procedure VECTOR can be used to specifically set up a one-dimensional array. The values stored in the elements must be specified when VECTOR is used. For instance the following sets up a Vector Y with four elements.

(SETQ Y (VECTOR 'THE 'BOOK 'IS 'HERE))   (8-3)

The four elements are THE, BOOK, IS, and HERE. Note that the operaation of MAKE-ARRAY and VECTOR differ considerably.

We have not considered all aspects of MAKE-ARRAY and VECTOR here. We shall discuss these procedures in greater detail subsequently.

The elements of an array can be accessed using the primitive function AREF. For instance,

(AREF Y 3)   (8-4)

will return the value of element number three of the Y array. This can be used in the usual ways. For instance,

(SETQ ZZ (AREF Y 3))   (8-5)

will bind ZZ to the value of element number three in the Y array.

The numbering of the elements of an array start with element number 0. Thus, if a vector is dimensioned to have 20 elements, they will be numbered from 0 to 19. The number of an element of a vector is called its *index*. The index for the elements of a two-dimensional array consists of a sequence of two numbers. For instance, if the element in row 3 and column 4 of a two-dimensional array called WW is to be accessed, the expression,

(AREF WW 2 3)   (8-6)

would be used. These principles can be extended to arrays of larger dimension.

Array data is entered, or changed using SETF. For instance, element 2 3 (row 3 column 4) of the array that is assigned to WW will be changed, or set equal, to 34 by executing:

(SETF (AREF WW 2 3) 34)   (8-7)

An element of an array can be a list, or any other data object. For instance, evaluation of,

(SETF (AREF Y 2) '(THE BOOK IS HERE))   (8-8)

results in the list '(THE BOOK IS HERE) being stored in element number 2 of the array that is assigned to Y. Note that this array is referred to as array Y.

```
DEFUN ENTER-NAMES(ARR &AUX DIM X)
    (SETQ DIM (ARRAY-LENGTH ARR))
    (DO ((I 0 (+ I 1)))
        ((= I DIM))
        (PRINT '(THERE ARE ,(- DIM I) ELEMENTS VACANT))
        (PRINT '(ENTER ID NUMBER AND NAME))
        (TERPRI)
        (SETQ X (READ))
        (COND ((< X 0) (RETURN))
              (T (SETF (AREF ARR I) (LIST X (READ))))))
    )
)
```

```
(DEFUN FIND-ID (ARR ID-NUMB &AUX DIM X)
    (SETQ DIM (ARRAY-LENGTH ARR))
    (DO ((I 0 (+ I 1)))
        ((= I DIM))
        (SETQ X (AREF ARR I))
        (COND ((LISTP X)
                (COND ((EQUAL ID-NUMB (CAR X)) (PRINT (CADR X))))
              )
              (T (TERPRI)
                 (PRINT '(THERE ARE ,(- DIM I) ELEMENTS REMAINING IN LIST))
                 (RETURN)
              )
        )
    )
)
```

Figure 8.1. The procedures ENTER-NAMES and FIND-ID that manipulate arrays

In figure 8.1 we illustrate some procedures that manipulate arrays. Suppose that we have a one-dimensional array of 20 elements that is an index file for a database. Each element of the array consists of a list of two elements. The first element of the list is a person's ID number and the second element is the person's name. We assume here that the first and last names are combined into a single atom. Consider the primitive function ARRAY-LENGTH that is used in figure 8.1. It returns the dimension of the array whose name is its argument. Thus, the array ARR will have DIM elements. The maximum size of an array is limited by the amount of memory that is available. If the array is to be called Y and it is to have 20 elements (numbered from 0 to 19), then it can be set up by evaluating:

(SETQ Y (MAKE-ARRAY 20))   (8-9)

The first procedure of figure 8.1 is called ENTER-NAMES. It is used to initially enter data into the array. ENTER-NAMES interacts with the person entering the initial data. The person entering the data is prompted to enter the ID number and name. Just prior to this he is told how many empty elements are available. If all DIM ID numbers and names have been entered or if the person entering data enters a negative ID number, the procedure will terminate. This procedure is used only to enter data initially. If additional data is to be entered after the procedure has been run, SETF should be used. This assumes that there are available elements of the array. If the procedure ENTER-NAMES is rerun, the old data will be written over.

The procedure uses a DO loop that loops DIM times. Note that the backquote is used in the output of the number of empty elements remaining in the array. X will be assigned the first item of data that is entered. This should be the ID number. The predicate NUMBERP could be used to test that the correct type of data is entered. We have not done this to avoid obscuring the procedure with unnecessary detail. The COND construction is used to test for a negative ID number. If the entered number is negative, then the procedure will end because of the RETURN. If the entered number is nonnegative, then the second item of data, the name, will be read. The SETF expression will then cause the list of data to be stored in the proper element of the array.

The second procedure, FIND-ID, finds the name associated with an ID number. The procedure uses a pair of nested COND expressions. X is set equal to one element of the array on each pass through the loop. If X is not a list, it is assumed that data has not been entered into that element or into any succeeding elements of the array. The procedure terminates and the number of elements that are available for additional data is output. Note that the procedure does not terminate after the ID number is found. In this way, if a duplicate ID number exists, it will be found. In addition, if the entire list was not searched, the number of remaining elements could not be output. The procedure FIND-ID can be easily modified, if this type of operation is not desired.

There are certain optional parameters that can be included when an array is initially specified using MAKE-ARRAY. These specifications are preceded by a colon. We shall illustrate these options. The element type can be specified using :ELEMENT-TYPE, For instance,

$$\text{(SETQ Y (MAKE-ARRAY 20 :ELEMENT-TYPE 'SINGLE-FLOAT))} \tag{8-10}$$

establishes Y as an array of 20 elements in which each element must be of type SINGLE-FLOAT. An error will result if an element of a type other than SINGLE-FLOAT is entered into the array. If an ELEMENT-TYPE is not specified, then the data types in the element are arbitrary. Indeed different data types can be stored in different elements of the same array.

The initial value of all the elements of the array can be specified at the time that the array is established. If all the elements are to have the same initial value, then :INITIAL-ELEMENT is used. For instance,

$$\text{(MAKE-ARRAY 20 :ELEMENT-TYPE 'SINGLE-FLOAT}$$
$$\text{:INITIAL-VALUE 32.7)} \tag{8-11}$$

would be used to set up a one-dimensional array of 20 elements. The elements could store only data of type SINGLE-FLOAT; the initial value of the data stored in each of the 20 elements would be 32.7. If an ELEMENT-TYPE is specified, then the INITIAL-ELEMENT must conform to this specification. Note that, for the sake of brevity, we have not assigned this array to a variable.

If the initial values of each of the elements of the array are to be different, then these values can be specified in the MAKE-ARRAY expression. In this case the :INITIAL-CONTENTS specification is used. All of the elements of the array must be specified in a list. For instance,

$$\text{(MAKE-ARRAY 4 :INITIAL-CONTENTS '(1 2 3 4))} \tag{8-12}$$

would be used to set up a four-element array. Element number 0 would store 1; element number 1 would store 2, etc. When the INITIAL-CONTENTS of a multidimensional array are specified, that specification is in the form of a list of lists. The number of elements in the main list is equal to the first dimension, for instance,

```
(MAKE-ARRAY '(2 3) :INITIAL-CONTENTS
    '((HOUSE BOOK TABLE)
      (ONE TWO THREE)))                              (8-13)
```

If there are additional dimensions, then there will be further nesting of the lists, for example,

```
(MAKE-ARRAY '(4 3 2) :INITIAL-CONTENTS
    '(((A B) (C D) (E F))
      ((G H) (I J) (K L))
      ((1 2) (3 4) (5 6))
      ((7 8) (5 1) (3 7))))                          (8-14)
```

Note that :INITIAL-CONTENTS should not be specified if :INITIAL-ELEMENT is specified. That is, these specifications are mutually exclusive.

A *fill pointer* can be specified for a vector, that is for a one-dimensional array. Fill pointers make it convenient to enter data into the array. This entering of data is referred to as filling the array. If it exists, the fill pointer points at an element of the array. Data can be entered into this element of the array and then the fill pointer is incremented so that it points at the next element of the array. We shall clarify this with several examples. The fill pointer is set up using :FILL-POINTER, in conjunction with MAKE-ARRAY, at the time that the vector is established. For instance, the following sets up a vector of 15 elements with a fill pointer pointing at element number 0:

```
(SETQ FF (MAKE-ARRAY 20 :FILL-POINTER 0))           (8-15)
```

If the last 0 were replaced by 3 the fill pointer would point at element number 3. Assume that (8-15) has been evaluated. Now if we want to enter data into element 0 of vector FF, we can use the procedure VECTOR-PUSH. For instance, if the list (THE BOOK) is to be entered into that element, the following expression would be evaluated:

```
(VECTOR-PUSH '(THE BOOK) FF)                        (8-16)
```

The value 0 will be returned; this is the element of the FF vector that was modified. Now the fill pointer points at element number 1. If another VECTOR-PUSH expression is evaluated, such as,

```
(VECTOR-PUSH 44 FF)                                 (8-17)
```

then 1 will be returned, 44 will be stored in element number 1 of vector FF and vector FF's fill pointer will point to element number 2. Note that the use of the fill pointer simplifies some of the bookkeeping details. If you attempt to put more elements than have been dimensioned into a vector using VECTOR-PUSH, of SETF for that matter, an error will result. Note that a vector will have a fill pointer only if the :FILL-POINTER term is included in the MAKE-ARRAY expression and if the value following :FILL-POINTER is not NIL.

If the elements of a vector are not initialized when the array is set up, the vector is said to have an *active length* of zero. Each time that VECTOR-PUSH is evaluated, the active length is incremented (by one). The active length cannot exceed the dimension of the array. In general, the active length of a vector is determined by the first element of the array that is changed from an uninitialized value. Note that if you use SETF to change an element's value and subsequently use VECTOR-PUSH, unpredictable results may occur with some Lisp systems.

The procedure VECTOR-POP is used to read, but not to change, a vector. If,

(VECTOR-POP FFF)   (8-18)

is evaluated, the value stored in the element of FFF pointed at by the fill pointer will be returned and the value of the fill pointer will be decremented (by one). VECTOR-PUSH and VECTOR-POP can be used only if a fill pointer has been set up when the array was established.

We have indicated that the dimensions of an array are fixed. However if a vector has a fill pointer, then its dimensions can be changed using the procedure ADJUST-ARRAY. The use of ADJUST-ARRAY follows that of MAKE-ARRAY. The dimension, specified as an argument of ADJUST-ARRAY, becomes the new dimension of the vector. Remember that the vector must have been set up with a fill pointer if ADJUST-ARRAY is to be used with that vector.

There are a number of functions that are supplied with Common Lisp systems that supply information about arrays. The function FILL-POINTER returns the value of the fill pointer (the element pointed at) for the specified array. For instance,

(FILL-POINTER FF)   (8-19)

returns the fill pointer of the FF vector. We have already discussed the function ARRAY-LENGTH that returns the total number of elements allowed in an array. There are other functions that are supplied with Lisp systems that are used with arrays. Consult your Lisp manual to determine those that are supplied with your system. Some Lisp systems use procedures that differ from the ones discussed here. However, the general principless should apply to all Lisp systems.

8-2. Characters

All text is made up of collections of *characters*. Collections of characters are called *strings*. Both characters and strings are Lisp data types. We shall discuss characters in this section. Strings will be discussed in the next section.

A character is stored using a numeric code. (Actually, this statement is true for all data types.) In many systems, each character is represented by its ASCII code. (ASCII stands for American Standard Code for Information Interchange.) This is a code of 128 numbers, each representing one of the standard characters. The ASCII codes are given in Table 8.1.

Table 8.1. The ASCII Codes

Code	Character	Code	Character
0	null	64	@
1	Ctrl A	65	A
2	Ctrl B	66	B
3	Ctrl C	67	C
4	Ctrl D	68	D
5	Ctrl E	69	E
6	Ctrl F	70	F
7	Ctrl G	71	G
8	Ctrl H	72	H
9	Ctrl I	73	I
10	Ctrl J	74	J
11	Ctrl K	75	K
12	Ctrl L	76	L
13	Ctrl M	77	M
14	Ctrl N	78	N
15	Ctrl O	79	O
16	Ctrl P	80	P
17	Ctrl Q	81	Q
18	Ctrl R	82	R
19	Ctrl S	83	S

Code	Character	Code	Character
20	Ctrl T	84	T
21	Ctrl U	85	U
22	Ctrl V	86	V
23	Ctrl W	87	W
24	Ctrl X	88	X
25	Ctrl Y	89	Y
26	Ctrl Z	90	Z
27	ESC	91	[
28	FS	92	\
29	GS	93	]
30	RS	94	^
31	VS	95	_
32	Space	96	`
33	!	97	a
34	"	98	b
35	#	99	c
36	$	100	d
37	%	101	e
38	&	102	f
39	'	103	g
40	(	104	h
41	)	105	i
42	*	106	j
43	+	107	k
44	,	108	l
45	-	109	m
46	.	110	n
47	/	111	o
48	0	112	p
49	1	113	q
50	2	114	r
51	3	115	s
52	4	116	t
53	5	117	u
54	6	118	v
55	7	119	w
56	8	120	x
57	9	121	y
58	:	122	z
59	;	123	{

Code	Character	Code	Character
60	<	124	|
61	=	125	}
62	>	126	~
63	?	127	DEL

The ASCII codes from 1 to 26 are the control codes. These are generated on most terminals by simultaneously pressing the control key and the key in question. Some of the control codes have special significance. For instance, Ctrl-M represents a carriage return and Ctrl-J represents a line feed. There are other schemes for representing characters. However the ASCII code is very widely used.

Each character has a numeric representation. If we were representing simple collections of characters, such as a computer program, then each character would be represented by its ASCII code. However, there are more complex representations of text. For instance, in the usual textbook some characters may be printed in the standard Roman font, while others are printed in italics, and still others are printed in boldface. In addition, the size of the font can vary. Also, computer terminals often supply *graphics characters*. These are a collection of shapes that are used to draw figures on the screen of the terminal. Moreover, there are foreign language fonts. Therefore, the system must know a great deal of information about any given character.

A single 8-bit byte can be used to represent 256 different numbers. If all the information about a character is to be carried in its code, then one byte will not be large enough to store all the necessary data. Note that one byte is large enough to store the ASCII code for any single character. Common Lisp provides two modes of character storage. In one mode only one byte can be used and only the ASCII, or other similar, code for the character is stored. In the other mode, more than one byte must be used and much more information is carried with the coded representation of the character. The first mode has the advantage of conserving storage space. The second mode has the advantage that more information is carried by the representation of a character. This additional information is not always needed. For instance, suppose that you are working with a word processor that is being used to type business letters. All the text may be printed using a single font. Thus, it is not necessary to provide font information. Even if different fonts are used, it is not necessary to include the font information with each character. A special character, or a sequence of characters, could be inserted into the text to indicate where font changes are to be made. In such a situation, there usually are long sequences of text without font changes. Thus, the inclusion of the special characters into the text would not substantially increase the total amount of text. In this case, storage space would be conserved if the font information were not included with each character. These special character sequences often start with the ESC (ASCII 27) which is called *escape*. The sequences are called *escape sequences*.

Characters in common Lisp have three possible attributes, *code*, *font*, and *bits*. The code is the numerical representation of the character, e. g., the ASCII code. The font is a number that represents the font type. The bits allow additional information to be associated with each character. If a character has only the code specified, then it is called a *standard character*.

Every character is represented by a code that consists of a number. The primitive function CODE-CHAR can be used to establish the numerical code. The form of its use is:

(CODE-CHAR char bits font)   (8-20)

In this expression char, bits, and font should be replaced by appropriate numerical values. Of course, these numerical values can be represented by variables. For instance, suppose that we wish to bind the atom ZZ to the character c, with a bit value of 1 and a font value of 1. Evaluation of the following will accomplish this:

(SETQ ZZ (CODE-CHAR 99 1 1))   (8-21)

Note that the ASCII code for c is 99. The value returned will depend upon the Lisp system. Typically, 355 would be the value assigned to ZZ. The character can be output using FORMAT. For instance,

(FORMAT T "~C" ZZ)   (8-22)

will result in the output of c.

The bits and font arguments of (8-20) are optional. For instance,

(CODE-CHAR 99)   (8-23)

simply will return 99.

There are various primitives that are used to manipulate characters. For instance, CHAR-UPCASE will convert a lowercase letter into the corresponding uppercase letter. For example if (8-21) is executed,

(CHAR-UPCASE ZZ)   (8-24)

will (typically) return 323, which represents an uppercase C with bit and font values of 1. If the bit and font values of ZZ were zero then the value of ZZ would be 99 and the value returned by (8-24) would be 67, which is the ASCII code for C. If ZZ represented anything but a lowercase letter, then CHAR-UPCASE would return the unmodified value of ZZ. There is a function called CHAR-DOWNCASE whose operation is similar to CHAR-UPCASE except that it converts an uppercase letter into the corresponding lowercase letter.

Some characters are given names. For instance, ASCII 32 is called Space. It represents a blank space and ASCII 13 is called Return. The function NAME-CHAR can be used to determine these names. For instance if we evaluate the following sequence,

(SETQ X 32)	(8-25a)
(CHAR-NAME X)	(8-25b)

the word Space will be returned. Note that we have set X equal to the character value simply by binding it to 32. (The ASCII code for a blank space is 32.) CODE-CHAR need only be used when font and bits are specified. Note that in some Lisp systems CHAR-NAME will not return a character. For instance, if X had been bound to 99 (8-25b) would not return c. Note that we have assumed that ASCII codes are used. If your system uses a different coding scheme, then some numerical values may be different from those given here.

Consider table 8.1. The numbers have lower codes than do the uppercase letters. In turn, the uppercase letters have lower numerical codes than do the lowercase letters. The digit 0 has a lower code than does the digit 1, the letter A has a lower code than B, etc. This type of ordering occurs in essentially all coding schemes. There are primitives that compare characters on the basis of their codes. For instance, CHAR= will return true if all its arguments are the same character and NIL otherwise. The primitive CHAR/= will return true if all of its arguments are unequal and NIL otherwise. The procedure CHAR> will return true if each of its arguments is greater (has a higher code value) than the argument to its right. For most Lisp systems, these predicates consider only the code component of the character value in their comparisons. The bit and fonts are ignored. Thus, CHAR> functions in a manner that is analogous to >, except that the code value of the character is taken. For instance, the numerical value of ZZ produced when (8-21) is evaluated is 355. Now suppose that we evaluate,

(SETQ XX 102)	(8-26)

and then evaluate:

(CHAR> XX ZZ)   (8-27)

T will be returned. Note that although ZZ is bound to 355, the code value of ZZ is 99. Thus, the code value of XX is greater than the code value of ZZ. The predicates CHAR<, CHAR>=, and CHAR<= perform comparisons with the code component of characters that are analogous to those performed by <, >=, and <= with numbers, respectively. The primitive CHAR-CODE will extract the code value from the numeric value generated by CODE-CHAR. If there are no font or bits attributes, then these values will be equal.

There are other predicates that are available. STANDARD-CHAR returns true if its argument is a standard character (no bit or font values). ALPHA-CHAR-P, LOWER-CASE-P, and UPPER-CASE-P return true if their arguments are alphabetic characters, lowercase characters, and uppercase characters, respectively. The predicates DIGIT-CHAR-P and ALPHANUMERICP return true if their arguments are digits and letters, respectively. The predicates discussed in this paragraph have a single argument. There are other primitives that are available. Consult your Lisp manual to determine those that are available for your system. Note that some Lisp systems may use functions whose names differ from the ones that we have discussed here. Consult your Lisp manual to determine the forms used by your Lisp system.

8-3. Strings

Characters are usually combined into *strings*. For instance this sentence is composed of a string of characters. There is a Lisp data type called string. A string is actually a vector, each of whose elements is a character. (The characters can be extracted using AREF.) Strings can be set up in several ways. The procedure MAKE-STRING can be used. This is used in a manner similar to MAKE-ARRAY. For example, the evaluation of,

(SETQ A (MAKE-STRING 8))   (8-28)

results in A being bound to a vector with 8 elements. Each element can store a character. The option of entering an initial element is allowed. This follows the use of :INITIAL-ELEMENT with MAKE-ARRAY. Element values can be read and changed using AREF and SETF, just as with other arrays.

When strings are written, they are delimited by (double) quotation marks. Note that the quotation marks are not stored in memory. Most Lisp systems allow you to use a simple SETQ statement to set up a string and enter the character values. For instance, the evaluation of,

    (SETQ A "THE BOOK")   (8-29)

results in an array named A storing the string "THE BOOK."
  There are a number of primitives that can be used with strings. STRING will return the value of a string. For instance, if (8-29) has been evaluated then,

    (STRING A)   (8-30)

will return "THE BOOK". If the argument of STRING stores a character, then STRING will return that character, as a string (i. e., enclosed in quotation marks). If STRING's argument is an integer, then the character, that corresponds to that integer, will be returned as a string. (Note the integer will be processed by CODE-CHAR before it is processed by string.)
  There are procedures that will remove characters from the beginning and/or end of a string. STRING-LEFT-TRIM is used to "trim" characters from the left side of a string. The general form of its use is,

    (STRING-LEFT-TRIM trimstring string)   (8-31)

The argument trimstring contains the characters that are to be removed from the left side of string. For instance, if we evaluate the sequence,

    (SETQ X "THE BOOK IS HERE")   (8-32a)
    (STRING-LEFT-TRIM "TH" X)   (8-32b)

Then the string "E BOOK IS HERE" will be returned. If the trim string does not match the left end of the string, then no characters will be trimmed from the string. If only the leftmost characters of the trim string match the leftmost characters of the string, then only these characters will be trimmed. For instance, if (8-32b) is replaced by,

    (STRING-LEFT-TRIM "TQE" X)   (8-32c)

the string "HE BOOK IS HERE" will be returned. There are two other trimming primitives, STRING-RIGHT-TRIM and STRING-TRIM; they result in trimming from the right side and from both sides of the string, respectively.

There are primitives that change the case of the characters in a string. STRING-UPCASE and STRING-DOWNCASE return strings with all the letters of their arguments replaced by the corresponding uppercase or lowercase letters, respectively. For instance, if X is as established in (8-32a),

  (STRING-DOWNCASE X)   (8-33)

will return, "the book is here." Note that the string stored in X is unchanged by this operation. The starting and ending points of the operation can be optionally specified using the words :START and :END. For example,

  (STRING-DOWNCASE X :START 3)   (8-34)

will return "THE book is here". That is, the operation of STRING-DOWNCASE will not be performed on the characters numbered 0, 1, or 2 of the string.

There are predicates that are used to compare strings. These are *lexicographical comparisons*. For instance, if string A would precede string B in an alphabetical listing, then string A is lexicographically less than string B. The ordering of characters is based on their ASCII codes. Note that the uppercase letters have lower ASCII codes than the corresponding lowercase letters. Some of the string comparisons ignore the case differences. That is, for comparison purposes, the lowercase letters are converted to uppercase letters, or vice versa. Some case sensitive predicates are STRING=, STRING/=, STRING>, STRING>=, STRING<, and STRING<=. These predicates take two strings as arguments. The predicates return true if the two strings are lexicographically, equal, not equal, the first greater than the second, the first greater than or equal to the second, the first less than the second, and the first less than or equal to the second, respectively. Note that these predicates are case sensitive. Some Lisp systems provide case insensitive predicates. For example, STRING-LESS-P is equivalent to STRING<, except that STRING-LESS-P is case insensitive.

There are optional start and end specifications that may be included with these predicates; these are similar to those used with STRING-DOWNCASE, but they can be specified for each string. For instance,

```
(STRING= "THE BOOK" "HEAVY WEIGHT" :START1 1 :END1 2
         :START2 0 :END2 1)
```
(8-35)

will return true because only the second and third characters of string 1 will be compared with the first and second characters of string 2. Note that the first character of a string is numbered 0.

The primitive STRING-SEARCH can be used to determine if one string is contained in (i. e., is a substring of) another string. For example,

```
(STRING-SEARCH "BOOK" X)
```
(8-36)

will return 4. Remember that X stores "THE BOOK IS HERE". Thus, the substring "BOOK" is part of A. Its starting position, 4 in this case, is returned. If there is no match, then NIL will be returned. The predicate STRING-SEARCH* is a case insensitive form of STRING-SEARCH.

One string can be appended to another one with the STRING-APPEND procedure. For instance,

```
(STRING-APPEND X " NOT ON THE CHAIR")
```
(8-37)

will return "THE BOOK IS HERE NOT ON THE CHAIR." Note that the strings that are the arguments of STRING-APPEND are not modified.

We have discussed many string procedures here. Most of these are included in the Common Lisp standards. However, the string procedures provided by Lisp systems vary greatly. Consult your Lisp manual to determine the form of the string procedures provided by your system.

```
(DEFUN ALPHA(ARRIN &AUX ARR LAST NUMB TMP MARK)
    (SETQ ARR (MAKE-ARRAY (ARRAY-LENGTH ARRIN)))
    (DO ((I 0 (+ I 1)))
        ((= I (ARRAY-LENGTH ARR)))
        (SETF (AREF ARR I) (AREF ARRIN I))
    )
    (TERPRI)
    (SETQ LAST "zzzzzzzzzzzzzzzz")
    (SETQ NUMB (ARRAY-LENGTH ARR))
    (DO ((I 0 (+ I 1)))
        ((= I NUMB))
        (SETQ TMP LAST)
        (DO ((J 0 (+ J 1)))
            ((= J NUMB))
            (COND ((STRING< (AREF ARR J) TMP)
                    (SETQ TMP (AREF ARR J))
                    (SETQ MARK J)
            ))
        )
        (PRINC (AREF ARR MARK))
        (TERPRI)
        (SETF (AREF ARR MARK) LAST)
    )
)
```

Figure 8.2. An alphabetizing procedure

As an example of string manipulation let us write a procedure that alphabetizes a set of strings and outputs the result to the terminal. The procedure is illustrated in figure 8.2. We assume that the strings in question are stored in a single array. This is actually a two-dimensional array. Each element of the array is a string which is, in turn, a one-dimensional array.

We must consider something before we start. When a variable is passed to a procedure as an argument, the variable is evaluated and its *value* is actually supplied to the procedure. The variable name, X for example, in the formal parameter list represents a local variable of the procedure. If X is modified, the variable passed to the procedure will not be modified. On the other hand, when an array is set up using MAKE-ARRAY, the situation is somewhat different. For instance, suppose that we evaluate:

(SETQ AA (MAKE-ARRAY 5))   (8-38)

In this case, the value stored by AA is the address of the array. Suppose that AA is the argument of a procedure wherein AA corresponds to XX in the formal parameter list. XX will then store the same address as AA. Thus, if the procedure modifies XX it will also modify AA. In addition, if we evaluate,

(SETQ BB AA)   (8-39)

BB will then store the same address as does AA. Thus, AA and BB will represent the same array. Any modification of AA will change BB and vice versa. Finally, if a string is set up using SETQ the picture is somewhat different. If we evaluate (8-32a), the variable X actually stores "THE BOOK IS HERE" and not an address. Thus, if X were the argument of a procedure, corresponding to Y in the formal parameter list, a modification of Y would not modify X.

Now let us continue with the discussion of figure 8.2. The array containing the strings to be alphabetized is called ARRIN. The procedure will modify the array containing the strings to be alphabetized. We do not want to change the array that is passed to the procedure. Thus, another array must be established. The array ARR is set up. Its dimension is the same as that of ARRIN. The first DO loop sets each element of ARR equal to the corresponding element of ARRIN. This is done on an element-by-element basis because, as noted previously, using SETQ to bind ARR to ARRIN would not set up a different array.

Now let us consider the alphabetization procedure. LAST is bound to a string of z's. Thus, LAST will be the last string in a typical alphabetical list. There is a pair of nested loops. At the start of the outer loop, TMP is bound to the value of LAST. Now the inner loop is entered. TMP is compared with each string (element of the array ARR) in turn. If the element of the array ARR is lexicographically less than TMP, then TMP is replaced by that element. Thus, after the first pass through the inner DO loop, the value of TMP will be that of the string that is lexicographically first. In addition MARK will be equal to the index of that string (i.e., its position in the array). After the cycling of the inner loop is complete, the value of,

(AREF ARR MARK)   (8-40)

is output. This is the same as the current value of TMP. Next, the element corresponding to MARK is assigned the value of LAST. Thus, the element that was lexicographically first becomes lexicographically last. Now, the outer loop cycles again and the procedure is repeated with the modified array ARR. In this case, the string that was lexicographically second will be output and then replaced by the value of LAST. When the cycling of the outer loop is complete, the entire alphabetized set of strings will have been output.

Exercises

Check any procedures that you write by running them on your computer.

1. What is meant by an array.

2. Set up a vector with five elements. Each element of the vector is to be a list containing 10 numbers. Write a procedure that returns a five-element vector, each element of which is to contain the average of the numbers in the corresponding element of the vector that was passed to the procedure.

3. Repeat exercise 2, now assume that the information is contained in a two-dimensional array with five rows and 10 columns.

4. Modify the procedure of exercise 2 so that it can be passed a vector of any dimension.

5. Modify the procedure of exercise 4 so that the lists that are stored in the vector can be of arbitrary length.

6. Write the expression that will set up a vector of 10 elements, each of whose elements is the atom EMPTY.

7. Write the expression that will set up a five-element vector in which the initial values of the elements are 2, 4, 6, 8, and 15.

8. Write the expression that will set up a three-row two column array in which the initial value of each of the elements in the first row is 1; the initial value of each of the elements in the second row is 2; the initial value of each of the elements in the third row is 3.

9. Set up a 10-element vector with a fill pointer. Then write a procedure to fill this vector with the values 1, 2, ..., 10. Use VECTOR-PUSH in the procedure.

10. Write a procedure that uses VECTOR-POP to read the values of the elements of the vector of exercise 9. Each of these values and the corresponding value of the fill pointer should be output to the screen of your terminal.

11. What are the ASCII codes?

12. What is meant by an escape sequence.

13. Determine the numerical representation for lowercase d on your system. Then use CODE-CHAR to generate the code corresponding to d, with bit and font values of 1.

14. Write a procedure whose argument is an integer. The procedure should return the character corresponding to the code portion of that integer.

15. What is meant by a string?

16. Write a procedure that has two arguments that are strings. The procedure should output the string that is lexicographically first.

17. The lexicographical order of two strings is determined in the following way: The code values of the first two characters are compared. If the code value of the first character of string A is less than that of the first character of string B, then string A has a lower lexicographical order, than string B. If the code values of the first characters are the same, then the second characters are compared, etc. If string A is shorter than string B and the leftmost characters of string B are the same as string A, then string A is of lower lexicographical order than string B. Using this definition, write your own version of STRING>.

18. Repeat exercise 17, but now make the procedure case insensitive.

19. Use the procedure of exercise 18 to write a case insensitive alphabetizing routine.

20. Modify the procedure of figure 8.2 in accordance with the following information. The strings are to contain both first and last names. The names are to be separated by a single blank space, for instance, "TOM SMITH." The alphabetization procedure is to be based on the last names. The complete name is to be output.

21. Repeat exercise 20 but now have the alphabetization be based on the complete name last name first. The form of the input and output lists are the same as in exercise 20. Hint: the string to be alphabetized should be in the order: last name, blank space, first name.

9

Some Advanced Topics

In this chapter we shall consider some additional subjects. Topics such as object-oriented programming, messages and flavors will be discussed. We shall also consider packages and other related topics. We have not yet specifically discussed the storage of files which we shall do in this chapter. These topics will provide the reader with an understanding of some of the more powerful aspects of Lisp.

9-1. Object Oriented Programming

There are occasions when a similar, but not identical, operation is to be performed on various sets of data. Keeping track of which procedure to use can be both tedious and confusing. In this section we shall consider a technique that, in many circumstances, can eliminate these problems. For instance, suppose that a bank uses a Lisp program to maintain the records of its depositors. Some of the depositors have regular checking accounts for which there is no charge for checks and no charge for deposits. Other depositors have special checking accounts for which there is a charge of $0.75 for each check and $1.25 for each deposit. Thus, different deposit and withdrawal routines must be used for each kind of account. This means that the person running the program that updates customer accounts must remember to use one set of routines for one type of customer and another set of routines for another type of customer. It would be less confusing if this were not the case. That is, it should appear to the person running the program that he is using the same routines for both types of checking accounts. This could be accomplished if the data for each account contained the appropriate procedures to be used. If the corresponding procedures in different accounts could be accessed using the same instructions, then the person person running the program would not have to remember different procedure names or have to remember which customers had regular checking accounts and which had special checking accounts. A programming abstraction has been achieved. This type of abstraction wherein the data supplies the routines that operate upon it is called *object-orientated programming*.

```
(DEFSTRUCT CHECKBOOK
   (BALANCE 0.00)
   (CHECK 0.00)
   (DEPOSIT 0.00)
   (TAKEOUT 'CHECKBOOK_CHECK_TO_BALANCE)
   (PUTIN 'CHECKBOOK_DEPOSIT_TO_BALANCE)
   (MAKEDEPOSIT 'CHECKBOOK_ENTER_DEPOSIT)
 )


(DEFUN CHECKBOOK_CHECK_TO_BALANCE(NAME)
   (SETF (CHECKBOOK-BALANCE NAME)
      (- (CHECKBOOK-BALANCE NAME) (CHECKBOOK-CHECK NAME)))
   (SETF (CHECKBOOK-CHECK NAME) 0.00)
   (CHECKBOOK-BALANCE NAME)
)


(DEFUN CHECKBOOK_SPCHECK_TO_BALANCE(NAME)
   (SETF (CHECKBOOK-BALANCE NAME)
      (- (CHECKBOOK-BALANCE NAME) (CHECKBOOK-CHECK NAME) 0.75))
   (SETF (CHECKBOOK-CHECK NAME) 0.00)
   (CHECKBOOK-BALANCE NAME)
)


(DEFUN CHECKBOOK_DEPOSIT_TO_BALANCE(NAME)
   (SETF (CHECKBOOK-BALANCE NAME)
      (+ (CHECKBOOK-BALANCE NAME) (CHECKBOOK-DEPOSIT NAME)))
   (SETF (CHECKBOOK-DEPOSIT NAME) 0.00)
   (CHECKBOOK-BALANCE NAME)
)


(DEFUN CHECKBOOK_SPDEPOSIT_TO_BALANCE(NAME)
   (SETF (CHECKBOOK-BALANCE NAME)
      (+ (CHECKBOOK-BALANCE NAME) (CHECKBOOK-DEPOSIT NAME) -1.25))
   (SETF (CHECKBOOK-DEPOSIT NAME) 0.00)
   (CHECKBOOK-BALANCE NAME)
)
```

Figure 9.1. The definition of the structure CHECKBOOK and its procedures CHEEKBOOK_CHECK_TO_BALANCE, CHECKBOOK_CHECK_TO BALANCE, CHECKBOOK_DEPOSIT_TO_BALANCE, and CHECKBOOK_SDEPOSIT_TO_BALANCE.

An example will help to clarify this. Figure 9.1 contains a number of routines. The first of these is a DEFSTRUCT operation, A structure of type CHECKBOOK is defined here. It contains six slots. The last one can be ignored for the time being. It will be considered in the next section. The first slot stores the account BALANCE. It is this figure that is to be updated when checks are written and when deposits are made. The next two slots store the amount of the current check and the amount of the current deposit. These slots are called CHECK and DEPOSIT, respectively. The default values of these first three slots are all 0.00. There is a slot called TAKEOUT that has the default value CHECKBOOK_CHECK_TO_BALANCE. This is the name of a procedure. Similarly, the slot called PUTIN has the default value CHECKBOOK_DEPOSIT_TO_BALANCE. There is a procedure called CHECKBOOK_CHECK_TO_BALANCE that is used to update the balance when a check is written on a regular checking account, and there is a procedure called CHECKBOOK_SPCHECK_TO_BALANCE that is used to update the balance when a check is written on a special checking account. Similarly there are two procedures, CHECKBOOK_DEPOSITE_TO _BALANCE and CHECKBOOK_SPDEPOSIT_TO_BALANCE that are used to update the balance when a deposit is made into a regular checking account and into a special checking account, respectively.

Now suppose that two structures are to be set up. One called JOHN is to have a regular checking account while another called BILL has a special checking account. If we execute,

(SETF JOHN (MAKE-CHECKBOOK))   (9-1)

then the structure called JOHN will be set up. The values stored in each slot will be the default values. In particular, BALANCE, CHECK, and DEPOSIT will each store 0.00. TAKEOUT and PUTIN will store the atoms CHECKBOOK_CHECK_TO_BALANCE and CHECKBOOK_DEPOSIT _TO_BALANCE, respectively. Note that we do not store the actual procedures in each structure; only their names are stored there. It would be a waste of storage space if there were many structures (e. g., one for each depositor) and they each stored the same procedures. In addition, such structures would not be suitable for use when programs were compiled.

Now suppose that a deposit of $125.00 is made into JOHN's account. That amount is entered into the DEPOSIT slot of structure JOHN. This can be accomplished by executing:

    (SETF (CHECKBOOK-DEPOSIT JOHN) 125.00)   (9-2)

This is the usual procedure that is used to modify a slot value in a structure.

The balance is updated by running the procedure CHECKBOOK_DEPOSIT_TO_BALANCE. However, we do not want to use this name. Remember that the person running the program should use a single name for the operations appropriate to both regular and special checking accounts. In this case, the word PUTIN should be used for both regular and special checking accounts to indicate that the balance is to be updated after a deposit has been made. The PUTIN slot in structure JOHN stores the atom CHECKBOOK_DEPOSIT_TO_BALANCE. This atom will be used to call the proper procedure. For instance, to update the balance in structure JOHN, the following will be executed:

    (FUNCALL (CHECKBOOK-PUTIN JOHN) JOHN)   (9-3)

Note that because,

    (CHECKBOOK-PUTIN JOHN)

returns CHECKBOOK_DEPOSIT_TO_BALANCE, the correct procedure will be called.

The argument of the procedure CHECKBOOK_DEPOSIT_TO_ BALANCE is JOHN. In most Lisp systems, a structure is set up as an array. When an expression such as (9-1) is executed, the structure is set up and JOHN stores the address of the structure. When JOHN is used as the argument of a procedure, JOHN is evaluated and returns the address of the procedure. Thus, that procedure is passed the address of the structure called JOHN. The expressions within the procedure can then access and/or modify the structure.

The procedure CHECKBOOK_DEPOSIT_TO_BALANCE adds the amount stored in the DEPOSIT slot of the structure NAME to the BALANCE slot of that structure. Note that NAME is the formal parameter that corresponds to the argument, JOHN in this case. Next, the amount stored in the DEPOSIT slot is reset to 0.00 to prevent a user from inadvertently crediting the account twice, the updated balance is returned, and the procedure terminates.

The form of the name CHECKBOOK_DEPOSIT_TO_BALANCE has no significance to the Lisp system. We chose the name so that people reading the program would associate it with structures of type CHECKBOOK. Any other valid name could have been used.

When a check is written, its amount is entered into the CHECK slot. For instance, the evaluation of,

(SETF (CHECKBOOK-CHECK JOHN) 75.00)   (9-4)

enters $75.00 into the CHECK slot of the structure JOHN. The balance is updated by evaluating:

(FUNCALL (CHECKBOOK-TAKEOUT JOHN) JOHN)   (9-5)

The amount in the CHECK slot of JOHN will be deducted from the amount in the BALANCE slot; then the amount stored in the CHECK slot will be set equal to 0.00. Finally, the new balance is returned and output to the screen.

Now let us set up a structure called BILL for a person that has a special checking account. The procedures that correspond to PUTIN and TAKEOUT now are CHECKBOOK_SPDEPOSIT_TO_BALANCE and CHECKBOOK_SPCHECK_TO_BALANCE, respectively. Thus, the expression that sets up the structure is:

(SETF BILL (MAKE-CHECKBOOK
            :TAKEOUT 'CHECKBOOK_SPCHECK_TO_BALANCE
            :PUTIN 'CHECKBOOK_SPDEPOSIT_TO_BALANCE))
                                                        (9-6)

Note that the remaining slots are assigned their default values. Once the structure BILL is set up, the person running the program need not know whether BILL has a regular or a special checking account. If a deposit of $130.00 is to be made to BILL's account, the amount must first be stored in the DEPOSIT slot of structure BILL. This is accomplished by evaluating:

(SETF (CHECKBOOK-DEPOSIT BILL) 130.00)   (9-7)

The balance is updated by evaluating:

(FUNCALL (CHECKBOOK-PUTIN BILL) BILL)   (9-8)

The new balance of 128.75 is then output. Remember that $1.25 is deducted for each deposit to a special checking account. Suppose that a check for $40.00 is drawn to BILL's account. The evaluation of,

(SETF (CHECKBOOK-CHECK BILL) 40.00)   (9-9)

will cause this amount to be entered into the CHECK slot of structure BILL. The balance is updated by evaluating:

(FUNCALL (CHECKBOOK-TAKEOUT BILL) BILL)   (9-10)

The balance will be updated, the value stored in the BALANCE slot will become 0.00, and the new balance of 88.00 will be output. Remember that, for a special checking account, 0.75 is deducted from the balance each time that a check is cashed.

Note that the forms of the expressions (9-7) to (9-10) referring to the structure BILL are the same as those of (9-2) to (9-4) for the structure JOHN. Thus, even though structure JOHN and structure BILL each require that different procedures operate on them, the person running the program need not be aware of any difference. This abstraction is an important advantage of object oriented programming.

The procedures that we have used have been kept simple for illustrative purposes. In an actual banking program, a single operation would be used to update the balance and enter the amount of a check or a deposit. In addition, the form of expressions (9-2) to (9-4) or (9-7) to (9-10) are not obvious and, thus, could be confusing to a nonprogrammer. Macros could be written to simplify the forms of the expressions. Such macros will be discussed in the next section.

When an object-oriented program such as the one that we have discussed is written, the person running the program is given only as much information as he needs. For instance, because the structures BILL and JOHN are usually stored as arrays, the data they contain could be accessed and modified using AREF and SETF. *However, these procedures should not be used* . The form of the data storage need not be known by the person running the program. Indeed, the actual form of data storage may be highly system dependent.

The programmer also need not be aware of the form of the data storage. He need only know how to use the access procedures. If other procedures are used to access or modify data, errors can result because the specific form of data storage is not known. Suppose that AREF and SETF are used on the structures. The data can be changed improperly. This can actually prevent the program from functioning. For instance, suppose that the information in the

PUTIN or TAKEOUT slots is changed to numerical data. The program will no longer function.

Therefore, the user of the program should know only about the procedures that he is supposed to use. He is said to enter into a *contract* with the programmer. The user is supplied certain procedures and data structures. In return, the user agrees not to use any procedures but the ones supplied. If possible, the user should not be aware of any procedures that can access the data directly.

In this section we have illustrated object-oriented programming using a simple example. Of course, these ideas can be applied to much more complicated systems. However, the basic concepts presented here apply to more complicated systems as well.

9-2. Messages and Flavors.

The object-oriented programs discussed in the last section achieved the abstraction desired. However, the forms used to invoke the procedures, although not very complex, could be confusing. This would be especially true if the persons running the program were not programmers. For instance, the form of expression (9-4) that was used to store data in the CHECK slot of structure JOHN is different than the form of expression (9-5) that was used to update the BALANCE slot of structure JOHN. The person running the program should be able to use essentially the same form to invoke the various procedures. Although the form of the invocation would be the same, the name of the procedure and the data supplied would be different. An abstraction of this type is called *sending a message*. That is, the structure, or other data storage mechanism, is sent a message "telling it" to use a procedure that it stores to manipulate its data. Remember that the structure may not actually store the procedure; it may store only its name.

For instance, suppose that the PUTIN operation is to be performed on the structure called JOHN. The following would be evaluated,

```
(SEND-MESSAGE JOHN CHECKBOOK-PUTIN)          (9-11)
```

On the other hand, if 45.00 were to be entered into the DEPOSIT slot of JOHN, the following would be evaluated:

```
(SEND-MESSAGE JOHN CHECKBOOK-MAKEDEPOSIT 45.00)
                                              (9-12)
```

SEND-MESSAGE is a macro that the programmer must write. Once SEND-MESSAGE has been written, the person running the program need remember only a single basic form to perform any of the pertinent operations. Expression (9-12) makes use of the last slot of the structure CHECKBOOK discussed in the last section.

```
(DEFMACRO SEND-MESSAGE(TARGET OPERATION &REST OTHERS)
    (APPLY (EVAL (APPEND (LIST OPERATION) (LIST TARGET)))
                    (CONS (EVAL TARGET) OTHERS)
        )
    )
```

Figure 9.2. A message-passing macro.

The macro SEND-MESSAGE is illustrated in figure 9.2. At the start, ignore the &REST; we will consider it later. Consider (9-11); its evaluation should result in the same operation as does the evaluation of (9-3), which we repeat here:

$$\text{(FUNCALL (CHECKBOOK-PUTIN JOHN) JOHN)} \qquad (9\text{-}13)$$

The evaluation of,

$$\text{(CHECKBOOK-PUTIN JOHN)} \qquad (9\text{-}14)$$

results in CHECKBOOK_DEPOSIT_TO_BALANCE. Now let us consider figure 9.2. A macro is used to avoid evaluation of the arguments. The expression that calls the macro will be of the form of (9-11). TARGET will be passed JOHN, and OPERATION will be passed CHECKBOOK-PUTIN. When the arguments are substituted in,

$$\text{(APPEND (LIST OPERATION) (LIST TARGET))}$$

and it is evaluated, (9-14) will be returned. When that expression is evaluated, CHECKBOOK_DEPOSIT_TO_BALANCE is returned. This will be the first argument of APPLY. The second argument of APPLY will be (EVAL TARGET); this results in the address of the JOHN structure. Thus, the result will be the same as if (9-13) was evaluated. (Note that the actual form of the expression that is evaluated is different from that of 9-13.)

```
(DEFUN CHECKBOOK_ENTER_DEPOSIT(NAME AMT)
   (SETF (CHECKBOOK-DEPOSIT NAME) AMT)
)
```

Figure 9.3. The procedure CHECKBOOK _ ENTER _ DEPOSIT

Now let us extend these ideas. Suppose that an expression of the form of (9-12), rather than that of (9-7), is used to place an amount into the DEPOSIT slot of structure JOHN. The slot called MAKEDEPOSIT of the structure defined in figure 9.1 is used here. Its default value is CHECKBOOK_ENTER_DEPOSIT. That is, the seventh line in the DEFSTRUCT construction is:

$$\text{(WRITEDEPOSIT 'CHECKBOOK\_ENTER\_DEPOSIT)} \qquad (9\text{-}15)$$

A procedure called CHECKBOOK_ENTER_DEPOSIT must be written. This procedure simply enters data into the DEPOSIT slot. The procedure is shown in figure 9.3.

Now let us consider the complete form of the macro of figure 9.2. If the macro SEND-MESSAGE is passed more than two arguments, the additional arguments (&REST) will be placed in a list called OTHERS. Now consider the CONS statement. This will construct a single list from (EVAL TARGET) and OTHERS. This list will become the second argument of APPLY. Therefore, the desired arguments will be passed to the procedure that is the first argument of APPLY and thus, SEND-MESSAGE will function as desired. Thus, the evaluation of (9-12) would cause $ 45.00 to be entered into the DEPOSIT slot of JOHN.

FLAVORS

The abstraction that we have introduced can be a great help to programmers and nonprogrammers alike. All communication between the person using the program and the program is of the same form. There is no reason to remember various forms to use, and the chance for error has been reduced. This type of abstraction can be extended to still another level. For example, suppose that a slot called PARENT, in a structure called JOHN, stored the name of yet another structure. Suppose that the name of this other structure were SUPERROUTINES and that this structure stored other procedures (or their names). We could say that structure JOHN had inherited procedures from SUPERROUTINES. Message passing macros could be written so that SUPERROUTINES' procedures could be accessed as if they were JOHN's procedures. Thus, people using the program would not become confused. The versatility of object-oriented programming and message passing is increased by this type of operation. Suppose that SUPERROUTINES' procedures are used, not only for manipulating checkbooks, but also for other kinds of operations. Several different types of structures, not only those of type CHECKBOOK, could inherit SUPERROUTINES' procedures. This makes for a very versatile arrangement.

The concepts that we have discussed can be extended. For instance, SUPERROUTINES could inherit procedures from other structures. (Note that although we use the structure as an example, any other form of data storage could be used.) Indeed, we could pick and choose procedures that are eventually inherited by the structures that actually store the data, JOHN for example. This mixing of procedures is called the *flavors* concept. The flavor that a structure receives can be obtained from the mixing of procedures from several structures, that is, from the mixing of other flavors. We have indicated how such a mixing could be used with structures. Some Lisp systems provide procedures that automatically set up flavors and the procedures and macros to be used with them. Of course, if this is not the case you can write your own procedures and macros.

9-3. Packages

Consider that a team of programmers is working on a single large program. Each programmer is developing one or more procedures that will make up the program. Name *conflicts* can develop. For instance, suppose that one programmer writes a procedure to sum numbers and calls it ADD. Another, programmer might write a procedure with the same name that adds an atom to the end of a list. If the DEFUN expressions for both of the procedures called ADD are evaluated by the Lisp system, the one evaluated last will be the only one that can be used. Conflicts can also arise with variable names.

Such things as procedures, macros, and variables are referred to by symbols. For instance, the name of a procedure is a symbol. Common Lisp provides a mechanism called a *package* that addresses the problems that can occur when different procedures, or groups of procedures inadvertently use the same symbols. All symbols are not directly accessible at the same time. Each symbol is said to belong to a package. At any one time, only one package is the *active package* . Symbols in the active package can be referred to in the direct manner that we have used thus far. Special means must be used to refer to symbols that are in a package other than the active package.

When most Common Lisp systems start up, the active package is called USER. Thus far, all the user-defined procedures and variable have been part of this USER package. There are other packages that are usually present. A package named LISP contains the Lisp primitives; the SYSTEM package is used for system functions; the KEYWORD package contains all the keywords used by system or user defined procedures. These keywords always start with a colon. (Note that we shall also use the colon to reference a particular package. This is a different usage of colon.)

Users can define their own packages. When a package is set up, it can have one or more *nicknames* (an alias). The package name is usually long, in order to fully define the contents of the package. The nickname is a shortened form that makes it easier for the programmer to refer to the package. For instance, suppose that John Smith has written an editor and placed it in a package. The name of that package could be JOHN-SMITH-EDITOR, while the nickname might be JSED.

If you enclose some of your procedures in a package and it becomes the active package, it is most likely that you also would want to refer to the procedures in the LISP package. This can be accomplished when you set up the package. Packages are established using the MAKE-PACKAGE procedure. Suppose that you set up a package called JOHN-SMITH-EDITOR with the nicknames JSED and ED, and that package is to be able to directly refer to the symbols in the LISP and KEYWORD packages. The expression that accomplishes this is:

```
(MAKE-PACKAGE 'JOHN-SMITH-EDITOR
        :NICKNAMES 'JSED 'ED :USE 'LISP 'KEYWORD)
```
$$(9\text{-}16)$$

Note that there can be more than one nickname and more than one package to be used with the package being set up.

In Common Lisp, the address of the active package is stored in a variable called *PACKAGE*. SETF or SETQ can be used to store the value returned by MAKE-PACKAGE in a variable. If the variable *PACKAGE* is bound to this value, then the active package will become that defined by MAKE-PACKAGE.

When you write a package, you can declare that some of the symbols defined in it are to be used by other packages. The function EXPORT is used for this purpose. The form of EXPORT is:

(EXPORT '(ABC DEF))   (9-17)

It is good form to place the EXPORT expression near the start of a package so that users of the package can easily find the list of exported symbols. EXPORT has a second optional argument that is the name of the package from which the variables are to be exported. If no package is specified, then the current package is the one that is used. Note that you can EXPORT symbols from a package that is not the current one, or from one that you did not write. The symbols in the list all should be symbols of the package. EXPORT returns true if it functions properly. Note that the package must have been loaded into the system and that the symbols in the list that is EXPORT's first argument must be part of the package. Packages in Lisp do not provide the hidden features or protection that they do in some of the modern languages such as ADA or MODULA-2.

Suppose that you want to use exported symbols from a package called OTHER that is not the active package. You must indicate to the system that those symbols are to be found in that package. This is done by preceding the symbol by the name of the package, OTHER in this case, followed by a colon, :. For instance, if you want to refer to the exported symbol AAA in package OTHER you would write:

OTHER:AAA   (9-18)

Even if a symbol has not been exported from a package, it still can be referred to. The form follows that of (9-18) except that the colon is replaced by a pair of colons, ::. For instance, if BBB is an unexported symbol of OTHER it can be referred to by:

OTHER::BBB   (9-19)

When you have many references to a symbol in another package then it becomes tedious to have to write the name of the package every time that you write the symbol. The procedure IMPORT can be used to make specific symbols of another package directly available to the current package. For instance if AAA and BBB of OTHER are to become directly available to the current package, the following would be evaluated:

(IMPORT '(OTHER:AAA OTHER::BBB))   (9-20)

If you want to make *all* the symbols of another package available to the current package, then use the procedure USE-PACKAGE. For instance, all of OTHER's symbols will become available to the current package by evaluating:

    (USE-PACKAGE 'OTHER)   (9-21)

If any of these operations are to work, the package OTHER must have been loaded into the system prior to the evaluation of the pertinent expressions. Usually, packages are stored on the computer's hard disk and must be loaded specifically. The procedure REQUIRE can be used to perform this loading. For instance,

    (REQUIRE 'OTHER)   (9-22)

should be evaluated before referring to OTHER in any expression.

Sometimes you may have to to determine information about the current package. As mentioned, in most Lisp systems, there is a variable called *PACKAGE* that stores the address of the current package. If *PACKAGE* is entered at the top, or listener, level the address and possibly the string that is the name of the package will be output. The procedure PACKAGE-NAME will return the name of the package that is its argument. For instance,

    (PACKAGE-NAME *PACKAGE*)   (9-23)

will return the name of the current package.

There are many procedures and predicates that can be used with packages. Consult your Lisp manual to determine those that are available with your system.

9-4. THROW and CATCH

There are times when it is useful to terminate only a particular portion of a procedure. For instance, suppose that the improper entry of certain data will prevent some part of a procedure from functioning properly. It might be desirable to terminate only that part of the procedure that uses the improper data. We say that in this case an *error trap* has been set up. In general, an error trap causes control of the program to jump to some predetermined location instead of simply terminating. We shall consider these ideas in greater detail later in this section.

Lisp systems provide primitives called THROW and CATCH that can be used to perform operations of the type discussed in the last paragraph. CATCH is used to define a particular region within a procedure. The THROW expression lies within the region defined by the CATCH construction. We shall start with a simplified discussion and then generalize the ideas. The basic form of a THROW-CATCH construction is:

```
(CATCH tag1 ;   Start of CATCH construction
        ExpressionsA
        (COND ((test) (THROW tag2 (Expression1))))
        ExpressionsB
)             ; End of CATCH construction
ExpressionsC
```

$$(9-24)$$

Assume that this sequence is part of a procedure. Now let us consider some notation; tag1 and tag2 are values that are used to identify the THROW and the CATCH. They are referred to as *tags* and may, in fact, be variables. When circumstances are such that a THROW statement is executed, control will be transferred to the beginning of the CATCH construction whose tag has the same value as that of the THROW that has been evaluated. A THROW statement must be embedded within any CATCH construction to which it transfers control. In our simple example there is only one CATCH construction, but there can be CATCH constructions nested within other CATCH constructions. This is why tags are necessary. The transfer of control is not what one might expect. Let us consider it in detail. We shall assume in this discussion that tag1 and tag2 evaluate to the same value.

Suppose that the test of the COND is false. In that case, the THROW statement will not be evaluated. ExpressionsA and ExpressionsB will be evaluated and the CATCH construction will terminate. Next ExpressionsC will be evaluated.

Now let us assume that the test of the COND expression is true. When the CATCH construction is evaluated, ExpressionsA will be evaluated. Next, the COND expression will be evaluated. Because the test is true the THROW expression will be evaluated. This results in several actions. First Expression1 is evaluated in the usual way. In addition, the result of this expression is the value returned by the THROW expression. Next, control returns to the start of the CATCH construction. However, no further evaluation of any expression within the CATCH construction takes place. Instead, the entire CATCH construction terminates. The CATCH construction returns the value returned by the THROW expression. Note that ExpressionsB are never evaluated in this case. After the evaluation of the

CATCH construction terminates, ExpressionsC are evaluated. The test of the COND expression often tests for some error. Note that we have achieved the desired operation. If the test is true (i. e., the error has occurred), then a part of the procedure (e. g., ExpressionsB) is omitted from evaluation, but the overall procedure does not terminate.

The form of a THROW expression is:

(THROW tag Expression1)   (9-25)

In general, Expression1 must be a single Lisp expression. However, multiple expressions can be evaluated using PROG1, PROGN, or the backquote macro, see secs. 4-6 and 7-2.

Now let us consider a more complicated case in which there are nested CATCH constructions. Assume that they all have different tags. Now suppose that a THROW expression, that lies within the innermost CATCH construction is evaluated. Expression1 of that THROW expression will be evaluated and then control will jump to the start of the CATCH construction whose tag evaluates to the same value as does the tag of the THROW. The comparison is made using EQL. That CATCH construction will be terminated and the value returned by the THROW expression will be returned. Any CATCH expressions that are nested within the terminated one will be terminated also. If a THROW expression is not embedded in a CATCH construction whose tag is EQL to the tag of the THROW expression, then an error will result when that THROW expression is evaluated. Several of the nested CATCH constructions can have tags that are the same (EQL). If the tag of an evaluated THROW expression corresponds to one of these tags, then control will jump to the most recently evaluated CATCH construction.

```
(DEFUN TEST-THROW-CATCH(A B)
   (CATCH 'HERE
       (PRINT 'FIRST)
       (PRINT 'SECOND)
       (COND ((> A B) (THROW 'HERE (PRINT 'THROW1))))
       (PRINT 'THIRD)
   )
)
```

Figure 9.4. An illustration of THROW and CATCH

Let us clarify these ideas with an example. Figure 9.4 illustrates the procedure TEST-THROW-CATCH that is a simple illustration of the use of THROW and CATCH. The tag for both THROW and CATCH is the literal HERE. Note that the THROW is embedded within the CATCH and will be evaluated only if A and B, the arguments of the procedure, are such that A is greater than B. Suppose that,

(TEST-THROW-CATCH 2 3)   (9-26)

is evaluated. The condition of the COND expression will be false and the THROW expression will not be evaluated. The output will be:

FIRST
SECOND   (9-27)
THIRD
THIRD

That is, the expressions are evaluated as if the THROW and CATCH did not exist. Note that THIRD appears twice because PRINT both outputs its value and returns it. The procedure TEST-THROW-CATCH then returns this value.

Now suppose that,

(TEST-THROW-CATCH 3 2)   (9-28)

is evaluated. Now the THROW expression *is* evaluated and the output becomes:

FIRST
SECOND   (9-29)
THROW1
THROW1

As in the previous case, the expressions of the CATCH construction that occur before the THROW are evaluated. Thus, FIRST and SECOND are output. Next, because the test of the COND now returns true, the THROW is evaluated. Its Statement1, *see* (9-25),

(PRINT 'THROW1)   (9-30)

is evaluated, resulting in the output THROW1. This value (THROW1) is returned by the THROW statement. Control now jumps to the CATCH operation which immediately terminates and returns the value that was returned by the THROW construction. Thus, THROW1 is again output.

UNWIND-PROTECT

There are times when certain statements in the CATCH construction must *always* be evaluated, but, for programming reasons, they must be written after the THROW. Consider that a procedure that controls a printer performs the following operations:

Turn on printer
Print text
Turn off printer

Suppose that the printer runs out of paper. It sends a signal to the computer. This signal changes the value of a global variable. The "Print text" portion of the procedure tests this variable to determine if the printer is out of paper. If it is, then a THROW is evaluated to terminate operation. If the entire procedure terminated, then the printer would never be turned off. We would like to ensure that the last part of the procedure is always evaluated. Lisp supplies a primitive called UNWIND-PROTECT that gives us the ability to do just that. The general form of its use is:

```
(UNWIND-PROTECT
    (Expression1)                                    (9-31)
    (Expression2)
)
```

If Expression1 is interrupted by a THROW, GO, or RETURN, then Expression2 will be executed before the operation terminates. Note that Expression1 and Expression2 are single expressions. However, the programmer can group statements into a single "compound expression" by using the backquote macro or by using PROG1, or PROGN, see secs. 4-6 and 7-2.

```
(DEFUN UPTEST(A B)
   (CATCH 'HERE
     (UNWIND-PROTECT
         (PROGN (PRINT 'FIRST)
             (PRINT 'SECOND)
             (COND ((> A B) (THROW 'HERE (PRINT 'THROW1)))))
         )
         (PRINT 'THIRD)
     )
   )
)
```

Figure 9.5. An illustration of UNWIND-PROTECT.

To illustrate the use of UNWIND-PROTECT we shall rewrite the procedure of figure 9.4. Now the expression,

(PRINT 'THIRD)   (9-32)

will be evaluated even if the THROW is evaluated. The procedure is called UPTEST and is illustrated in figure 9.5. An UNWIND-PROTECT construction is embedded within the CATCH construction. The compound expression set up by PROGN corresponds to Expression1 of (9-31). Note that this consists of the first two PRINT expressions and the THROW expression. Expression2 corresponds to (9-32). Now suppose that,

(UPTEST 2 3)   (9-33)

is evaluated. The output will appear as,

```
FIRST
SECOND
THIRD                                                            (9-34)
NIL
```

This is essentially the same as (9-27) Note that NIL is returned in this case because UNWIND-PROTECT returns NIL if its protection feature is not utilized.

Now suppose that,

(UPTEST 3 2)   (9-35)

is evaluated. The output now will be:

FIRST
SECOND
THROW1   (9-36)
THIRD
THROW1

When the THROW expression is evaluated, the PRINT expression causes THROW1 to be output. Control then returns to the CATCH. The UNWIND-PROTECT causes the protected expression, (PRINT 'THIRD) in this case, to be evaluated. The CATCH construction then terminates, returning the value that was returned by the THROW. Thus, the second THROW1 is output. THROW and CATCH, in combination with UNWIND-PROTECT, are used in many error handling procedures.

9-5. Streams - Files

All the programs that we have worked with thus far have taken input from the keyboard and output data to the screen. It is often desirable to store data so that it can be used over again. For instance, if a database is entered from the keyboard, but not stored, then it would be lost when the computer was turned off. All the data would have to be entered again. Thus far, we have assumed that all information that was to be stored was entered into an editor that has provisions for storing data. We shall now discuss procedures that allow the programmer to write programs to store data directly and to retrieve that stored data.

Let us consider some basic concepts here. A *file* is set up to store the data. Such a file is probably stored on either a floppy disk or on a hard disk. We must consider the procedures for writing and reading such a file. Computers are directed by *operating systems*. These are programs that direct the standard tasks performed by the computer. In particular, the operating system oversees the reading and writing of disk files.

Each disk contains a *directory*, which is itself a file. The directory contains the names of the files that are stored on the disk. Other information that might be included is the length of the file and the date it was written and/or modified. The directory also contains other information used by the operating system (e. g., the position of the file on the disk).

Before a file can be written to or read from, it must be *opened*. We need not concern ourselves with the specific details of how the operating system opens a file. However, it involves such things as setting up the directory entry for the file, if it is a newfile. If the file has already been written to the disk, its position must be determined. There are various modes for opening a file. An existing file can be opened for reading or for appending data. In the second case new data will be added to the end of the file. If a file is opened for writing, then any data in that file will be overwritten and *all old data will be lost*. Not all Lisp systems allow a file to be opened to append data. In such cases, the file must be completely rewritten each time that it is changed.

After all the data has been written to, or read from, a file, that file must be *closed*. This signifies to the operating system that operations with that file are complete. In addition to the operations that we have discussed, the operations of opening and closing a file have particular significance to the Lisp system. We shall consider this in greater detail subsequently.

STREAMS

A *stream* is a Lisp object to which data is entered or from which data is output. For instance, when you type data from the keyboard that data is said to enter a stream. This is called the *standard input stream*. The Lisp system reads the characters from the input stream and interprets them appropriately. Similarly, there is a *standard output stream*. The Lisp system usually writes characters to the standard output stream. These characters appear on the terminal. Some of the actions involved here have not been considered. For instance, the output stream must interact properly with the terminal so that the appropriate characters are output to the screen. Similarly, the input stream must interact properly with the keyboard so that the signals from the keyboard are interpreted appropriately. The programmer need not be concerned with the details of this interaction. They will be handled by the system.

The streams can be redirected. For instance, the output stream can be redirected to an opened disk file. In this case, the output will not be to the screen but to the file. The Lisp system represents streams as variables. There are several variables that the system uses to represent standard streams. We shall consider some of these: *STANDARD-INPUT* represents the standard input stream from the keyboard. The primitive input functions, such as READ, take their input from this stream as a default. Although we have not considered this previously, a standard input primitive, such as READ, can take its input from a stream other than *STANDARD-INPUT*. We shall consider this in greater detail subsequently. Note that the variable *STANDARD-INPUT* begins and ends with an asterisk. This has no significance to the Lisp system, but indicates to the programmer that this variable has some special system significance. If you do not start or end any variables of the programs that you write with asterisks, you will probably not modify any system variables inadvertently. The system variables are global variables, so that procedures can modify them if necessary. You should not do this unless you fully understand all the implications. If a system variable is improperly modified, the system may not function at all and may, in fact, have to be rebooted. This may cause all the entered, and/or calculated, data to be lost.

The variable *STANDARD-OUTPUT* represents the output stream. Normally the output is sent to this stream. Procedures such as PRINT and PRINTC use this stream as a default. However, other streams can be used by these procedures.

There are other system variables that are used in conjunction with standard streams. The notation that we have discussed here are used by most Common Lisp systems. You should consult your Lisp manual to determine the variable names used by your system for the standard streams.

When a file is written to or read from, a new stream must be set up and associated with the file. We shall now discuss some procedures for setting up new streams. The stream must be related to a particular file. A computer may have several disk drives. The disk drive containing the disk that is to be used must be specified. A single disk may be divided into several directories. This may be a hierarchical structure. That is, one directory may contain another directory, etc. Remember that directories are files so that if one directory contains another one, the directory information about the the second directory file is contained in the first directory. In such cases, the first directory is said to be the *parent* of the second directory. Thus a directory may have several ancestors. If we want to place a file into a particular directory, then the location of that directory must be specified. Specifically, the disk drive containing the disk must be specified. In addition, any ancestors of the specified directory must be given. All of this information constitutes the *path* to the file. The form of the path varies with the operating system. Consult your operating system manual to determine how to specify a path in your system. Suppose that the disk drives are specified by a letter followed by a colon. The directories that are ancestors of the directory containing the file in question are specified by name and are separated by delimiters; let us assume that these are backslashes. Consider that the path for the file called TEST, that is in directory PROGS, that is, in turn, in directory ACTIVE on the hard disk that is in drive C is to be specified.

That path is represented by:

C:ACTIVE\PROGS\TEST   (9-37)

A problem can arise when this notation is used with those Lisp systems in which the backslash is used to represent a special character. In those systems the backslash must be replaced by two backslashes, and (9-37) would be written as,

C:ACTIVE\\PROGS\\TEST   (9-38)

The actual Lisp system's internal representation of the file name and the path that the Lisp system uses to reference the filename is in a form that is different from either (9-37) or (9-38). The primitive PATHNAME is used to set up that system representation. For example, the evaluation of,

(SETQ ZZ (PATHNAME "C:ACTIVE\PROGS\TEST"))   (9-39)

binds ZZ to the Lisp system representation of (9-37). Note that if your Lisp system uses the backslash as a special character, then the double backslash form should be used in (9-39).

The pathname can be used to open a stream. There are a number of primitives that can be used for this purpose. We shall consider several of them here. The simplest primitive is OPEN. For instance, if,

(SETQ XX (0PEN :DIRECTION :OUTPUT))   (9-40)

is evaluated, XX will represent the stream to the file specified by (9-38). The :DIRECTION can be specified in a number of ways. :OUTPUT indicates that data is to be written to the file. Other specifications are: INPUT, which indicates that data is to be read from the file; :IO, which indicates that data can be both read from and written to the file; and :APPEND which indicates that data is to be written onto the end of the file. If :OUTPUT is used with an existing file, the old file will be overwritten and all previous data will be lost. On the other hand if :APPEND is used with an existing file, the old data will remain intact and the new data will be written onto the end of the file. The default value for :DIRECTION is :INPUT. If a stream is opened for input, both :DIRECTION and :OUTPUT can be omitted from (9-40).

Once a file is opened for output, it can be written to by various primitives that we have already considered. For instance PRINT, PRINC, and PRIN1 all can be used for this purpose. The stream is specified after the item to be printed. For example the evaluation of,

  (PRINT 'HOUSE XX)   (9-41a)

will cause HOUSE to be output to the stream XX. Similarly the evaluation of,

  (PRINT 'BOOK XX)   (9-41b)

will cause BOOK to be output to the same stream. Note that the procedure PRINT will output its text on a new line just as if the output were to the screen. This means that the newline character is written to the stream and will appear in the disk file.

  After all the required data has been written to the stream, the stream must be closed. The primitive CLOSE will accomplish this. The form of its use is:

  (CLOSE XX)   (9-42)

After (9-42) is evaluated, all the data will be written to the disk file, the file will be closed, and the stream will no longer exist. Note that the data may not actually be written to the file each time that a PRINT expression is evaluated. In fact, it may be stored in the memory of the computer until a particular amount of data has accumulated and then output to the disk. Such data is said to be stored in a *buffer*. When an expression, such as (9-42) is evaluated, any data in the buffer is written to the file (stream), and the file is closed. Serious system errors can occur if you do not close a stream once it has been opened.

  Now let us open the file for reading. Because :INPUT is the default, the stream will be set up simply by evaluating:

  (SETQ YY (OPEN ZZ))   (9-43)

Note that we could have used XX as the variable name here (in place of YY) because the original stream has been closed. The file can now be read. Because the file consists simply of atoms that are delimited by new lines, the READ primitive can be used. For instance,

  (READ YY)   (9-44a)

will return HOUSE. If we subsequently evaluate,

(SETQ QQ (READ YY))   (9-44b)

QQ will be assigned the value BOOK. Note that although the default stream for READ is the *STANDARD-INPUT*, we have used YY rather than the default value. If an aditional expression of the form (9-44a) was evaluated, an error would result because the end of the file had been reached. Files containing text are usually ended with a special symbol called an *end-of-file* mark, abbreviated EOF. After the reading of a file is completed, that file should be closed. This is done by evaluating a statement of the form:

(CLOSE YY)   (9-45)

We have discussed several input and output primitives. There are others. The FORMAT procedure can be used to write to any stream. In sec. 2-8 we considered the use of FORMAT to output data to the screen. Let us briefly review this. Suppose that the following have been evaluated:

(SETQ X 3)   (9-46a)
(SETQ Y 5)   (9-46b)

A FORMAT expression that will output the values of X and Y to the standard output stream with suitable text is:

(FORMAT T "FIRST IS ~D SECOND IS ~D" X Y)   (9-47)

The T stands for terminal and indicates that the output stream is to be *STANDARD-OUTPUT*. If the T is replaced by another stream, then the output will be to that stream. For instance, if stream XX is opened for output as in (9-40), then evaluation of,

(FORMAT XX "FIRST IS ~D SECOND IS ~D" X Y)   (9-48)

will cause the data to be written to the stream XX, that is, to the designated file. All of the FORMAT directives discussed in sec. 2-4 apply here as well. There are other primitives that can be used to write to any stream. TERPRI will write a newline to any specified stream as well as to the default *STANDARD-OUTPUT*. The form of its use is:

(TERPRI XX)   (9-49) where XX represents the stream, as before. The primitive WRITE-CHAR is used to write a single character to a stream. The default stream is *STANDARD-OUTPUT*. For instance the evaluation of,

        (WRITE-CHAR 99 XX)   (9-50)

will cause the character c (ASCII 99) to be written to the stream represented by XX. There are other primitives that are used to write to a stream. For instance, WRITE-STRING, WRITE-LINE, and WRITE-BYTE will output a string, line and a single byte, respectively to the specified stream. The default stream is *STANDARD-OUTPUT*. WRITE-STRING and WRITE-LINE can use the :START and :END keywords, *see* sec. 8-3. For instance, the evaluation of,

        (WRITE-STRING "THE BOOK IS HERE" XX
                :START 1 :END 10)   (9-51)

will result in HE BOOK IS being output to the stream represented by XX. WRITE-LINE will append a newline character to the end of the line that it output.

There are primitives for the reading of data from a stream. In general, these correspond to the ones that write data to a stream. Let us consider some of these. READ-LINE causes a line to be read from the specified stream. A line is delimited by a newline character. Thus, READ-LINE is used to read lines of text generated by WRITE-LINE. READ-CHAR is used to read a character from the specified stream. READ-BYTE is used to read a byte from the specified stream. In all cases the default is *STANDARD-INPUT*. For instance the evaluation of,

        (SETQ AA (READ-LINE XX))   (9-52)

will bind AA to the line of text read from the stream represented by XX. There are many primitives that are used to read from or write to a stream. Consult your Lisp manual to determine those that are available with your system and for the options that are available.

```
(SETQ AA (PATHNAME "D:TEST.TXT"))

(WITH-OPEN-FILE (BB AA :DIRECTION :OUTPUT)
    (PRINT "THE BOOK IS" BB)
    (PRINT "ON THE TABLE" BB)
    (PRINT "NEAR THE DOOR" BB)
)


(WITH-OPEN-FILE (CC AA :DIRECTION :INPUT)
    (SETQ A (READ CC))
    (SETQ B (READ CC))
    (SETQ C (READ CC))
)
```

Figure 9.6. An illustration of WITH-OPEN-FILE.

Whenever a file is opened, it must be closed. Serious file system errors can result if you terminate operations while files are still open. Sometimes however, errors can result when you are writing to a disk, and some of these might cause your program to terminate before the appropriate CLOSE expression can be evaluated. Error trapping routines can be written using UNWIND-PROTECT to help ensure that all opened files will be closed. Because such routines involve the trapping of disk errors, a general understanding of the disk operations is needed to write them. Fortunately, Common Lisp provides a macro called WITH-OPEN-FILE that performs all these operations so that the programmer does not have to write the error trapping routines relating to disk operations. In addition, WITH-OPEN-FILE will open and close files under normal (error free) conditions. The use of WITH-OPEN-FILE is illustrated in figure 9.6. Three separate operations are listed there. In the first line AA is bound to a path name. Note that it is not necessary to do this because all occurrences of AA could be replaced by,

$$(PATHNAME \text{ "D:TEST.TXT"}) \qquad (9\text{-}53)$$

in the remainder of figure 9.6.

Now consider the first WITH-OPEN-FILE macro. The first line consists of:

$$(WITH\text{-}OPEN\text{-}FILE \text{ (BB AA :DIRECTION :OUTPUT)} \qquad (9\text{-}54)$$

This line consists of the atom WITH-OPEN-FILE followed by an atom, BB in this case. This atom will represent the stream to the file. That is, the macro will open the file using an OPEN expression of the form of (9-40). BB will replace the variable that corresponds to XX in (9-40). The path name follows. In this case we have used the variable AA, but this could be replaced by (9-53). The options that would be used in the OPEN expression then follow. In (9-54) we have used the :DIRECTION :OUTPUT option. Thus, the file will be opened for output. Note that all of this information is in the form of a list so that it is enclosed within a pair of parentheses. The first line is followed by a sequence of Lisp expressions. In this example each of these expressions writes data to the stream represented by BB. However, there can be other Lisp expressions, not related to writing to a stream, that could be included here. The macro then ends. When the macro is evaluated, the stream BB will be established; that is, the file will be opened. Next, the PRINT expressions will be evaluated. Then the stream will be closed and the macro terminates. If an error results during the evaluation of the macro an UNWIND-PROTECT construction would be used to attempt to close the stream.

The second WITH-OPEN-FILE of figure 9.6 opens the file for reading. Note that the :DIRECTION and :INPUT could be omitted because they are the default values. (If one is omitted, both must be omitted.) There are three READ expressions. Each will read one of the strings written to the file. For instance, after the macro is evaluated B will be bound to "ON THE TABLE". Again, the macro will close the stream just prior to the macro's termination. When the file is initially opened, there is a pointer that points to the start of the file. Data is always read starting from the pointer position. After each item of data is read, the pointer is moved past that data. The next evaluation of a READ will start with the data pointed to and will continue until a delimiter is reached. Thus the second string will be read. Note that, in this case, the data consists of strings enclosed in quotation marks. Newline characters are output by the PRINT procedure; these act as delimiters. If there was a fourth READ expression in figure 9.6, an error would occur because after the third READ the pointer points at the end of the file and there is no further data to be read.

```
(DEFMACRO STRUCT-BOOK-SAVE(NAME)
   (WITH-OPEN-FILE (SNAME (PATHNAME (STRING-APPEND "D:" NAME ".TXT"))
                          :DIRECTION :OUTPUT)
      (SETQ NAME (EVAL NAME))
      (PRINT (BOOK-COPYRIGHT NAME) SNAME)
      (PRINT (BOOK-COVER NAME) SNAME)
      (PRINT (BOOK-PUBLISHER NAME) SNAME)
      )
   (PRINT "DONE")
)


(DEFMACRO STRUCT-BOOK-SETUP(NAME)
   (WITH-OPEN-FILE (XNAME (PATHNAME (STRING-APPEND "D:" NAME ".TXT")))
      (SET NAME (MAKE-BOOK))
      (SETQ NAME (EVAL NAME))
      (SETF (BOOK-COPYRIGHT NAME) (READ XNAME))
      (SETF (BOOK-COVER NAME) (READ XNAME))
      (SETF (BOOK-PUBLISHER NAME) (READ XNAME))
      )
   (PRINT "DONE")
)
```

Figure 9.7. The macro STRUCT-BOOK-SAVE that is used to save a structure of type BOOK and the macro STRUCT-BOOK-SETUP that is used to set up a structure of type BOOK from data stored in a disk file.

As an example of the use of the operations that we have discussed, we shall write two macros. The first STRUCT-BOOK-SAVE is used to set up a structure of type BOOK. These structures were defined in figure 6.14. Note that structures of type BOOK have three slots, COPYRIGHT, COVER, and PUBLISHER. Now consider the first macro of figure 9.7. It is passed the name of the structure. This is called NAME. Consider,

(PATHNAME (STRING-APPEND "D:" NAME ".TXT"))   (9-55)

Suppose that the argument of STRUCT-BOOK-SAVE is LBOOK, then STRING-APPEND will return D:LBOOK.TXT. Note that we assume that all files are to be of this form. That is they will be stored on drive D and will have the extension .TXT. The name of the file is to be the same as the name of the structure. Thus, the appropriate file will be opened for output.

(Note that the primitive STRING-APPEND has been used to form a single string from substrings.) Next,

(SETQ NAME (EVAL NAME))   (9-56)

is evaluated. Now NAME will store the address of the structure. When,

(PRINT (BOOK-COPYRIGHT NAME) SNAME)   (9-57)

is evaluated, the value in the COPYRIGHT slot of the structure LBOOK will be written to the stream, that is to the file. Note that SNAME is the name used to represent the stream in the WITH-OPEN-FILE macro. We assume here that the DEFSTRUCT construction of figure 6.14 has been evaluated so that the access functions for structures of type BOOK are available.

The evaluation of the next two PRINT expressions causes the data in the COVER and NAME slots of LBOOK to be written to the file. The WITH-OPEN-FILE macro closes the stream and terminates. Finally "DONE" is output and the STRUCT-BOOK-SAVE macro terminates.

The macro STRUCT-BOOK-SETUP reads the data stored by STRUCT-BOOK-SAVE and sets up an appropriately named structure. We again assume that the DEFSTRUCT construction of figure 6.14 has been evaluated prior to running this macro. The details of the first line of the WITH-OPEN-FILE macro are the same as for STRUCT-BOOK-SAVE. We have called the variable that represents the stream XNAME. There is no significance to this change of name. It was done simply for illustrative purposes. Now consider:

(SET NAME (MAKE-BOOK))   (9-58)

Note the use of SET, rather than SETQ. Unlike the case of SETQ, the first argument of SET is evaluated. The structure that is set up is not to be bound to an atom called NAME, but is to be bound to the atom whose name is the value of NAME (i. e., that NAME is bound to). This is why SET is used here. Suppose that LBOOK were the argument of STRUCT-BOOK-SETUP. After (9-58) is evaluated, a structure called LBOOK will have been established. Initially, its slots will hold the default values. However, the data stored in the disk file will replace these default values. In order to use the access functions, NAME must be replaced by the address of the structure LBOOK. Thus, an expression of the form of (9-56) is evaluated. The three READ expressions now recover the data from the file, and this data is then entered into the appropriate slots.

We have discussed the basic ideas of files and streams in this section. Operations with files are dependent on both the Lisp system and on the particular operating system in use. Thus, file handling will vary from system. Consult your Lisp manual to determine the specific form of the procedures to use with your system.

Exercises

Check any procedures or macros that you write by running them on your computer.

1. What is meant by object oriented programming?

2. Modify the operations of figure 9.1, now assuming that the data is stored in an a-list.

3. Repeat exercise 2, now assuming that the data is stored in a p-list.

4. Set up a structure and any necessary procedures for an object-oriented program that keeps track of the amount owed by charge account customers of a store. Each customer's records must be maintained in a separate structure. Purchases are added to a monthly balance and payments are deducted from a running balance. There are two types of customers. Those with revolving accounts must pay a $ 1.25 service charge each month and a 2 percent charge is added to the outstanding balance at the end of each month. Those with regular accounts are expected to pay their full balance at the end of each month. There will be no charge unless this amount is not paid, in which case, a penalty of 5 percent of the outstanding balance will be added to the account. There should be several routines: one that adds purchases to the balance, another that determines the amount to be billed and one to process payments. To simplify matters, assume that all payments are received on the same day of the month and that the bills are generated after that day. The person running the program should not have to know the type of account possessed by each customer.

5. Repeat exercise 4 but use a-lists to store the data.

6. Repeat exercise 4 but use p-lists to store the data.

7. Define a macro so that message passing can be used with exercise 3.

8. Define a macro so that message passing can be used with exercise 4.

9. Define a macro so that message passing can be used with exercise 5.

10. Define a macro so that message passing can be used with exercise 6.

11. What is meant by a flavor?

12. Write a procedure that simulates error checking with disk operations. The procedure should have a single argument that represents an error signal. If the argument is 0, then the following should be output:

    File open
    Text being output
    File closed

This is the error free simulation. If the argument of the procedure is 1, then only,

    File open

should be output. This is the error simulation. Use THROW and CATCH in your procedure

13. Repeat exercise 12 but have,

    File open
    File closed

output when the argument of the procedure is a 1. Use UNWIND-PROTECT in your procedure.

14. Discuss files, streams, and the storage of data on disks.

15. Write a procedure or macro that will store the data for an a-list of exercise 2 in a disk file.

16. Write a procedure or macro that will store the data for a p-list of exercise 3 in a disk file. Note that SYMBOL-PLIST, or the equivalent, can be used to extract the data in a p-list.

17. Write a procedure or macro that will read the data written by the program of exercise 15 and then reconstruct the a-list.

18. Write a procedure or macro that will read the data written by the program of exercise 16 and then reconstruct the p-list.

19. Write a procedure or macro that will store the data for each structure of exercise 4 in a disk file.

20. Write a procedure or macro that will read the data written by the program of exercise 19 and then reconstruct the structure.

Index